Religion 6
for Young Catholics

Nihil Obstat given at Scranton, Pennsylvania, on the 20th day of November, 2001, by Rev. Msgr. David Bohr, S.T.D., Censor Librorum.

Imprimatur given at Scranton, Pennsylvania, on the 20th day of November, 2001, by the Most Reverend James C. Timlin, D.D., Bishop of Scranton.

The *nihil obstat* and *imprimatur* are official declarations that a book or pamphlet is free of doctrinal or moral error. No implication is contained therein that those who granted the *nihil obstat* or *imprimatur* agree with the contents, opinions, or statements expressed.

by the Seton Staff

The Seton Catholic Family Catechism Series
A Religion Series for Children Educated at Home by their Parents

Seton Press
Front Royal, Virginia

Seton Home Study School
1350 Progress Drive
Front Royal, VA 22630
(540) 636-9990
(540) 636-1602 fax

Internet: www.setonhome.org
E-mail: info@setonhome.org

Cover: *Finding in the Temple* by Philippe de Champaigne

Dedicated to the
Sacred Heart of Jesus

Contents

Preface

This book is written primarily for parents who are teaching religion to their children at home at least five days a week. It is part of a total program or course of studies for Catholic children offered by Seton Home Study School.

This book is only part of the Seton Fifth Grade religion program. It is to be studied in conjunction with the Baltimore Catechism No. 1, and a Bible history book.

In the Seton religion program, Lesson Plans are written for daily assignments in all three texts. These include study activities and memory work. They include supplementary helps, information about the saints through the liturgical year, and even helpful web site links.

For those enrolled in the Seton religion course, quarterly tests are available which are graded by Seton teachers. Report cards are returned to the parents with the religion tests, which include comments by the Seton teachers.

Seton Home Study School offers an approved Catholic program under the Bishop of Arlington.

For more information about enrolling in the Seton religion program, or in any other courses, please call 540-636-9990; or fax us at 540-636-1602; or e-mail us at info@ setonhome.org; or visit our web site at www.setonhome.org.

Introduction

Welcome to Sixth Grade Religion, and the study of our Catholic Faith!

In the *Catechism of the Catholic Church* of 1994, Pope John Paul II wrote that the new *Catechism* would follow the same structure as the *Catechism of the Council of Trent*. That earlier *Catechism* was the result of the Council of Bishops meeting in Trent from 1545 to 1563. Thanks to the work of holy bishops and theologians, such as St. Peter Canisius, St. Charles Borromeo, and St. Robert Bellarmine, many national catechisms, including the American *Baltimore Catechism*, were written based on the *Catechism of the Council of Trent*.

All of these catechisms consisted of four parts. The new *Catechism of the Catholic Church* calls these four parts the four "pillars" because it is on these four parts that the foundation and structure of the Catholic Faith is built. The Vatican dictates that each year, children must study the four "pillars" of the Catholic Church: the Creed, the Commandments, the Sacraments, and Prayers. In fourth grade, our focus was on the Apostles' Creed. In fifth grade, we concentrated on the Commandments. This year, after reviewing the Creed and the Commandments, we will spend two quarters learning about the Sacraments. The Vatican has said that we must review and learn about *all* aspects of our Faith *each year*, but we may concentrate on a certain area that is appropriate for the students.

This book is written to be an explanation of the Faith in coordination with *The New Saint Joseph Baltimore Catechism, No. 2.* You will notice that the answers to many of the questions are contained in this book. We chose this particular edition of the *Baltimore Catechism* because it has illustrations in color, explanations under many of the questions and answers, Biblical references, and end-of-lesson exercises for children. This book is used in Seton's program for sixth, seventh, and eighth grades. Because this is the first year the students are using the Number 2 edition, we are not trying to cover every single item in the book. The book may appear small, but it is loaded with Catholic doctrine. So we will cover basic introductory concepts, and ask the children in the lesson plans to memorize only the basic questions and answers. In the next two years, of course, answers to all the questions will eventually be memorized.

We begin with a prayer to ask our Lady to enlighten our minds: Hail, Mary, full of grace! The Lord is with thee; blessed art thou among women, and blessed is the Fruit of thy womb, Jesus. Holy Mary, Mother of God, pray for us sinners, now and at the hour of our death. Amen. Mary, Seat of Wisdom, pray for us. Amen.

Sooner or later, every human being asks the following questions: Who am I? Where did I come from? How did I get here? Where am I going? How do I get there? These five questions are the most important anyone can ever ask. Why? Unless we discover the answers to these questions, we will not be able to carry out our mission on earth. What is every person's mission or purpose? God answers these questions for us through His Holy Catholic Church, which was founded by His Son, Jesus Christ. The Holy Catholic Church teaches that our purpose is to know, love, and serve God on earth so that we may be happy with Him forever in Heaven.

How did we all come to be? We were called into existence out of love, because of the love of our parents and because of the love of God. God created us out of love with the consent of our parents. We now have a large responsibility, a large part to play in where we will go at the end of our time here on earth. We are responsible, with the help of divine grace, to live a holy life in obedience to God's laws. In order to attain Heaven and perfect happiness for all eternity with God, we need the help of divine grace. Where do we find that help? We find that help in the same place we learn the chief truths of divine revelation: the Catholic Church founded by Jesus Christ.

For the first quarter of Sixth Grade, we are going to review The Apostles' Creed, the official statement of truths that God revealed to the Apostles and members of His Catholic Church, through His Son, Jesus Christ. Thus we find the chief truths of divine revelation in the Catholic Church. We know that God, the Supreme Being, created us out of love to show us His goodness. He created us that He might share with us His everlasting happiness in Heaven. We know that to reach Heaven with God, we must know, love, and serve Him while we live in this world.

What *means* do we have to know, love, and serve God? The Catholic Church, founded by Jesus Christ provides the means. Why is it important to learn truths? It is important to learn the truths in the Creed that we might grow in our *knowledge* of God. The more we *know* God and His truths, the more we will *love* Him, and want to attain eternal life and true happiness by *serving* Him, by being obedient to His laws. Thus the Catholic Church points the way to eternal life.

Our parents have shared and continue to share the Catholic Faith with us. We, too, have a serious responsibility, not only to live the Faith ourselves, but also to share our precious Catholic Faith with others. For our own salvation and for the salvation of others, we need to learn the truths revealed by Jesus Christ by learning the Apostles' Creed.

Like one billion others who are members of the Catholic Church in the world, we must continually work at learning, understanding, and loving the truths of Jesus Christ as stated in the Apostles' Creed.

God All-Knowing and All-Wise, have mercy on us.

We begin our study of the Apostles' Creed with some brief comments. The Apostles' Creed can be traced all the way back to the twelve Apostles who walked and learned with Jesus Christ. The Apostles taught all the truths of this prayer, The Apostles' Creed, to new converts who learned the Creed before they were baptized. The fact that we have had this prayer for so long is living proof of the strength and continued existence of the Catholic Church for these past 2000 years.

The Apostles' Creed is a summary of the truths of our Faith. Our Faith is the basis for living a holy life. The twelve articles of The Apostles' Creed were revealed to us by God. We say a form of The Apostles' Creed—the Nicene Creed—at every Sunday Mass. Every Catholic should memorize this wonderful prayer of our Faith word for word. It should be easy to memorize since we are saying the Creed when we attend Mass on Sunday, and also at the beginning of each Rosary.

The word "Creed" comes from the Latin word *Credo* which means "I believe." Every time we say the Creed, we are pleasing God by publicly professing our belief in twelve basic truths revealed by Him. Each truth or "article" of the Creed is what we *must believe* if we are true followers of Jesus Christ, the Son of God. What does it mean to believe? There are two kinds of belief or faith: human and divine. Human faith means that we believe what people tell us; divine faith means that we believe what God tells us. There is a difference. People do not always tell the truth, but God *always* tells the truth. God can neither deceive nor be deceived.

Because God Himself, Who can never deceive, revealed these truths of The Apostles' Creed, we believe them totally and completely, without hesitation. Though we *believe,* our minds still want to be informed or enlightened so that we are moved to *act* on what we believe and know and understand. We cannot really love without *knowing* the object of our love. This is especially true when we speak about God, Whom we must *know* before we can really love Him. Our salvation depends upon knowing, loving, and serving God. In the Bible, we read the words of Jesus Christ, "He who believes and is baptized will be saved" (Mark 16:16). When we say The Apostles' Creed, we are informing our minds so that our wills can love God even more.

One good way to memorize The Apostles' Creed is to think about the words of the prayer in the Presence of God. Become aware that you are in God's Presence, then take a few minutes to slowly recite each article of the Creed. Ask Jesus to help you understand what each article means.

In the Apostles' Creed we find the following truths:

· The world did not always exist. God, Who has no beginning, created the world out of nothing.

· The Son of God became Man; Jesus Christ is God-made-Man. He was born of the Virgin Mary, died on the Cross, rose from the dead, and will come as our Judge at the end of the world.

· Jesus Christ sent the Holy Spirit, Who gives life to the Church Jesus founded. We receive all the supernatural graces we will need through the Church, and we are saved through these graces.

Here are the twelve articles of the Creed:

- "I believe in God, the Father Almighty, Creator of Heaven and earth,"
- "And in Jesus Christ, His only Son, our Lord,"
- "Who was conceived by the Holy Spirit, born of the Virgin Mary,"
- "Suffered under Pontius Pilate, was crucified, died and was buried. He descended into Hell,"
- "The third day He rose again from the dead."
- "He ascended into Heaven, sits at the right hand of God, the Father Almighty."
- "From thence He shall come to judge the living and the dead."
- "I believe in the Holy Spirit,"
- "The Holy Catholic Church, the Communion of Saints,"
- "The forgiveness of sins,"
- "The Resurrection of the body, and"
- "Life everlasting. Amen."

Father, from Whom are all things, have mercy on us.

True (T) or False (F)

_____ 1. The Apostles' Creed should be memorized.

_____ 2. The Apostles' Creed can be traced back to the Apostles.

_____ 3. In the early Church, new converts memorized the Creed first before they were baptized.

_____ 4. The Apostles' Creed is a prayer.

_____ 5. We begin the Rosary with an "Our Father."

_____ 6. The word "Creed" comes from the Greek word for "I believe."

_____ 7. There are exactly twelve articles in the Apostles' Creed.

_____ 8. We are not required to believe all the articles in the Creed.

_____ 9. Human faith is the same as divine faith.

_____ 10. God can neither deceive nor be deceived.

Today we begin with the first article of the Creed: "I believe in God, the Father Almighty, Creator of Heaven and earth."

Who is God? When we talk about God, we are talking about Someone entirely different and apart from anything or anyone in the universe. God is the Creator of everyone in the universe. God has always existed, and always will exist. God has endless existence. He had no beginning and He has no end. Our human language fails us when we try to describe God.

The Catholic Church has found some words to describe God. The Catholic Church describes the qualities or characteristics of God. Today we will learn about some of God's characteristics. However, since God is perfect, we call His characteristics "perfections." We could say "Tommy is

kind." One of his characteristics is kindness. God, however, is perfect kindness. He does not *have* kindness, He *is* perfect kindness.

God is *infinitely perfect*. This is one of the most important things the Church teaches us about God. We human beings have good qualities, but they are limited. We are not perfect in any way. We are not perfect in our thoughts or acts or emotions, nor are we physically perfect. We have a need to eat and sleep. Some of us need to wear glasses or braces. God, however, has no limitations or imperfections. He is perfect in everything, so the Church says He is all-perfect or infinitely perfect.

God is *eternal*. This means God had no beginning and will have no end. The Catholic Church teaches us that God *must* exist. He cannot *not exist*. You and I do not *need to* exist; we live only because God called us into existence so that He could love us and we could love Him. We have a beginning date, when God created us. As you know, however, we will continue to exist forever and ever and ever. God made us so that even though our bodies will die, our souls will continue to exist. *We, all of us who exist, will continue to exist forever.* God, our loving eternal Creator, however, always was, and He always will be.

God is *all-good*. This means God is infinitely good and loveable. God loves us as a father loves His children. God loves us more than all the fathers put together in the whole world could love their children. God takes care of all our needs with a father's love and protection.

God is *all-knowing*. God knows all things and there is nothing He does not know. We creatures, created by God, must learn from our parents, and others such as priests, teachers, the internet, and books. God, however, knows everything, absolutely everything that exists, even if it exists only in someone's mind. God knows all that has happened in the past, all that is happening in the present, and all that will happen in the future.

God is *all-holy*, *all-merciful* and *all-just*, and all His perfections are equal. This means God is not more of one perfection than He is of another. He is not, for example, more merciful than He is just, or more just than He is merciful. He is equally perfect, totally perfect, in all of His perfections.

God is *all-present*. This means He is everywhere at the same time. We creatures are either here or there. We cannot be in more than one place at a time. God, however, is all-present. He sees all things. God sees us and knows what we are thinking and doing at all times.

God is *pure Spirit*. We cannot see Him with our earthly eyes because God has no body. He is pure Spirit. When my body dies and I, as a soul with my mind and will, go to Heaven, I will then "see" God because my soul is a spirit also.

God, our Creator, has such love for us, we cannot even begin to understand such great love. However, the Church has named it. The Church has called God's loving care and protection for us *Divine Providence*. St. Thomas Aquinas was given a great knowledge about God by God Himself. St. Thomas Aquinas said that by Divine Providence, God watches over and governs everything and everyone He has made.

Father Everlasting, have mercy on us.

7

Multiple Choice

_____ 1. God is the Being Who
   a) always was. b) always will be.
   c) cannot *not exist.* d) a, b and c.

_____ 2. Human language
   a) describes exactly Who is God.
   b) fails us in describing Who God is.
   c) can in no way tell us about God.

_____ 3. When we say that God is eternal, we mean
   a) that He had a beginning but no end.
   b) has an end, but no beginning.
   c) He has no beginning and no end.

_____ 4. God is all-good
   a) and loves us more than all fathers in the world put together.
   b) loves us like a human father.
   c) loves us only when we are good.

_____ 5. God is all-knowing. That means
   a) He does not know our thoughts.
   b) He does not know the future.
   c) He knows all things, past, present, and future.

_____ 6. God's mercy is
   a) equal to His justice.
   b) more powerful than His justice.
   c) less powerful than His justice.

_____ 7. Because God is our Creator, we are His
   a) slaves.
   b) independent creatures.
   c) dependent creatures.

_____ 8. God
   a) may exist. b) cannot *not exist.* c) exists with help.

_____ 9. Divine Providence means
   a) some things just happen.
   b) we need not study.
   c) God's loving care for us.

_____ 10. God's characteristics are
   a) His perfections.
   b) His best qualities.
   c) His personality.

Reason, revelation, and *faith.* These three words explain how we come to know about God. Through *reason* and *faith,* we can learn about God. Divine *Revelation* comes from God and completes our knowledge of God.

First, we will discuss *reason.* Each person is composed of a body and soul. The soul is composed of an intellect and a will. By the intellect, we reason; by the will, we choose to do this or that. The soul is the spiritual part of us that will never die; this is the part of us that is separated from our bodies when we die. However, at the end of time, God will reunite each person's body and soul.

Reason is part of our intellect and one of the things that make us truly human and different from the animals. What is reason? Reason is that part of the intellect or mind that informs us about what is real, what is true, what are the facts. We reason that one plus one equals two. We reason that the rain that falls from the skies comes from dark clouds. We reason that if we do not sleep enough at night, we will be tired the next day.

By our reason, we can know and understand the fact that *there must be a God.* When we look around at our beautiful world, the sky, trees, flowers, mountains, rivers, and oceans, we *know, we reason, we figure out* that they did not come into existence by themselves.

Did you know that, with rare exception, all peoples of all times, even from the very beginning of the human race, believed that there was a God? Adam and Eve and their descendants, and, after the great Flood, Noah and his descendants certainly passed on the knowledge of God. However, even primitive persons could *reason* that there must exist a Creator-God. They would look to the heavens, see the regular movement of the sun, moon, and stars. They could and did come to the conclusion intellectually that there must be a God.

How can each person *reason* that there must be a God? We can reason that there must be a God because nothing can cause itself. The sun, the moon, and the stars could not cause themselves. The earth could not create itself. The first bird, the first fish, the first animal, could not create itself. How do we human beings *know* that nothing can cause itself? By the aid of our human intellect, our reasoning power, and from what we see happening around us, we know that nothing can cause itself. Everything we see must have had a beginning. Everything must have been created at some point in time long ago by Someone with an Intellect Who had no beginning. And this Someone is Who we call God.

It is with our *natural reason* that we human beings can come to know that there is a God, Who is self-existing, all-wise, and almighty, Who created the world around us. It is through natural reason that all human beings can and do come to know of God's existence.

However, human beings could not reason that God loves us and that He wants to be our Savior. God needed to tell us this. That is why God used *supernatural* means to reveal Himself to us. We call this Divine Revelation.

What is Divine *Revelation*? "Reveal" means to show or to inform someone about something he did not know. In this case, God *revealed* to the human race something we *could not* know without His help. God revealed to the human race far more about Himself than man could ever come to know on his own, using his human reason. We receive the truths of *revelation* through the Word of God in the Bible, and through the Catholic Church which was founded by Jesus Christ, the Son of God made Man.

God uses our *reason, Divine Revelation,* and the gift of *Faith* to reveal Himself to us. The *Catechism of the Catholic Church* tells us:

"Our Holy Mother, the Church, holds and teaches that God, the first principle [the First Cause or Creator] and last end of all things, can be known with certainty from the created world by the natural light of human reason. Without this capacity, man would not be able to welcome God's revelation. Man has this capacity because he is created 'in the image of God'" (n. 36).

We see we can learn of God's existence through human reason. We can learn about God and His perfections through Divine Revelation, that is, through the Bible and the Catholic Church. The third way we learn about God is through the gift of *Faith.* The gift of Faith is belief because we believe what God has told us through His Apostles and His Catholic Church.

We should pray for an increase in *Faith,* which we receive when we are baptized. Say the Act of Faith every day: "O my God, I firmly believe that You are one God in three Divine Persons, Father, Son and Holy Spirit. I believe that Your divine Son became Man, died for our sins, and will come again to judge the living and the dead. I believe these and all the truths which the Holy Catholic Church teaches because You have revealed them, Who can neither deceive nor be deceived. Amen."

Father, our Creator, have mercy on us.

Matching

_____	1. Reason	1. Supernatural
_____	2. Revelation	2. Creator
_____	3. Faith	3. Man
_____	4. God	4. Statement of belief in God
_____	5. Man	5. Received at Baptism
_____	6. Primitive people	6. Founded by Jesus Christ
_____	7. Cannot create themselves	7. Composed of body and soul
_____	8. Created in the image of God	8. Natural
_____	9. Act of Faith	9. Sun, moon, stars
_____	10. Catholic Church	10. Reasoned that there was a God

Today we will learn more about Divine Revelation. Divine Revelation refers to what God has revealed to us, and has been passed down from generation to generation. For instance, God revealed to Adam and Eve that He would send a Savior. That is why the Hebrew or Jewish people were waiting and expecting the Savior from God.

When God revealed truths about Himself or His laws, they were written down. For instance, Moses wrote down what God revealed to him, and we can read what Moses wrote in the first five books of the Bible. Besides knowing God from our natural reason, we can find truths about God which He revealed to certain persons. These are called supernatural revelations which God has revealed, and are written down in Sacred Scripture.

What is *Sacred Scripture*? The word "sacred" means holy. The words of Sacred Scripture are holy because God Himself gave them to us. The word "scripture" means written. Sacred Scripture is the Bible, holy written words revealed by God. The word "Bible" means book. The Bible contains seventy-three books and is the inspired Word of God. These are words and concepts "revealed" to the sacred writers. God gave His Sacred Word, Holy Scripture, to the Church to teach us about Himself in order for us to become holy and to be able to spend eternity in perfect happiness in Heaven with Him.

Sacred Scripture was inspired by God, and is the revealed Word of God. This is why we refer to it as Divine Revelation. What does that mean? It means that, although God is the Author of the Bible, He used certain holy men to write only what He wanted them to write. He gave them special "light" for their minds and inspirations for their wills. Each of the writers of the Bible used his own language, style, and writing ability, but each wrote only what God wanted him to write.

As we have seen, the Bible is divided into two parts. *The Old Testament* was written before Jesus, the Son of God, was born. The *New Testament* was written after Jesus Christ ascended into Heaven, at the end of His visible stay on earth. The first four books of the New Testament are the Gospels of Matthew, Mark, Luke, and John, who were apostles of Jesus Christ.

Where was the Bible written? Look at a world map, find the Mediterranean Sea, and then move your finger to the right. There you will find an area called the Holy Land. That is where most of the words of Sacred Scripture were written by writers inspired by the Holy Spirit.

The Catholic Church, inspired by the Holy Spirit, determined long ago which ancient books were divinely inspired. The 73 books of the Old and New Testaments make up the Bible. It is important to read only a Catholic Bible, such as the Douay-Rheims version of the St. Jerome Latin Vulgate. Protestants removed certain books of the Bible when they "protested" against certain Catholic Church doctrines. Since the Catholic Church is the Church founded by Jesus Christ, only the Catholic Church can be the official interpreter of the Bible. The Church encourages us to read the Bible every day. We receive special graces when we read the Bible for 15 minutes.

Sacred Tradition is the other way that God revealed His plan to the human race. What is *Sacred Tradition*? It is the oral and written preaching of the Apostles under the inspiration of the Holy Spirit. It is everything revealed that is not written in Sacred Scripture. It has been handed down from the Apostles who were the first hearers of Christ's message. They lived, walked, talked, and ate with their Master, Jesus Christ.

From the Apostles, the message of salvation was passed to the *Fathers of the Church* who carried on their message to the present day. What are some examples of Sacred Tradition? The Apostles' Creed and all the writings of the Fathers of the Church are examples of Sacred Tradition. Like Sacred Scripture, the Church honors the word-of-mouth truths revealed by God. Both Sacred Scripture and Sacred Tradition must be believed and embraced by everyone who is Catholic because, together, they are our Catholic Faith.

God Most High, Who inhabits eternity, have mercy on us.

Fill in the Blanks

1. Divine Revelation is composed of _____ _____ and

   _____ _____.

2. The word sacred means _____.

3. Another word for Sacred Scripture is the _____.

4. The Catholic Bible contains _____ books.

5. The Scripture writers were _____ by God to write only what He wanted them to write.

6. The _____ Testament was written before the Son of God became man.

7. The _____ Testament was written after Jesus ascended into Heaven.

8. _____ _____ was handed down to us from the Apostles.

9. As Catholics, we must believe both _____ _____ and

   _____ _____.

10. The Catholic Church is the official interpreter of the _____.

We are still on the first article of the Creed: "I believe in God the Father Almighty, Creator of Heaven and Earth." We have learned about some of God's attributes or perfections. Today we will learn about the Blessed Trinity. We will never fully understand the Blessed Trinity because it is a supernatural mystery. What is a supernatural mystery? This is a mystery which could not even be imagined *before* God revealed it, and *after* He revealed it, we still cannot fully understand the mystery. We can, however, understand some few things about the Blessed Trinity. We begin by defining the words "person" and "nature."

What is a *person*? Person answers the question "who." Who are you? You are an individual with a special name like John or Mary. You are unique. Unique means there is no one like you who ever lived or who ever will live. What is a *nature*? Nature answers the question "what." What are you? You are a not a dog or a pencil or a car. You are a human being with an intellect and a free will.

We use those same words when we speak about God. God is one divine *nature* Who is three separate and distinct divine *Persons*. Another way to say it is: the Father is not the Son or the Holy Spirit; the Son is not the Holy Spirit or the Father; the Holy Spirit is not the Father or the Son. They are individual Persons, a community or Family of three Persons Who share one divine nature. Each of the three Persons of the Blessed Trinity is equal to the others.

Over the years since Jesus Christ's visible stay on earth, there have been many misunderstandings about the Blessed Trinity. In fact, there have been some heresies about the Blessed Trinity. Heresies are formal denials of truths by a baptized person about certain Church teachings, called doctrines or dogmas. A heretic, a person who denies a doctrine, is in serious danger of losing his soul. Each time a heresy arose, a Church Council met and, with the help of the Holy Spirit, cleared up the confusion.

One of the first heresies, Arianism, took its name from a man named Arius who lived from 256-336. He declared that Jesus Christ was *not divine*, was *not* the Son of God, and that there are *not* three distinct Persons in God. The First Council of Nicaea met in 325. About two hundred bishops from all over the world met in what is called a "solemn session." They re-affirmed what the Catholic Church had been teaching from the beginning: that Jesus Christ *is* divine, that Jesus Christ *is* the Son of God, and that there *are* three divine Persons in one God.

Beginning with the early Christians following the Ascension of Jesus into Heaven, many Christians were killed by the Roman leaders for outwardly demonstrating their faith in Jesus Christ. The ancient Romans hated the new Christians because of their belief in Jesus Christ as King.

St. Cecilia, one of the first Christians, lived from 230 to 250. Like all Christians of that time, her young life was marked by persecution for her strong faith in Jesus Christ. Her faith was so strong, in fact, that early in her life, she decided never to marry because she wanted to belong completely to Jesus Christ, so much did she love Him. She believed what the early Church taught: that there are three divine Persons who have one divine nature. She was killed for her Catholic Faith. She died with three fingers extended on one hand and one finger on the other— *representing three divine Persons in one God. With the last act of her will, she was proclaiming the Blessed Trinity even unto her death.*

*"Holy Trinity, Father, Son, and Holy Spirit,
I adore Thee with all my heart. Amen."*

True (T) or False (F)

_____ 1. We can fully understand the Holy Trinity.

_____ 2. Person answers the question "who."

_____ 3. Nature answers the question "when."

_____ 4. God is one divine Person.

_____ 5. The three Persons of the Blessed Trinity share one divine nature.

_____ 6. Each of the three Persons of the Blessed Trinity is equal to the other two.

_____ 7. A heresy is a formal refusal by a baptized person to accept a doctrine of the Church.

_____ 8. The first Church Council was Vatican Council II.

_____ 9. St. Cecilia gave up her life for faith in Jesus Christ.

_____ 10. St. Cecilia died declaring her belief in Three Persons in One God.

We continue to study the first article of the Creed: "I believe in God, the Father Almighty, *Creator* of Heaven and earth." What does it mean to *create*? Do we create a picture with paints? Does Mother create a new dress when she sews? Does a carpenter create a new house?

When we paint a picture, we must use paper, brushes, and paint. Those are things that already exist. When Mother sews a dress, she needs a sewing machine, fabric, and thread. When a carpenter builds a house, he needs many things such as wood, nails, and cement. Painting a picture, making a dress, and building a house are not acts of creation because we must begin with things already in existence in order to make them.

Creation is something entirely different. *Creation means making something out of nothing.* It means starting with nothing and ending with something. No one in this world can do that. That is why we say that *only God can create.* When God creates, He uses nothing, He starts with nothing. There is only one Creator, and that is God.

When we say that God created Heaven and earth, which Person of the Blessed Trinity actually did the creating? Does this mean that God the Son and God the Holy Spirit did not create? No. Remember in our last lesson, we learned that the Blessed Trinity has one divine nature. What one Member of the Blessed Trinity does, all three Members do because they have one divine nature. In human language, we do "say" that God the Father created the world, God the Son redeemed the world, and God the Holy Spirit sanctifies us or makes us holy. However, *all three Persons* of the Blessed Trinity create, redeem, and sanctify, because the one God does these things.

What is a creature? A creature is any being created by God, everything from the tiniest one-celled animal to the tallest tree, from the single cell to the highest mountain. We know that God created the entire universe, the world, and everything in the world. God created many different kinds of creatures, but not all creatures are on the same level. The lowest level of creatures God made are what we call inanimate objects like rocks, mountains, and minerals. Although they are creatures, they are not living beings. These inanimate objects give form, shape, and beauty to our earthly world.

The next level of creatures God made is living things such as plants and trees. They are higher than inanimate objects because they are living things. Although they do not move from place to place, they grow in response to the sun's light and heat, and they give even more beauty to the world. The third level of being is animals. Animals move and breathe, eat and sleep, but they do not think and reason. They are the workers and companions of men, providing entertainment, enjoyment, and help.

The final level of creatures on earth is man. Only one creature on earth, man, has been gifted with the greatest ability of all: to think and choose. Man has intellect and free will. Man has reason, intelligence, and the ability to choose. Like animals, man is a living creature who breathes, moves, eats, and sleeps. Unlike animals, however, man is a rational being, with an intellect and a free will.

All creatures depend on God, not only for their existence, but also for continuing in existence. God did not create the world and then abandon His creation. He lovingly keeps and sustains everything, especially us, in existence. He watches over us with loving care and protection.

All of creation glorifies God. Everything from the tiniest atom to the largest beautiful mountains and oceans is a tribute to God's creation. How blessed we are!

God the Father, Power Infinite, have mercy on us.

Across

3 to make something out of nothing (6)

5 All three Persons of the Blessed Trinity share one ___ nature. (6)

6 We attribute the work of salvation to God the ___. (3)

7 objects that are not living beings (9)

10 Three Persons in one God (7)

11 gives the ability to choose (4,4)

12 gives the ability to think (9)

13 any being created by God (8)

Down

1 We attribute the work of sanctification to God the ___. (4,6)

2 only man is this type of being (8)

4 God keeps everything in ___. (9)

8 workers and companions of man (7)

9 God watches over us with ___ care. (6)

11 We attribute the work of creation to God the ___. (6)

Today we will learn about a very popular and fascinating topic: angels. The word "angel" means one who is sent or messenger. Who are angels? Angels are persons like us. They have an intellect and a free will. Unlike man, though, angels are pure, created spirits. They have no bodies, so they do not depend on matter, like food and water, for their existence or activity. We often see angels pictured with bodies. That is because when angels have appeared to people, they have taken the form of a human body so they could be seen.

There are other ways angels and humans are different. Angels have very high intelligence, far higher than any human being. Human beings must read, study, and experience life to learn. Angels do not need to study to acquire their vast knowledge the way we do. Angels also have great power. They can move instantly from place to place just by thinking about it. The good angels are very holy and do not commit sin.

How do we know that angels exist? The main reason we believe in angels is because they are so often mentioned in the Bible. The Bible tells us that there are many more angels than there are people. In the Bible, the Apostle Paul tells us, "…you are come to Mount Zion and to the city of the living God, the Heavenly Jerusalem, and to the company of many thousands of angels" (Hebrews 12:22).

We frequently read about angels in Sacred Scripture. From the very first book of the Bible, Genesis, we can read about angels. We read about God sending an angel to help people. In Exodus, we read about the angel God sent with Moses and his people as they traveled. God sent the angel Raphael to help Tobias to find a wife and to find medicine to help his blind father. In the New Testament, we read about the Angel Gabriel who appeared to Mary, the angel who appeared in a dream to Joseph, the angels at the birth of Jesus, and the angel who was in the Garden of Gethsemane with Jesus.

Do angels have names? Yes. The inspired writers of the Bible have revealed three important angels. Michael is the angel who defeated the devil in the Book of Apocalypse or Revelation (12:7-9). Gabriel was the angel who announced to Mary that she was to be the Mother of God (Luke 1:11-20, 26-38). Raphael was the angel who helped Tobias: "I am the angel Raphael, one of the seven angels who stand before the Lord" (Tobias 12:15).

There are nine choirs or levels of heavenly beings: seraphim, cherubim, virtues, powers, principalities, dominations, thrones, archangels, and angels. Each of these levels has a special status and special powers. They are all united in praising and worshiping God.

St. Michael, defender of the people of God, pray for us.

St. Michael, who drove Lucifer and his rebel crew from Heaven, pray for us.

St. Gabriel, who foretold to Zachary the birth and ministry of St. John the Baptist, pray for us.

St. Gabriel, who announced to Blessed Mary the Incarnation of the Divine Word, pray for us.

St. Raphael, who led Tobias safely through his journey to his home again, pray for us.

St. Raphael, who restored sight to Tobias the elder, pray for us.

All you holy Angels, who stand around the high and lofty throne of God, pray for us.

Matching

_____ 1. "Angel"	1. Annunciation
_____ 2. Pure spirits	2. Fought bad angels
_____ 3. Proof of angels' existence	3. Moses with angel
_____ 4. Raphael helped _____.	4. Have intellect & free will
_____ 5. High intelligence	5. Tobias
_____ 6. Exodus	6. Sacred Scripture
_____ 7. Angels	7. Means messenger
_____ 8. Gabriel	8. Quality of angelic spirits
_____ 9. Choirs of angels	9. Angels
_____ 10. Michael	10. Nine

In our last lesson, we learned about angels in general. Today we will learn that there are good angels and bad angels. We know that when God created angels, He gave them a free will. In man, our free will enables us to either love God by doing His will, or to commit sin by going against what He wills.

Angels, however, were created with very high intelligence, much higher than man's intelligence. Angels were not given the chance to sin again and again, as we so often do. Since angels have no bodies, they do not have as many "inclinations" toward sin as we do. Nor do angels have a weakened nature as we do. In fact, with their high intelligence, they were able to see and understand the consequences of sin much more clearly than we can.

When the angels were created, they could not behold the face of God until they passed a test. Sadly, some of them did not pass the test. We know that St. Michael the Archangel led the good angels, and Lucifer led the bad angels. The angels led by Lucifer committed a sin of pride and disobedience. They did not want to serve God. They turned away from God in revolt. In effect, they chose not to stay in Heaven, and chose Hell. Today, the bad angels are in Hell, and will spend all eternity there.

The angels who remained faithful to God entered into the Beatific Vision where they behold God face to face. They spend eternity loving, praising, and adoring the God Who created them. At the same time, they have a very big job to do. They are God's special messengers who serve as our guardian angels.

The bad angels, or devils, try constantly to tempt us to sin. They know our special weaknesses and they use that information to lure us into sin, to tempt us to sin.

We must remember that, with God's grace, we can resist temptations. The chief way we resist temptation is by the reception of the Sacraments of Penance and the Holy Eucharist, and by prayer. Whenever we are tempted to sin, we should pray for God's grace to help us. We should pray especially to our Guardian Angel to protect us from sin.

What is a guardian angel? God knows our weak human nature and our need for help throughout our lives. The moment we come into existence, God sends each of us our own guardian angel who will always be with us. The guardian angels enlighten our minds when we are in darkness. They also guard and protect us from danger. They are constantly helping us. We should remember our guardian angels in prayer each day. Each day we should pray to our guardian angel and thank him for his help.

Here is the Guardian Angel Prayer:

Angel of God, my guardian dear,

To whom God's love commits me here;

Ever this day be at my side,

To light and guard, to rule and guide.
Amen.

Fill in the Blanks

1. God gave angels a free _____.

2. There are _____angels and _____angels.

3. The angels have very high _____.

4. Angels have no _____.

5. The bad angels constantly try to _____us into sin.

6. The good angels were led by _____.

7. We can resist temptation by reception of the Sacraments of _____and the _____and by _____.

8. The angels in Heaven behold God _____ _____ _____.

9. Everyone has a _____angel.

10. We should say the Guardian Angel Prayer every_____.

Today we want to think about the Creation of Man, the meaning of "Man," and how the sin of Adam and Eve affected mankind.

What is Man? The Church teaches that Man is a creature composed of body and soul, made in the image and likeness of God. God created Man in His image. What does that mean? It means that God created us with an intellect and a free will. Our intellect has the power of reasoning and of knowing what is real and true. Our will is the power of our soul which tends toward a good and away from an evil. The purpose of the will is to choose, to want, to hope, to say yes or no, to love, and to enjoy.

God gave certain gifts of the intellect and of will to Adam and Eve. However, when they sinned these gifts of the intellect and will were lost, not only for them, but for us, their descendants. We would have inherited these gifts if Adam and Eve had not sinned.

One gift which Adam and Eve received which was lost is the gift called *infused knowledge.* Did you ever wonder what it would be like if you did not need to study so hard to learn? In other words, wouldn't it be wonderful if we could know things without having to study? Adam and Eve, our first parents, had this gift of infused knowledge. Do you remember in the Bible that Adam named all the animals, and probably the trees, the fruits, and the minerals? He did not need to take any science classes, but knew the names of the animals automatically. Not only did he know their names, but he knew the nature of the animals and plants, just like we would study in a biology textbook.

Adam and Eve also enjoyed the gift of *freedom from unruly desires of the will.* In other words, *their reason had control over their emotions.* We, on the other hand, have trouble with our emotions. For instance, we know with our intellect that we should control how much chocolate we eat, but our wills are weak, we crave sweets, and we enjoy eating too much! This is because we have darkened intellects and weakened wills. We must constantly beg God's grace for help to overcome our weaknesses of the flesh, of the mind, and of the will. The seven capital sins of anger, envy, pride, covetousness, lust, gluttony, and laziness are a result of our emotions and passions not being controlled by our reason. Adam and Eve had no such unruly desires before they sinned.

Adam and Eve also enjoyed the gift of *bodily health.* That means they did not suffer and experience pain or sickness. They never became tired, or hurt themselves in an accident. They never had the flu or a cold. They never got a stomachache from eating too much spicy food. In addition, their bodies would never die. All this changed, of course, after they committed Original Sin.

Above all the gifts God gave to Adam and Eve, the highest gift they received was *Sanctifying Grace.* Sanctifying Grace made them children of God and gave them a right to Heaven as children inherit what their parents give them. Adam and Eve lost Sanctifying Grace when they sinned. When we are born with Original Sin, it means we are born without Sanctifying Grace. We are not born as children of God; we are not born with a child's right to Heaven.

God, in His mercy and goodness, has allowed us to gain back one of these special gifts: Sanctifying Grace. We must be baptized, however, in order to receive Sanctifying Grace. God has allowed us to increase Sanctifying Grace in our souls whenever we receive one of the Sacraments worthily.

Our souls, consisting of our intellect and will, will never die. Our souls will live forever. We know, of course, that our bodies must die someday. However, at the end of time, our bodies will be reunited with our souls, and will live forever as God intended. Our resurrected bodies, reunited with our souls, will be in a *glorified state*. What does that mean? We know what this means because Jesus rose from the dead with a glorified body, and walked the earth among His Apostles and disciples for forty days!

Blessed glorified bodies will have:

· **Impassibility**, which means it will no longer be subject to pain or sickness;

· **Brightness**, which means our bodies will shine like the sun;

· **Agility**, which means the body will be able to move easily and quickly; and

· **Subtlety**, which means the body will be completely obedient to the soul, completely obedient to our intellect and will.

Even though we have lost the gifts given to Adam and Eve before their sin, we are able to obtain Sanctifying Grace in Baptism, and we can look forward to receiving the other special gifts with our glorified bodies at the end of time. How blessed we will be to be able to live with God like that for all eternity!

Through Thy holy Angels, we beseech Thee Lord, hear us.

True [T] or False [F]

_____ 1. Adam and Eve had the gift of infused knowledge.

_____ 2. Adam automatically knew the names of all the animals.

_____ 3. Adam and Eve were free from unruly emotions.

_____ 4. We did not inherit the gift of reason and free will.

_____ 5. Adam and Eve enjoyed bodily immortality before they sinned.

_____ 6. The highest gift Adam and Eve received was Sanctifying Grace.

_____ 7. Man is composed of body and soul.

_____ 8. God created each of us with an intellect and a free will.

_____ 9. Love is an act of the will.

_____ 10. We will have glorified bodies as soon as we die.

In our last lesson, we studied the meaning of Man. Man is a creature of God, composed of body and soul. We learned that we are all made in the image of God, meaning that we have an intellect by which we can reason, and a will, by which we can choose. We also learned that God gave our first parents, Adam and Eve, special gifts. These were gifts for both their bodies and their souls.

The chief gift given to Adam and Eve was Sanctifying Grace. Sanctifying Grace made them children of God and gave them the right to Heaven. Other gifts bestowed on them by God were perfect happiness in the Garden of Paradise, great knowledge or infused knowledge, control of their passions by their reason, and freedom from suffering and death.

The Fall of Man happened when Adam and Eve disobeyed God and ate of the forbidden fruit of the tree of knowledge of good and evil. Because of this sin, Adam and Eve lost Sanctifying Grace, thus losing their right to Heaven. They also lost their special gifts. They were even driven from the Garden of Paradise.

Imagine for a moment that Adam and Eve had not sinned, had not disobeyed God. They would have continued to enjoy complete happiness with God in the Garden of Paradise. They would have kept their gifts of immortality, infused knowledge, and freedom from unruly or uncontrolled emotions and passions. Amazingly, because Adam and Eve are our first parents, we, too, would be enjoying the same gifts right now. We would never experience pain or disappointment; we would be living in peace and harmony with everyone, and we would never get sick or die.

Something that took an instant to happen changed this earthly world until the end of time. We remember the story well. God loved Adam and Eve so much, He wanted them to prove their love for Him. He gave them an opportunity to freely choose Him. Among all the trees in the Garden of Paradise, God forbade them to eat of only one tree: the tree of the knowledge of good and evil. The choice they made—of following their own wills rather than the will of their Creator— caused an immediate and permanent change in mankind. We call this sin Original Sin.

Because of Adam's sin, we are born without the gifts given to Adam, which we should have inherited. Because of Adam's sin, we now inherit Original Sin, which means we are born without Sanctifying Grace.

Such is the power of our free wills that we can choose sin, we can choose between good and evil! Because we are human like Adam and Eve, we, too, have the same power of choosing between what is good and what is evil. God's will is always what is good; our will—when it is not in agreement with God's will—is bad. The consequence of Adam and Eve's disobedience is that we all inherit Original Sin. We have inherited their fallen nature. Adam and Eve lost the grace needed for Heaven for themselves and for all of us.

The Church's teaching on Original Sin was challenged in the late fourth century. An Irish monk named Pelagius refused to believe what the Church had been teaching for four hundred years. Instead, Pelagius taught that Adam would have died even if he had not sinned. Pelagius was denying the gift of bodily immortality, which was a gift given to Adam and Eve. Pope Innocent I condemned Pelagius as a heretic. The Catholic bishops at the Council of Carthage met and confirmed the Church's teaching on Original Sin. The Council declared that Adam was indeed the first man and had been created to live forever.

When he sinned, Adam lost his right to Heaven and his punishment was bodily death. The Council also declared that Adam's sin was passed on to the whole human race. The death of the body of each of us is the punishment for Adam's sin.

Adam's sin has directly affected us in the following ways:

· The loss of the gift of Sanctifying Grace;

· Suffering and bodily death;

· Inheritance of Original Sin; and

· The loss of infused knowledge

Our first parents received wonderful gifts given to them by God. First, they were given *natural* gifts, the gift of the ability to reason, to think; that is, the gift of an intellect. Second, they were given the gift of the ability to choose, the gift of a free will.

Third, Adam and Eve were given the gift of natural immortality. This means that they would live forever, their bodies would not die. However, when Adam and Eve sinned, God took away the gift of natural immortality for their bodies. Their souls, being spirits, would never die. However, our bodies must die, and it is our resurrected glorified bodies which will live forever.

Fourth, Adam and Eve were given *supernatural* gifts. These were the gifts of Sanctifying Grace, the virtues of faith, hope, and charity, and a right to Heaven. These supernatural gifts were lost when they sinned, and we inherited that loss. Through Baptism, however, these supernatural gifts are given back to us.

Holy Trinity, One God, have mercy on us.

Across

3 This heretic taught that Adam would have died even if he had not sinned. (8)

5 the gift of the ability to think and reason (9)

6 God __ Adam and Eve very much. (5)

8 Because of their sin, we inherit __ __. (8,3)

10 Adam and Eve ate of the __ fruit (9)

11 If Adam and Eve had not sinned, we would never __. (3)

13 Adam's sin was a sin of __. (12)

15 chief gift given to Adam and Eve (11,5)

17 Through Baptism, the __ gifts are given back to us. (12)

Down

1 This council upheld the Church's teaching on Original Sin. (8)

2 We have __ our First Parents' fallen nature. (9)

4 God forbade them to eat of the tree of __ of good and evil. (9)

5 They had gift of __ knowledge. (7)

7 They had __ from suffering and death. (7)

9 Our resurrected __ bodies will live forever. (9)

12 In the Garden, Adam and Eve had __ happiness. (7)

14 the gift of the ability to choose (4,4)

16 __ and Eve (4)

27

The world became a dark and dismal place after Adam and Eve sinned. After their fall from grace, they immediately lost many of the gifts God had given them. Their sin cast a long shadow over the world. What had been a bright and beautiful harmonious world filled with lovely flowers, trees, plants, and friendly animals of every kind, became a place where people experience deep pain, sadness, and separation. Everyone would experience bodily death. Even good people who died could not go to Heaven because, after Adam's sin, Heaven's gates were closed by God the Father. However, a tiny light shone through the darkness. That light was God's promise of help by a Redeemer.

We human beings are very needy of everything, and God gives us everything we need. In the Bible, we read, "All good things come from God." Everything God has given us is a free gift, given with love. God has given us our lives and everything we own. That is why no one has a *right* to anything because everything we have and everything we are are gifts from God. Many of our gifts were lost after Adam's sin, but not everything was lost. We still have our intellects, though they are darkened, and we still have our wills, though they are weakened. However, mankind stood in need of help after Adam's Original Sin.

God, Who is all-merciful, did not leave us in our darkened and weakened state because He still loved us. In the very first book of the Bible, we read God's promise to the human race regarding Lucifer, the head of the fallen angels: "I will put enmities between you [Lucifer] and

the woman, and (between) your seed and her seed; she shall crush your head, and you shall lie in wait for her heel" (Genesis 3:15). What does that mean?

The Church teaches that these words of God in the Garden of Paradise were the promise of a Savior or Redeemer for mankind, who would be born of a woman many years in the future. A Redeemer would come to us through a woman. He would undo the sin of Adam and Eve. The "woman" was to be the only human who was preserved from the first moment of her existence from Original Sin, Adam's sin which we inherit. This woman is Mary. We also call her the Second Eve because she lived the way Eve should have lived, being obedient to God. Mary's preservation from Original Sin is called her Immaculate Conception. Mary was conceived and born with Sanctifying Grace. The Angel Gabriel addressed her as "Mary, Full of Grace."

The punishments we inherited from Adam's sin, from Original Sin, are bodily death, suffering, ignorance, and a strong inclination to sin. Mankind needed Someone to change things, to help us resist sin. That is why God sent His Son, Jesus Christ, to save us from our sins and to re-open the gates of Heaven.

Why was Mary conceived and born without Original Sin? Mary was conceived and born without Original Sin because she was to be the Mother of the Son of God, Jesus Christ, the Second Person of the Blessed Trinity. Her soul needed to be immaculate and pure because she was the first "tabernacle" for Jesus Christ. Mary's soul was always turned perfectly toward the will of her divine Son.

The angel Gabriel appeared to Mary when she was a young girl, probably only about fourteen years old. Holy Mary immediately submitted her will to the will of God. At that moment, the Holy Spirit came over her and Jesus began to live. Mary was not only born without Original Sin, she did not commit a single sin during her life because she was not under the influence of a weakened, fallen human nature.

St. Michael, most powerful Prince in the armies of the Lord,
pray for us.

Matching

2	1. World before sin	1.	Mankind's state after the fall
5	2. Adam's fall	2.	Harmonious
1	3. Darkened intellect; weakened will	3.	Mary preserved from Original Sin
10	4. God's Promise	4.	Appeared to Mary
8	5. Mary	5.	Brought darkness to the world
3	6. Immaculate Conception	6.	Leader of the bad angels
9	7. Always loves us	7.	Inherited from Adam
4	8. Angel Gabriel	8.	Second Eve
6	9. Lucifer	9.	God
7	10. Original Sin	10.	A Redeemer

In the lessons for this week, we have been discussing God's creation of our first parents, Adam and Eve. We discussed how God asked Adam and Eve to obey Him by not eating of the fruit of the Tree of Knowledge of Good and Evil. We discussed their disobedience and their Original Sin, and the fact that we have all inherited Original Sin and the consequences of Original Sin.

In the last lesson, we learned about the Blessed Virgin Mary, the Mother of God. She was preserved from Original Sin through the merits of Jesus Christ. We call this privilege her Immaculate Conception.

Mary, according to the *Catechism of the Catholic Church,* "was enriched by God with gifts appropriate to such a role" which was to be the Mother of the Savior (CCC 490). The angel Gabriel at the Annunciation salutes her as "full of grace." The *Catechism* points out that through the centuries, the Church has taught that the Blessed Mother was redeemed from the moment of her conception.

Pope Pius IX proclaimed in 1854: "The most Blessed Virgin Mary was, from the first moment of her conception, by a singular grace and privilege of Almighty God and by virtue of the merits of Jesus Christ, Savior of the human race, preserved immune from all stain of Original Sin" (CCC 491).

The *Catechism* further declares that "By the grace of God, Mary remained free of every personal sin her whole life long" (CCC 493).

When the angel Gabriel announced to her that God wanted her to be the Mother of the Savior, she immediately responded "Let it be done to me according to your word." She immediately gave her consent. In speaking of Mary, St. Irenaeus said, according to the *Catechism*, that Mary "Being obedient, she became the cause of salvation for herself and for the whole human race" (CCC 494).

Fathers of the Church compare the disobedience of Eve with the obedience of Mary. While Eve disbelieved God and bound the human race by sin, Mary trusted God and helped loose the human race by her faith. One of the phrases used by the Fathers of the Church is "Death through Eve, life through Mary" (Ibid.).

Our Lord and the Blessed Mother want the world to know that Mary never had Original Sin. The Blessed Mother appeared to St. Catherine Laboure, in 1830, at a convent in France. The Blessed Mother told Catherine that she wanted a special medal designed in order to give graces to people. Mary appeared to Catherine as she wanted the medal designed. Mary stood with her arms outstretched, and coming from each of her fingers were rays representing graces she wanted to give the people of the world. Around her image were the words: "O Mary conceived without sin, pray for us who have recourse to thee."

One of the most famous appearances of Our Blessed Mother was at Lourdes, France, in 1854, to a young girl named Bernadette. The Blessed Mother appeared to her several times, but did not say who she was. Finally, she told Bernadette: "I am the Immaculate Conception." Since then, there have been many miracles at Lourdes. People attend the shrine at Lourdes and are cured often through the prayers and the miraculous water coming from a spring dug by St. Bernadette at the instruction of the Blessed Mother.

Prayers from Masses for the Immaculate Conception teach us the doctrines and promote love, praise, and devotion. "O God, by foreseen merits of the death of Christ, You shielded Mary from all stain of sin and preserved the Virgin Mother Immaculate at her Conception so that she might be a fitting dwelling place for Your Son. Cleanse us from sin through her intercession so that we also may come to You untainted by sin. Through Jesus Christ, Our Lord. Amen."

Another Mass prayer expresses our love: "Blessed are you, O Virgin Mary, by the Lord the most high God, above all women upon the earth. You are the glory of Jerusalem, you are the joy of Israel, you are the honor of our people. You are all-beautiful, O Mary, and there is in you no stain of Original Sin. Amen."

The soul of the Virgin Mary whom God had chosen from all eternity to be the Mother of God, the Mother in the flesh of the Incarnate Word, was created full of grace and free from Original Sin. Her parents were Joachim and Anne. "God heard the prayers of Joachim and Anne, for Anne conceived the Mother of God without Original Sin. Today, the great mystery which has been announced from all eternity appears in the arms of Anne. Mary, the Maiden of God is prepared to be a dwelling of the King of Eternity.

"The honorable couple Joachim and Anne have given birth to Mary the lamb, who in turn will give birth in a manner beyond understanding to the Lamb of God, Who is to be sacrificed for all mankind."

O Purest of Creatures

O purest of creatures! Sweet Mother, sweet Maid!

The one spotless womb wherein Jesus was laid!

Dark night has come down on us Mother and we

Look out for thy shining, sweet Star of the Sea!

Deep night has come down on this rough spoken world,

And the banners of darkness are boldly unfurled.

And tempest-tossed Church all her eyes are on Thee,

They look to thy shining, sweet Star of the Sea!

The Church does what God had first taught her to do,

He looked over the world to find hearts that were true.

Through the ages He looked, and He found none but thee,

And He loved thy clear shining sweet Star of the Sea.

He gazed on thy soul, it was spotless and fair,

For the empire of sin, it had never been there!

None had ever owned thee, dear Mother, but He,

And He blessed thy clear shining, sweet Star of the Sea.

Father Faber, 1920

Actual sins are sins that we ourselves commit. Because of Original Sin, we have a weakened human nature. We have intellects that are darkened and wills that are weakened. Consequently, we are tempted to break the laws of God.

We have seen how Adam and Eve were sent out of the Garden of Paradise because of their sin of disobedience to the command of God. Adam and Eve did not obey God's command. They ate the forbidden fruit. Adam and Eve were not able to pass on Sanctifying Grace to the future members of the human race. What they did pass on to us was a weakened human nature.

Suppose a child builds a tower out of blocks. The tower is strong because it has a good foundation but another child comes and knocks it down. The tower has lost its wholeness as a tower. The blocks are all over the floor. It was much the same with Adam and Eve who were whole before their fall from Sanctifying Grace, before they "fell apart." After committing Original Sin, they were then subject to all the weaknesses of fallen human nature. We have inherited their weakness. The loss of the gift of Sanctifying Grace from Original Sin makes all of us weak in our resistance to committing Actual Sin.

Actual Sins are those that we ourselves commit. There are two kinds of Actual Sin: mortal sin and venial sin. Mortal sin is a very serious offense against the law of God. It is more deadly than a serious bodily disease. Why? Because a serious disease harms only the body which has *natural* life. But our souls have *supernatural* life. Mortal sin kills the supernatural life of God in the soul. That means we lose God's friendship.

Mortal sin deprives us of Sanctifying Grace and makes us enemies of God. Does that mean God

does not love us anymore? No, absolutely not. God loves us with an everlasting love. Nothing we can ever do can make Him stop loving us. God is all merciful, but we separate ourselves from Him when we choose to commit mortal sin.

Mortal sin takes away the merits of all our good actions. No matter how much good we do, when we are in mortal sin, nothing good that we do has value. Let us look even more closely at mortal sin. When Jesus Christ died on the Cross for our sins, He died for every sin ever committed by every human being from the beginning of the earthly world all the way to the end of time. When we gaze upon a crucifix and see such infinite Love, we should never again want to commit a single sin.

We know that mortal sin is a grievous offense against the law of God. However, three things are necessary to make a sin mortal. First, the sin of thought, word, or action must be seriously wrong. For example, stealing a large amount of money would be serious, or stealing from a poor widow would be serious.

Second, for a sin to be mortal, the sinner must realize the sin is seriously wrong. The sinner must have sufficient reflection, that is, the sinner must have thought about committing the sin. In other words, before actually stealing the money, the person intends to steal. There is sufficient reflection if a man purchases a gun a week before he murders; there is no reflection if a man, in a moment of anger during a fight, picks up a weapon lying nearby and murders someone.

Thirdly, for a sin to be mortal, the sinner must fully <u>consent</u> to commit the sin. If a teenager is running down the street with his gang, and they suddenly turn to damage a car, the teen may not have fully consented. However, he should have run away from the gang.

It is a horrible thing to commit even one mortal sin. God is merciful, however, and if the sinner is sorry and confesses his sin in Sacramental Confession, he will be forgiven and restored to Sanctifying Grace. Once a person realizes he has committed a mortal sin, it is important to go to Confession as soon as possible.

Not all sin is serious. We call less serious offenses against the law of God venial sins. If even one of the conditions for mortal sin is absent, the sin is only <u>venial</u>. We use the word "only" with reservation because all sin offends God. What is venial sin? Venial sin is a less serious offense against the law of God. The life of God remains in our souls, but venial sin darkens our intellects and weakens our wills even more than before. Every time we commit a venial sin, we are making it easier to establish a bad habit, which could later lead to mortal sin.

Holy Mary, Queen of Angels, pray for us.

Fill in the Blanks

1. Adam and Eve were sent out of the Garden of <u>Paradise</u>

2. Adam and Eve gave in to the temptation of <u>disobedience</u>

3. Sins that we ourselves commit are called <u>actual</u> sins.

4. Mortal sin destroys the life of <u>God</u> in our souls.

5. Mortal sin takes away the <u>merits</u> of our good actions.

6. The most awful consequence of mortal sin is that we lose <u>sanctifying grace</u>.

7. The first condition for mortal sin is that the thought, word, or deed must be <u>seriously wrong</u>.

8. The next condition for a sin to be mortal is <u>sufficient reflection</u>

9. The final condition for mortal sin is full <u>consent</u> of the will.

10. If only one condition for mortal sin is absent, the sin is <u>venial</u>.

33

Actual sin is sin that we ourselves commit. In our last lesson, we discussed mortal sin and its consequences. On God's earth, there is nothing more horrible or more frightful than mortal sin. Yet in the world today, there is too much tolerance toward serious sin. We hear things like, "You can do as you wish if it feels right for you." When we look about us, we see many examples of a casual attitude toward serious sin, especially on television, on the radio, in the news, newspapers, and magazines. We know from the Bible and the Church that mortal sin is so offensive to God that there is a special place called Hell for unrepentant sinners.

We might think, "I commit only venial sins. They are not bad." No, they are certainly not as bad as committing mortal sins, but they are bad and offensive to God. Venial sins committed often can become a bad habit which can lead into mortal sin. Moreover, venial sins must be expiated (made up for) either in this life, or in Purgatory. Most of all, because we love God, we certainly do not want to commit even a single venial sin.

What are the ways to avoid committing sin? Our first line of defense against venial sin is to pray every day, and to receive the Sacraments of Penance and the Holy Eucharist frequently. We need grace to be strong against the temptation to sin. Without the help of divine grace, we would not be able to resist sin at all. We should keep in mind that the Holy Spirit dwells within us when we are in the state of grace. That should make us never want to commit sin. The moment we are tempted to sin, we should immediately pray for grace to eliminate that thought before it becomes a sin in our thoughts and words or our actions. Avoiding near occasions of sin, like bad movies or bad companions, will certainly help to keep us out of sin. Finally, playing sports or having hobbies can keep us occupied with healthy thoughts and actions.

The Church teaches that we must avoid *the near occasions of sin*. The near occasions of sin are all persons, places, or things that usually lead us into sin. We should stay away from bad companions, bad movies, bad pictures or video games, bad magazines, malls or any place, like movie theaters, where people may be speaking or acting against a Commandment of God.

Because of the weak human nature we inherited from Adam and Eve, the seven capital sins are often within us. The capital sins are the main reasons *why* we commit other sins. The capital sins are: pride, covetousness or avarice (greed), lust, anger, gluttony, envy, and sloth or laziness. Most people are burdened by at least one of the capital sins. For example, Joe always has trouble getting up in the morning. He puts off what he knows he should do. The particular sin Joe has to resist is sloth, and because every sin has an opposite virtue Joe should try to become more busy for God. Another example is Jennifer, who cannot resist overeating. Whenever she even sees cake or cookies, she will eat even after she is full. Jennifer needs to practice temperance, the opposite of gluttony.

We should keep in mind that temptation itself is not a sin. As long as we resist temptation, far from being a sin, it can become an occasion of grace as we fight the temptation. God will give us that grace, however, only if we ask for it.

Angels of Heaven, pray for me.

True (T) or False (F)

_F_ 1. Venial sins are just as serious as mortal sins.

_T_ 2. Venial sin weakens us.

_T_ 3. Nothing in the world is as bad as mortal sin.

_F_ 4. Mortal sin is the same as Original Sin.

_T_ 5. The best way to avoid any sin is through prayer and the Sacraments.

_F_ 6. An example of a near occasion of sin is a bad movie.

_F_ 7. There are five capital sins.

_T_ 8. Sloth is the same as laziness.

_T_ 9. Every capital sin has an opposite virtue.

_F_ 10. Temptations are always sinful.

Today we will learn about the second and third of the twelve articles of the Apostles' Creed: "I believe in Jesus Christ, His only Son, Our Lord: Who was conceived by the Holy Spirit, born of the Virgin Mary…"

After Adam sinned, God did not abandon mankind. God made a promise to Adam and Eve that He would send a Savior into the world to save mankind, to free mankind from sin, and to reopen the gates of Heaven.

As we have seen, after Adam sinned, the world became a very dark and dismal place. All the gifts God had given to Adam and his wife were lost when they committed the first sin. Then something wonderful happened: God promised to send His Son Who would save the human race from their sins.

At exactly the right moment in time, the Son of God would become man, just like us in all things but sin. If we stop to think about that, we can hardly understand it. Why would God stoop to become a man? The Incarnation—God-become-Man—is a supernatural mystery which we will never fully understand. One thing we do know is that the Incarnation proved God's love for us. We read in the Bible, "For God so loved the world, that He gave His only Son, that whoever believes in Him should not perish but have eternal life" (John 3:16).

The Savior of all men is Jesus Christ. Who is Jesus Christ? He is the Second Person of the Blessed Trinity Who has two natures: human and divine. Although Jesus Christ, like the Father and the Holy Spirit always was and always will be, He was not always Man. He became Man at the time of the Incarnation. By the power of the Holy Spirit, Jesus was conceived in the holy womb of the Blessed Mother Mary. We know the story best by reading it in the Gospel of Luke.

"In the sixth month, the angel Gabriel was sent from God to a city of Galilee named Nazareth, to a virgin betrothed to a man whose name was Joseph, of the house of David; and the virgin's name was Mary. And he came to her and said, 'Hail, full of grace, the Lord is with you!'" (Luke 1:26-28)

The angel's announcement to Mary was the fulfillment of the promise of God to Adam of a Savior. The Incarnation, the Son of God become Man, is the greatest event of human history! The world held its breath waiting for Mary to say, "Behold, I am the handmaid of the Lord; let it be done to me according to your word" (Luke 1: 38).

What does the Incarnation really mean? It means God-become-Man. It means that Adam's sin—which had plagued the human race for centuries—was no longer a death sentence. If Jesus Christ had not become Man to save us from our sins, the gates of Heaven would still be closed. God-become-Man reopened Heaven for us so that it would be possible for us to live with Him forever.

The Holy Family is the model for all families of all times. They give us the best example of the virtues of humility, charity, obedience, and patience. Why *humility*? Because the most important family of all time lived in a small practically unknown town in the Middle East, called Nazareth. Because Jesus, the Son of God, lived the first thirty years of His life hidden as the humble Son of a poor carpenter.

The Holy Family lived in *charity*. Jesus, the Second Person of the Blessed Trinity, is Love itself. We can only barely imagine what it must have been like to live in the same town with the Boy Jesus and the Man Jesus. Before His public ministry, from outward appearances, He seemed to live like any other boy or man of His time. However, Jesus was perfectly holy, perfectly obedient to His parents, and was in perfect union with God the Father and God the Holy Spirit. For those who knew Him, His kindness and charity to those around Him would have so impressed them; they themselves would have been called to a higher standard of charitable living.

The Holy Family lived in *obedience* to the will of God. They lived all the virtues to perfection, and all the Commandments to perfection. Remember that Jesus called us not only to obey the Commandments, but to practice the Beatitudes. The saints became saints because they went beyond the Ten Commandments. They followed the command to "Be you therefore perfect, as also your heavenly Father is perfect."

The Holy Family lived with patience, knowing the kind of pain and suffering which would bring an ending to Jesus' life on earth. They knew that the will of God the Father would be fulfilled perfectly by His Son Jesus dying on the Cross as the Redeemer of mankind.

Jesus, Mary and Joseph should be our perfect models of humility, charity, obedience, and patience.

Holy Family, pray for us.

38

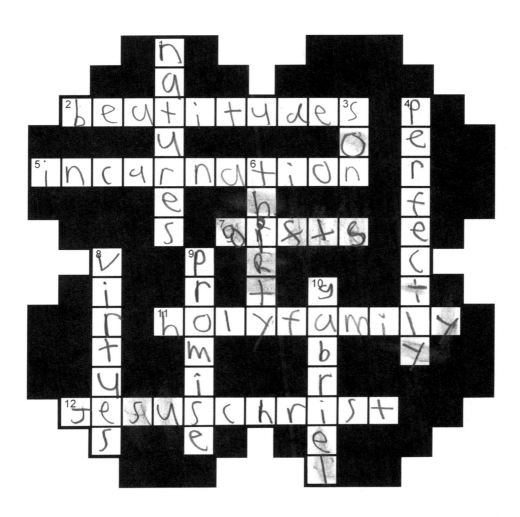

Across

2 Jesus called us to practice the __. (10)

5 the mystery of God being made man (11)

7 On account of their sin, Adam and Eve lost all their __. (5)

11 The __ __ is the model for all families of all times. (4,6)

12 __ __ is the Savior of all men. (5,6)

Down

1 The Second Person of the Blessed Trinity has two __. (7)

3 "For God so loved the world that He gave His only __." (3)

4 Jesus was __ holy and obedient to His parents. (9)

6 Jesus lived the first __ years of His life hidden as the humble Son of a poor carpenter. (6)

8 The Holy Family lived all the __ to perfection. (7)

9 God made a __ to Adam and Eve that He would send a Savior. (7)

10 The Angel __ announced to the Virgin Mary that she was to be the mother of God. (7)

The Incarnation means that the Son of God became man. The chief teaching of the Catholic Church about Jesus Christ is that He is the Son of God become man. He is God because He has the same divine nature as God the Father. He is man because He is the Son of the Blessed Virgin Mary and has a soul and a body like ours.

Jesus is only one Person, the Second Person of the Blessed Trinity. However, He has two natures: the nature of God and the nature of man. The Son of God was not always man, but He became man at the Incarnation. By the Incarnation is meant that the Son of God, keeping His divine nature, took to Himself a human nature, that is, a body and a soul like ours.

The Son of God became man when He was conceived and made man by the power of the Holy Spirit in the womb of the Blessed Virgin Mary. The angel Gabriel explained this when he said to Mary: "The Holy Spirit shall come upon thee, and the power of the most High shall overshadow thee. And therefore the Holy [One] which shall be born of thee shall be called the Son of God (Luke 1:35)."

Jesus had no human father, but St. Joseph was the spouse of the Blessed Virgin Mary, and the guardian or foster father of Jesus Christ. Jesus was born of the Blessed Virgin Mary in Bethlehem about two-thousand years ago. Jesus was perfectly obedient to Mary and Joseph, as the Bible says: "He was subject to them" (Luke 2:51).

In the words of the Creed, we state our belief: "For us men and for our salvation, He came down from Heaven; by the power of the Holy Spirit, He became incarnate of the Virgin Mary, and was made man."

The Son of God became man in order to save us, to take away our sins. He also became man to show us how much He loves us.

A third reason He became man is to show us how to be holy. Jesus is our model to live out the Beatitudes, which He gave us on the Sermon on the Mount. Jesus was showing us that we can do more than obey the Ten Commandments. We can be meek and humble of heart. We can love one another as He loved us.

A fourth reason the Son of God became man was to make us sharers in His divine nature through Sanctifying Grace and through receiving Him in the Sacrament of the Holy Eucharist.

As the *Catechism of the Catholic Church* teaches: He became truly man while remaining truly God. Jesus Christ is true God and true man (CCC 464).

"O Little Child, lying in a manger, by means of a star, heaven has called and led to You the three kings. They were astounded to behold not scepters and thrones but extreme poverty in a stable. They found You wrapped in swaddling clothes not royal colors. And yet the splendor of Your Divinity shone forth, O Lord!

"The earth offers a cave to the Incarnate God. Angels sing His glory along with the shepherds from the fields. Behold the image of God the Father has come down in the form of a servant. He has come down to us from a mother all-pure, and yet he has remained unchanged.

"He has remained true God as He was before, and has taken on Himself what He had not been, becoming Man out of His love for man.

"O Christ Our God, your kingdom is eternal. You have become incarnate of the Holy Spirit, being made Man through the ever-virgin Mary. Your coming, O Christ, has shed upon us a great light, O You Light of Light and Radiance of God the Father!

"You have illumined the whole creation! Everything that breathes sings to You a hymn of praise. You are the Image of God the Father's glory, You are eternal God, Who have existed before all the ages!

"O Jesus, what shall we offer You for Your coming on earth as a Man for our sake? Every creature that exists owes its existence to You and gives thanks to You. The angels offer hymns of praise, the heavens give a star, the three kings present their gifts, and the shepherds bring their wonder! The earth provides a cave and the desert a manger! As for us human creatures, we offer You a Mother, a most pure and most holy and most immaculate Mother!

"You were born in a cave hidden from the eyes of men, but the heavens revealed You to all by means of a star. You have shone forth from Your Mother, O Christ, Sun of Justice. A star found You in a cave, You Whom nothing can contain! A star led the three kings to adore You. With them, we worship You, O Giver of Life.

"When the Magi, the three kings from the East, learned that the heavenly King was born on earth, they followed the brilliant star. They hastened to Bethlehem and offered Him a variety of gifts of gold, frankincense, and myrrh. They worshipped Him in profound adoration; for in the Infant lying in a manger in a cave, they saw God Who is beyond time.

"Today a great and wonderful event occurs: The Word of God becomes incarnate, and yet is not separated from God the Father. Angels sing hymns of glory together with the shepherds, and we the faithful join our voices to theirs, singing out: Glory to God in the highest, and peace on earth to men of good will.

"When the Lord Jesus was born in Bethlehem, the Magi came from the East. They adored Him as the Incarnate God. They opened their treasures with eagerness and offered Him precious gifts: pure gold to the King of the Universe; frankincense to the God of all; and myrrh to the Immortal as if He were mortal, He Who was to remain three days in the tomb.

"All you nations come! Let us adore Him Who was born to save us all from sin! Glory be to the Father, and to the Son and to the Holy Spirit. Amen."

Adapted prayers from the Eastern Liturgy for Christmas

Today we will discuss the reason why the Second Person of the Blessed Trinity, the Son of God, became Man. The Son of God became Man so that He could suffer and die for us to save us from our sins, to show His love for us, and to open the gates of Heaven for us.

By the Redemption is meant that Jesus Christ, as the Redeemer of the whole human race, offered His sufferings and death to God the Father as a proper and fitting sacrifice in satisfaction for the sins of men. He regained for all of us the right to be children of God and heirs of Heaven.

Today we will tell three small stories. These stories will help us better understand the sin of Adam, the humanity of Jesus Christ, and God's loving and amazing response to us.

Suppose a child strikes a friend. It is certainly wrong to harm another person, especially a friend. Suppose that same child strikes his mother. That is far more serious than striking a friend because of the person sinned *against*. The child owes so much more to his parents than he owes his friend.

Now consider the sin of Adam. It was the most serious kind of sin. Why? Because of the Person sinned *against*. The one sinned against makes a big difference. Adam's sin was direct disobedience against God. Of course, every sin is against God and offends God. Adam's Original Sin, however, would affect every human being who would ever live. Original Sin was so serious that only a *divine* "solution" would be sufficient. The sin against Divinity Itself could be repaired only by a Divine Person. Only a Divine Person, Jesus Christ, obeying the will of His Father, could take away the sin against God.

Let us consider what is meant for God to become man. Suppose someone suggests that I become an ant, a tiny creature whose only function is to find its next meal. That is silly and unthinkable, we might say. A human is far above a tiny ant in intellect and will. Think about this. When God became Man, He was infinitely far above us, much farther from man than a man is from an ant. God is so far above humanity, that there is no comparison possible. Yet the Son of God became a man like us in all things except sin. God loves us so much that He was willing to become a human being, like one of the creatures He created! There is no way to express in human language the magnificent love that God has for us!

Let us suppose there was a cruel judge who one day had to hear the case of a thief who had stolen money, but the thief had done more than steal. He had stolen money from a *poor* family. The thief had taken all the money the poor family had in the world; and the thief was not sorry he had done it! The judge sentenced the thief to death. Suddenly, just before the guards took the thief away, a man in the courtroom stood up and yelled, "Stop! I will pay the price for that man! I will give back to the poor family all the money the thief stole. Then I will take the thief's place, accept his sentence of death, and die for the thief."

"What?" we might say, "That is very unfair and unjust. That man did not commit the crime, so why should he die for the unrepentant thief?" But that is what happened when Jesus Christ died for our sins. We are the sinners, Jesus is the innocent One. What Jesus did for us is even more incredible than what the man did in the story. Jesus Christ is *totally innocent*. Yet He chose to become a man, suffer on the Cross, and die for us on the hill of Calvary (or Golgotha). It was on Good Friday about 2000 years ago that Jesus saved us from our sins and reopened the gates of Heaven for all of us.

Now we can better appreciate our redemption! In the first analogy, we see that the sin of Adam was so great that it could be removed only by *supernatural divine* intervention. In other words, *only God* could take away our sin. In the second analogy, we see that God becoming a man was the greatest act of love that ever could or would be in human history. In our last analogy, we see an incredibly loving God, Who came down from Heaven, became a man, saved us from our sins, and made it possible for us to become holy. We certainly did not *deserve* what God has done for us.

What is the best way to respond to God's incredible love for us? The best way to say Thank You to Jesus for all he has done for us is by being willing to share in His sufferings. How do we do that? We can do that by offering up all our own small daily trials and sufferings, and uniting them to Him out of love and thanks, praise and adoration for what He has done for you and me.

Sweetest Jesus, have mercy on me.

Matching

10	1. Second Person of the Trinity	1.	Christ died for our sins
1	2. Redemption	2.	The place where Christ died
	3. Adam's sin	3.	Gates reopened by Christ's sacrifice
8	4. God	4.	Good Friday
	5. Calvary/Golgotha	5.	By offering up our trials and pains
	6. Heaven	6.	Required divine intervention
4	7. Day Christ died	7.	Sins against our Creator
5	8. How we return our love to God	8.	Far above any human being
7	9. Most serious kind of sin	9.	The will of His Father in Heaven
	10. Jesus Christ perfectly obeyed	10.	Became Man

By the Redemption is meant that Jesus Christ as our Redeemer, offered His sufferings and death to God the Father as a proper and fitting sacrifice in satisfaction for the sins of men. He regained for us all the right to be children of God and heirs of Heaven.

The chief sufferings of Jesus were His bitter agony of soul in the Garden of Gethsemane, His bloody sweat, His cruel scourging, His crowning with thorns, His crucifixion and death on the Cross. This happened on Good Friday, on Golgotha or Calvary, a hill outside of Jerusalem, about two-thousand years ago.

We learn from the sufferings of Jesus how much God loves us to be willing to suffer so for us! We also learn how evil sin must be for such suffering to be required to save us from our sins.

Almost a hundred years ago, a group of priests who were teaching children about the Redemption explained this mystery as follows.

The mystery of the Redemption is the mystery of Jesus Christ dying on the Cross for the salvation of all men. This is a mystery because we cannot understand how God could become a man, and then become a victim for us to atone for our sins. He literally paid a ransom for us. Jesus freed us from the slavery to which sin had reduced mankind. The price He paid for our ransom is His own precious blood.

Because sin is an infinite offense against God, only God could offer infinite satisfaction. Jesus suffered for us as a man, yet as God, His sufferings were of infinite value. By His passion and death, Jesus made superabundant satisfaction for our sins. He proved His love for us, and He merited so many graces for us, even our own sufferings are sanctified.

Jesus, the Son of God, was willing to suffer so much for us to teach us the horror of sin, to inspire us to have a horror for sin, and to encourage us, by His example, to suffer to expiate our own sins and the sins of others. We know that we must suffer and do good works ourselves because Jesus taught us: If any man will come after Me, let him deny himself, and take up his cross daily, and follow Me.

As Jesus carried His Cross, He was exhausted. He had been beaten by the soldiers to such an extent, He has lost a great amount of blood. The soldiers had forced a crown of thorns on His head, which also caused substantial bleeding. By the time He carried His Cross, Jesus was already severely wounded. He fell several times under the weight of the Cross.

One time when He fell, Veronica, a woman in the crowd, ran up to Him and wiped His face. St. Francis of Assisi wrote the following: "Veronica, impelled by devotion and compassion, presents her veil to Jesus to wipe His disfigured face. Jesus imprints on it His holy countenance, a great reward for so small a service. What return do you make to your Savior for His great and manifold benefits? Most merciful Jesus! What return shall I make for all the benefits Thou has bestowed upon me? Behold, I offer to Thee my heart; imprint on it Thy sacred image, never to be erased by sin."

Dear God, I wonder, when You climbed
The hill of Calvary—
Where were the children that You used
To take upon Your knee?
Where were they? In among the crowd?
And did they, too, not care
What happened to You, God, dear God,
But only came to stare?
Where were the children that You loved?
They do not seem to be
Around as You begin to climb
The hill of Calvary!
O God, I wish that I had been
A child that day! I might
Have done some little thing for You,
To make the cross more light!
I might have given You a glass
Of water on the way—
I might have whispered, as You passed,
"I love You so today!"
I might have done this—and yet—O
Perhaps I would have hid
Among the people and done just
What other children did.

Perhaps, by Mary Dixon Thayer

Today we continue to study The Apostles' Creed. The next article reads: "He descended into hell. On the third day, He rose again from the dead." After Jesus died, His Body was taken down from the Cross and placed into a tomb. For three days, mankind awaited the greatest event which would ever occur in human history: the glorious Resurrection from the dead of Our Lord and Savior Jesus Christ.

The Church teaches that when Jesus Christ died on the Cross, His soul separated from His body. Then His soul descended to a place the Church calls the Limbo of the Fathers. The word "hell" in this article of the Creed does not mean the place of the damned, but rather the place of the dead. That was where the souls of the good and just people were awaiting their redemption. The gates of Heaven had been closed after Adam's sin. The good and just souls had not yet received their Heavenly reward for living good lives. However, when Jesus died on the Cross, God the Father re-opened the gates of Heaven. Many good and just souls were waiting for that to happen. Certainly the souls of Joseph, the foster-father of Jesus, as well as Abraham and Moses and many others were waiting for Heaven to reopen.

It is on Easter Sunday that we celebrate the feast of the Resurrection of Our Lord and Savior Jesus Christ. What is the Resurrection? The Resurrection is not just a story. The Resurrection is

an actual historical event. That means it *really happened.* The Resurrection is when the human body and the soul of Jesus Christ, which had been separated by His death on the Cross, were reunited. We must keep in mind that death is a punishment for Original Sin. Because Jesus was sinless, He did not need to die like the rest of the human race. But He *chose* to suffer and die out of love for the will of His Father and out of love for each one of us. Jesus Christ, the Son of God, Who was born in Bethlehem, lived for thirty-three years preaching and teaching, and then died on Good Friday on the Cross. Then Jesus rose from the dead on Easter Sunday morning.

Why did Jesus Christ rise from the dead? The Resurrection of Jesus Christ was proof that He had defeated sin, the original cause or reason for our bodily death. How magnificent! We were freed from possible eternal death and now could enter the gates of Heaven and receive eternal life!

Jesus rose from the dead to prove that He is the Son of God. During His visible stay on earth, Jesus performed many miracles to prove that He is the Son of God. He restored sight to the blind,

He cured the paralyzed so they were able to walk. He healed the deaf so they were able to hear. He calmed storms with a single command, and fed thousands of people by multiplying bread and fish. He changed water into wine at the wedding feast of Cana. He raised the dead to life, such as Lazarus, and the young son of the widow, and the young daughter of Jairus. His own Resurrection was the greatest miracle of all, which proved to thousands of people at that time that Jesus Christ is God. Billions of people have now accepted the Risen Jesus Christ as Our Lord and Savior, as the Son of God.

Finally, Jesus Christ's Resurrection from the dead is a promise to all of us of our own resurrection from the dead on the Last Day. When we die, our souls will separate from our bodies, but only for a time. At the end of time, each person who lived on earth will have his soul and body reunited. We will once again walk and talk and see and hear. Glorified means our bodies will be immortal and never die again. They will be beautiful and never will experience pain again. Best of all, we will live happily with God forever in a magnificent eternity.

Jesus, Redeemer of the world, have mercy on me.

Fill in the Blanks

1. On the __third__ day, Jesus rose again from the dead.

2. When Jesus died on the Cross, His __body__ separated from His __soul__.

3. The word "hell" in the Apostles' Creed means __place__ of the __dead__.

4. Heaven was __closd__ after Adam's sin.

5. We celebrate the Resurrection on __easter__ Sunday.

6. The Resurrection of Christ is an __historical__ event, which means it really happened.

7. At the Resurrection of Christ, His __soul__ and __body__ were reunited.

8. The Resurrection proved that Jesus Christ is __GOD__.

9. The Resurrection is a promise of our own __resurrection__ from the dead.

10. If we do the will of God on earth, we will be __happy__ with Him in Heaven.

Today we will discuss the next article of the Apostles' Creed: "He ascended into Heaven, and is seated at the right hand of God, the Father Almighty. From thence He shall come to judge the living and the dead." What is the Ascension of Jesus Christ into Heaven? Forty days after His Resurrection from the dead, Jesus rose or ascended into Heaven. Jesus had just finished telling His disciples that they would receive power from the Holy Spirit. Here is what St. Luke wrote about the Ascension:

"And when He had said this, as they were looking on, He was lifted up, and a cloud took Him out of their sight. And while they were gazing into Heaven as He went, behold, two men stood by them in white robes and said, 'Men of Galilee, why do you stand looking into Heaven? This Jesus, Who was taken up from you into Heaven, will come in the same way as you saw Him go into Heaven'" (Acts 1:9-11). Many people watched Jesus rise high above the clouds and disappear into Heaven.

The next sentence in the Creed is: "(He) is seated at the right hand of God, the Father Almighty." What does that mean? This means that since Our Lord Jesus Christ is God, He is equal to the Father, and sits beside Him. As Man, Our Lord Jesus Christ shares in the glory of God the Father above all the saints who lived in the world. Sitting at the right hand of the Father means also that Our Lord Jesus Christ has supreme authority as King over all creatures of the earth.

Jesus will "come again to judge the living and the dead." What does that mean? The Church teaches that there are two judgments for each one of us: the Particular Judgment and the General Judgment. What is the Particular Judgment? The Particular Judgment means that the moment each person dies, he or she will be judged immediately by Jesus Christ. God will judge each person the moment his or her soul separates from his body. Those who have died in the state of grace, but in need of purification, will be sent to Purgatory to be made pure. Souls that are perfectly pure, such as martyrs, go directly to Heaven. Those who die with mortal sin on their souls are sent to eternal punishment in Hell.

The General Judgment at the end of time, at the end of this earthly world, will be for the entire human race at the same time. The General Judgment will be for every human being who ever lived. Why, we might ask, must there be another Judgment? The General Judgment also is called the "social judgment," because each person will see how his own sins and good acts have influenced others.

Every sin hurts the world. At the General Judgment, each of us will have a clear understanding of the harm our sins have done. At the same time, we will see how our acts of goodness and sacrifices have benefited others. The entire twenty-fifth chapter of the Gospel of Matthew describes the end times. The stories of the five foolish virgins, the master (Jesus) who returns from a journey and wants an account of what his servants have done, and the story of the sheep and the goats are all parables or stories to explain how the Final or Last Judgment will be an account of our life-long acts. All of those parables illustrate the certainty of a Final Judgment on the whole human race. At Mass, when we say, "Christ has died, Christ is risen, Christ will come again," we are praying in hope for the day when Christ will come, give the Final Judgment, and take us to be with Him forever.

Jesus, Living Bread from Heaven, have mercy on us.

True (T) or False (F)

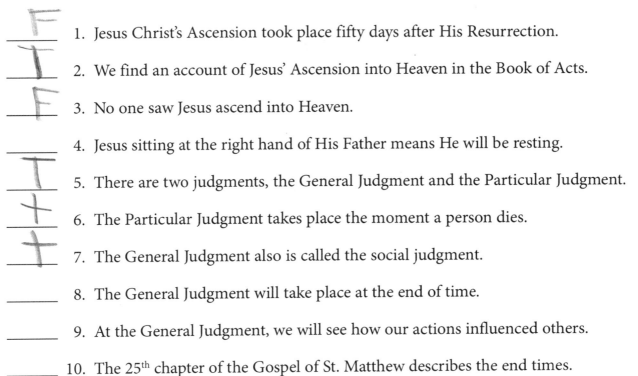

_____ 1. Jesus Christ's Ascension took place fifty days after His Resurrection.

_____ 2. We find an account of Jesus' Ascension into Heaven in the Book of Acts.

_____ 3. No one saw Jesus ascend into Heaven.

_____ 4. Jesus sitting at the right hand of His Father means He will be resting.

_____ 5. There are two judgments, the General Judgment and the Particular Judgment.

_____ 6. The Particular Judgment takes place the moment a person dies.

_____ 7. The General Judgment also is called the social judgment.

_____ 8. The General Judgment will take place at the end of time.

_____ 9. At the General Judgment, we will see how our actions influenced others.

_____ 10. The 25th chapter of the Gospel of St. Matthew describes the end times.

Today we will learn about two topics that go together: the Holy Spirit and Divine Grace. Why do they go together? They go together because the Holy Spirit comes to live in our souls the moment we are baptized. The Holy Spirit gives us Divine Grace when we are baptized. The Holy Spirit is the life of our soul.

We must use careful language when we are speaking about God. Who is the Holy Spirit? The Holy Spirit is God, the Third Person of the Blessed Trinity.

We say that the Holy Spirit *proceeds* from the Father and the Son. What does that mean? The Father and the Son love each other so much that their love for each other *is* the Third Person. The Holy Spirit *is* the love between the Father and the Son, yet all three Persons are equal. There is much that we do not understand about the Holy Trinity. That is why we say that it is a "strict" mystery. A strict mystery is something we did not know at all before it was revealed and, even after it has been revealed, we cannot fully understand it. We accept it with our faith because it was revealed to us by Jesus Christ.

The Holy Spirit is our supernatural life. What does that mean? It means that when we are baptized, the Holy Spirit comes to dwell in our souls and, as long as we are in the state of grace, He will never leave us. The Church allows us to say that the "Holy Spirit is the soul of our soul."

The Holy Spirit is also the life of the Church. Just as the Holy Spirit lives in all souls in the state of grace, so the Holy Spirit dwells in the Church. When members of the Church receive the Sacraments, they receive Sanctifying Grace from the Holy Spirit through the Church.

What is grace? Grace is a *supernatural gift* of God. We remember that before we were baptized, we had only *natural* life. Then when we were baptized, grace flowed into our souls. We then had *supernatural* life in our souls. That supernatural life is what we *must have* in our souls when we die. In fact, at the moment of our death, if we are not found with the supernatural life of grace in our souls, we cannot enter Heaven. It is simply impossible to bring only our natural selves into a place where our supernatural powers are necessary to see the things of God.

Divine Grace gives us the powers that enable us to live in Heaven. What are those powers? They are the powers of *knowing* and *loving*. We cannot have true, pure, and complete knowledge and love in our natural life. Our natural life gives us intellect and will, but intellect and will do not allow us to share in the life of God Himself. Only divine, supernatural grace allows us to know, understand, and love the things of God and of Heaven.

What are some of the other effects of Sanctifying Grace? Divine Grace makes us holy and pleasing to God, and makes us His adopted children. Divine Grace also makes us temples of the Holy Spirit. What does that mean? It means that the Holy Spirit actually *dwells* in our souls. That is the best reason why we should lead holy lives.

We might say that divine grace is the greatest gift anyone can ever receive. Yes, indeed! We can thank our loving God for the greatest gift we could ever receive.

Holy Spirit, Spirit of wisdom and understanding, have mercy on us.

Multiple Choice

_b_   1. When we are baptized, the Holy Spirit comes to live in our
        a) hearts.   b) souls.   c) bodies.

_c_   2. The Holy Spirit is the _____ Person of the Blessed Trinity.
        a) First
        b) Second
        c) Third

_a_   3. The Holy Spirit is the
        a) the life of the soul.
        b) the life of the body.
        c) the life of the free will.

_c_   4. The Holy Spirit proceeds from
        a) the Father.
        b) the Son.
        c) the Father and the Son.

_b_   5. The Holy Spirit comes to live in our souls
        a) when we are born.
        b) when we are baptized.
        c) when we die.

_b_   6. In this lesson, Grace is
        a) what we say before we eat.
        b) a supernatural gift of God.
        c) a girl's name.

_b_   7. Before we are baptized, we are living
        a) a supernatural life.
        b) a natural life.
        c) a prosperous life.

_____   8. In order for us to reach Heaven, we must
        a) have the supernatural life of grace in our souls when we die.
        b) not exercise our free will.
        c) say our prayers at least once a week.

_d_   9. Divine grace makes us
        a) holy and pleasing to God.   b) God's adopted children.
        c) temples of the Holy Spirit.   d) a, b and c.

_____   10. Intellect and will are
        a) good to have.
        b) natural powers of the soul.
        c) supernatural powers of the soul.

In the last lesson, we learned about Sanctifying Grace which we receive at Baptism and through the other Sacraments. Today we will talk about another kind of grace called Actual Grace. What is Actual Grace? Actual Grace is a supernatural help from God. Actual Grace is like a temporary burst of strength from God. We pray for Actual Graces that are light for our minds and strength for our wills to help us through difficult situations and temptations. Actual graces are transient, which means they leave after they have helped us. Actual graces are sent to us from God when we ask for them, usually in prayer.

Katie is going to take a test. She has studied long and hard for her test and feels that she is ready. However, she is very nervous about it because it is important for her final grade. Just before she takes the test, she prays and asks God for light for her mind to help her remember what she has learned. She has prayed for actual grace to help her through this difficult test. She then remembers all she has learned and is able to answer the test questions. Actual Grace helped Katie.

Nicholas has been wanting a new skateboard. He doesn't have enough money saved to buy it right now. One day at the mall, he sees a skateboard in a store display. It is red, his favorite color. He sees that the salesman is busy with a customer. It would be very easy to take the skateboard without being noticed, but something in his heart nags at him. It is his conscience telling him that it is wrong to steal. He wants to ignore his conscience. Then he remembers something his father told him about grace. He quickly says a prayer to his guardian angel to help him resist the temptation to steal. Nicholas decides to obey the Commandment of God, and walks away full of joy and peace because he resisted the temptation. Actual Grace helped Nicholas.

Actual graces help us on our way to Heaven. They are invaluable spiritual aids but they require our cooperation. What does that mean? It means that we must pray and ask for God's help. God wants us to ask Him for help. The Blessed Mother told St. Catherine Labouré that there are many graces available, but people do not ask for them. God has given each one of us a free will to choose to do good and to ask for God's help.

In our examples above, Katie freely chose to pray for God's help. Nicholas could have ignored his conscience, which was shaped by his love for God. Both Katie and Nicholas have grown closer to God because they chose to do good. That made them more pleasing to God because they cooperated with graces by exercising their wills for God.

What are the ways of obtaining actual graces? An important way to obtain Actual Grace is to pray for God's help when we are in a particular difficult situation. When we read the lives of the saints, we can see that they prayed continually, every day in fact, for help in the daily trials of each day. Children often need help in their studies, in being obedient in doing work or in doing their chores for their parents, in keeping their room clean, and in keeping respect for other members of the family. Children should begin the habit of praying every time a difficult situation arises.

Whatever we do, even the smallest task, ought to be done in the best way possible out of love for God. St. Thérèse of Lisieux is often called the saint of the "Little Way." That means she became holy by offering the smallest tasks to God. Whether she was sweeping the floor, washing the windows, or doing the dishes, she was offering her task with a heart filled with love for God. St. Thérèse is our model for living a holy life by offering our daily tasks to God.

St. Thérèse wrote in her autobiography: "How good God is! How well He fits our trials to our strengths!"

O Divine Infant Jesus, adored by the shepherds, have mercy on us.

Matching

_6_	1. Actual grace	1.	Actual Grace for the mind
_1_	2. Light	2.	Should be done out of love for God
_4_	3. Strength	3.	Fits our trials to our strengths
_10_	4. St. Thérèse	4.	Actual Grace for the will
_3_	5. God	5.	Wrong
_9_	6. Prayer	6.	Temporary supernatural help
_2_	7. Ordinary actions	7.	Can be overcome by prayer
_5_	8. Stealing	8.	Permanent supernatural help
_7_	9. Temptations	9.	Important way to obtain Actual Grace
_8_	10. Sanctifying Grace	10.	"Little Way"

We have seen that the *supernatural* life is far above our *natural* life. The moment we are baptized, our souls are filled with the new supernatural life of God. It is then possible to become holy and to enter Heaven. At Baptism, we receive certain powers we did not have before. In our natural lives, we cannot love as God wants us to love. However, in our supernatural life, we can love God better. We even can love our enemies, something that would be impossible without God's supernatural life in us.

When we are baptized, we receive the three theological virtues of faith, hope and charity. What is a virtue? A virtue is a good habit which helps a person to act according to his right reason. What is a *theological* virtue? It is a good habit of the mind or will that is supernaturally infused into the soul. What is the difference between a virtue and a theological virtue? A virtue is any good habit that helps a person to act well. Theological virtues have God as their object. In other words, they come from God and they go back to God when we practice them.

What is faith? We can use the word faith in several ways. I have faith that when I board an airplane that it will take me where I want to go. That is *natural* faith, which is better called trust or belief in people or things. It is not the same thing as the *theological virtue* of faith which relates to trusting God and not people. Although people usually speak the truth, it is possible that people can lie, but God can never lie. The theological virtue of faith, which is in the intellect, means that we firmly believe everything God has revealed to us through His Church. He cannot ever deceive us, nor can He be deceived. The virtue of Faith assures us that God is our final Authority in all things.

What is hope? Once again, we are not speaking about simple human hope. I hope to go on my vacation or I hope to get a new bicycle for Christmas. That is hope on a *natural* level. The *theological virtue* of hope—which is in our wills—is far above our own human nature. The theological or supernatural virtue of hope means that we are able to rely on God's infinite mercy. We can rely on His promises to obtain pardon for our sins and everlasting life with Him in Heaven, if we but call on Him in prayer.

We are intellectually weak, and if we had to rely upon ourselves, we would soon lose hope of ever reaching Heaven. However, with the theological virtue of hope, we trust that God will be faithful to His promises and give us the grace we so desperately need to become holy and to reach Heaven. The virtue of hope makes a person desire eternal life with God. The virtue of hope gives us the assurance that we *will* have the means to obtain Heaven on God's promise to us.

What is charity? Charity is love but the word "love" means different things to different people. We may say that we "love" chocolate ice cream or that we "love" our puppy, but we dare not say that we love God in the same way. That is why there is a special word for love of God: charity. Charity is *supernatural* love of God.

The virtue of charity also refers to love of our neighbor, not for anything our neighbor might have done for us, but purely out of love for God and those He created. Charity is in our wills and goes with the virtue of faith. We cannot love what we do not know in our intellects. The virtue of faith helps us to know God and the more we know Him, the more we are able to love Him through the exercise of the theological virtue of charity.

We should daily say an act of charity:

"O my God, I love Thee above all things, with my whole heart and soul, because Thou art all-good and worthy of all love. I love my neighbor as myself for the love of Thee. I forgive all who have injured me, and ask pardon of all whom I have injured.

Holy Spirit, Spirit of Grace and Prayer, have mercy on us.

Fill in the Blanks

1. The supernatural life is ___far above___ our natural life.

2. We receive the supernatural life in the Sacrament of ___baptism___.

3. The three theological virtues are ___faith___, ___hope___ and ___charity___

4. The theological virtues have ___GOD___ as their object.

5. When I believe that an airplane will take me to my destination, that is ___natural___ faith.

6. The theological virtue of faith is in the ___soul___.

7. The theological virtue of hope helps me to ___rely___ on God's infinite mercy and promises.

8. The theological virtue of charity is in the ___wills___.

9. The theological virtue of charity helps us to love ___GOD___ above all things.

10. The theological virtue of charity helps us to love even our ___enemies___

55

Those who receive Sanctifying Grace in Baptism receive the three theological virtues of Faith, Hope, and Charity. They also receive the seven Gifts of the Holy Spirit. As with the theological virtues, they are supernatural, meaning they are above our own nature. These Gifts of the Holy Spirit make us more aware of the will of God, and more prepared to do the will of God.

What are the seven Gifts of the Holy Spirit? They are wisdom, understanding, counsel, fortitude, knowledge, piety, and fear of the Lord. We will take a closer look at each one.

Wisdom is the first and highest of all the Gifts of the Holy Spirit. It makes the soul open and quick to respond to God in reflecting on divine things. In other words, the gift of wisdom helps us to judge correctly the things of God so that we might be better able to deal with our trials here on earth.

Understanding is the gift that gives us better insight and appreciation of the mysteries of our Faith. Some effects of this gift are clear insight into revealed truth even without fully understanding, and also a stronger belief in God's revealed word.

Counsel is the gift that helps a person to judge quickly and correctly what should be done in difficult situations. Counsel also helps us to guide other people wisely when they ask for our help.

Fortitude is the gift that gives a person special strengths of the will. All of the martyrs demonstrated fortitude when they proved their love for God by suffering and dying for Him. This gift helps us to undergo trials with great courage and to do the will of God even when it is very difficult.

Knowledge is the gift that makes the virtue of faith stronger. It makes us see everything with *supernatural vision* and from the viewpoint of eternity. This gift helps us to see God working in even the smallest event. Knowledge helps a person tell the difference between temptations and inspirations of grace.

Piety is the gift that helps us to love God deeply and to love those who are consecrated to God, such as the Pope, bishops, priests, and religious. This gift also helps us to be obedient to God and to do what He wills because of love for Him.

Fear of the Lord is the Gift of the Holy Spirit that gives us a deep respect for God's majesty. When we commit sin, this gift helps us to have a great sorrow for our sins. This gift helps us not to fear punishment, but to be sorrowful at having offended God, Who is our Creator . This gift gives us a deep sense of God's greatness and majesty. This gift gives us a deep sorrow when we have offended God even in small sins.

The effects of the Gifts of the Holy Spirit are the fruits and the beatitudes. The fruits of the Holy Spirit show outwardly that a person is experiencing God's presence in his or her soul. The following are the fruits of the Holy Spirit: charity, joy, peace, patience, benignity (or kindness), goodness, long-suffering, mildness, faith, modesty, continency, and chastity. All of these fruits show God and the world that a person is living a deeply Christian life.

When Jesus Christ gave His Sermon on the Mount, He began with the famous Eight Beatitudes. These Eight Beatitudes are the most important part of His talk to the thousands of people who had gathered to hear Him speak (Matthew 5:3-11). The beatitudes are the ways Jesus Christ tells us to live out the Ten Commandments. What does that mean?

"Blessed are the poor in spirit, for theirs is the kingdom of Heaven." This beautiful first Beatitude teaches us that if we are detached from all creatures or things, we are promised happiness with God in Heaven. To be "poor in spirit" or detached from earthly gifts does not mean that we must not own anything. It means that whatever we own, we must not be so attached to it that we love God less.

The first beatitude relates to the First Commandment. How? The First Commandment is: "I am the Lord thy God, thou shalt not have strange gods before Me." This means that nothing and no one should come before our love for almighty God. It is the same with all the beatitudes. They are eight promises of happiness provided we do the will of God and practice the virtues.

There are seven other Beatitudes. They are wonderful words of Jesus to all of us, teaching us how to be more holy, and telling us the wonderful heavenly reward that God has planned for those who are holy.

Now we will discuss the Moral Virtues. We have already learned that Virtues are good habits that help a person to act according to what is God's will. Their immediate object is not God—like the theological virtues—but people and things that lead to God.

There are four virtues to which all other virtues are related. The four chief Moral Virtues are called Cardinal Virtues. The Cardinal Virtues are *prudence, justice, fortitude,* and *temperance.*

What is prudence? *Prudence* is correct knowledge about things that ought to be done, as well as things that should be avoided. John has a decision to make. He must decide whether or not he should tell his parents about his friends who stole money from the collection basket at church. The virtue of prudence will help him to make the right decision.

Justice is the virtue that recognizes everyone's rights. Justice is a willingness to give God and neighbor their due. It includes fairness in dealing with others. Justice makes us realize that on Sunday, Holy Mass and prayer must come first because God is due our worship and praise. In Justice, we must attend Mass and not attend a beach party. Justice also makes us realize that if our parents are sick, we must help at home and not go bowling with our friends.

Fortitude is the virtue that makes us strong in spirit. Fortitude makes us ready and willing to face difficulties in doing our duties. In the example above, John knows that when he tells his parents about his friends' stealing the money, he will lose their friendship. John knows, however, he can have peace and happiness with God by being strong and choosing to do the right thing.

Temperance is the virtue that controls our natural desire for pleasures of all kinds. We know, for example, that we should not overeat and that if we do, we will get sick or injure our health. The virtue of temperance helps us to control our natural desire for eating too much, or drinking too much. It can refer to other pleasures as well. This virtue helps a person to not spend so much time in playing that his school work suffers. This virtue helps a man who likes to play cards or sports, to stop after a reasonable time and take care of his family and other responsibilities. This virtue helps a person realize that he must not spend a long time on the computer and neglect his chores or schoolwork.

Holy Spirit, shed Thy light into our souls.

The next part of the Creed we will study is the Catholic Church. We say we believe in the one, holy, Catholic, and apostolic Church.

Our study of the Catholic Church naturally follows from our study of the Holy Spirit because the Holy Spirit is the *soul* or the life of the Church. This article of the Creed teaches us that there is a Catholic Church, which is also the Communion of Saints. This means the people, who are members of the Church, are in union, they are in a community, they are in communion, with each other. The Church is a society of people who have been baptized and profess their faith in Jesus Christ. They share the same Faith, the same Sacrifice, and the same Sacraments. They are under the authority of the Holy Father, the Pope, and all the bishops who are in communion with him.

The word "Church" means several things. Most of us think of Church as the place we go to Mass. The church *is* a building, a holy building, in fact, because Jesus Christ dwells in the tabernacle there. However, the Church is much more than a building. The Church is also *the society or congregation of people* that Jesus Christ founded during His visible stay on earth. Finally, the Church is the *Mystical Body* of Christ. This means that the Church is a *spiritual body*, with Jesus Christ as the spiritual head, and its members as the parts of the Body.

Let us recall what a physical body is like. A human body has a head, a trunk, arms, and legs. What does mystical mean? *Mystical* means spiritual mystery. The Mystical Body of Christ, which is the Church, has a Mystical spiritual Head Who is Jesus Christ. Since we cannot see Him with our eyes, Jesus gave us someone we can see: a visible head of the Church, the Pope. The rest of the body of the Church is her millions of members.

The Mystical Body of Christ, the Church, has three divisions for the millions of its members; each member belongs to one of the divisions.

The *Church Triumphant* are all those members of the Church who are now in Heaven, enjoying face to face the Beatific Vision of God. They overcame temptations during their lives on earth and merited their heavenly reward with the help of divine grace. We can pray and ask these souls in Heaven to pray for us.

The *Church Suffering* are all those members who have been saved but who are in Purgatory awaiting release from the temporal punishment still due to their sins. They are happy because they know they are saved and are being purified so they can enter Heaven. Our prayers and sacrifices will help them on their way to Heaven.

The *Church Militant* consists of all members of the Catholic Church here on earth. We are still struggling with the world, the flesh, and the devil, working out our salvation.

When did the Church come into being? When Jesus Christ died on the Cross, when the Blood and Water flowed from the side of Jesus Christ, the Church came into existence. Jesus had spent three years preparing for the founding of His Church. He gave it life at His death.

Like any human body, the Church has a soul—the Holy Spirit, the Third Person of the Blessed Trinity. The Holy Spirit manifested Himself publicly on Pentecost Sunday, fifty days after Jesus rose from the dead. The Holy Spirit came down from Heaven in the form of tongues of fire on the heads of the Apostles. God the Father and God the Son sent the Holy Spirit to live in the Church, and to give life to the Church on earth.

Why did Jesus Christ found the Catholic Church on earth? Jesus Christ founded the Church so that all people could have eternal life with Him in Heaven. Salvation is found only in the Catholic Church, the one true Church. The Holy Spirit gives life to its members by giving them Sanctifying Grace, a sharing in the life of Christ. The Holy Spirit gives Sanctifying Grace when the Church members receive the Sacraments.

You can see how important it is to pray for non-Catholics so that they join the Catholic Church and obtain Sanctifying Grace. Of course, those who received a valid Baptism in a Christian Church have received Sanctifying Grace and have had Original Sin removed. However, if they never join the Catholic Church, they never experience "the fullness of grace and truth that Christ has entrusted to the Catholic Church" (*Catechism of the Catholic Church*, no. 819).

Holy Spirit, Spirit of peace and patience, have mercy on us.

Matching

_7_ 1. The Catholic Church	1. Visible head of the Church
_10_ 2. Jesus Christ	2. Souls in Purgatory
_1_ 3. Pope	3. Fifty days after the Resurrection
_2_ 4. Church Suffering	4. Soul of the Church
_8_ 5. Christ's death on the Cross	5. Church members on earth
_3_ 6. Pentecost	6. Sent Holy Spirit
_9_ 7. Church Triumphant	7. Jesus Christ founded
_6_ 8. Father and Son	8. Church came into existence
_4_ 9. Holy Spirit	9. Souls in Heaven
_5_ 10. Church Militant	10. Invisible Head of the Church

We continue our study of the Apostles' Creed by studying what we mean by the Catholic Church. Today we will learn about the functions of the Church. What does the Church *do* with the help of the Holy Spirit? The Church *teaches, sanctifies,* and *rules* her faithful members. As we have seen in our last lesson, the Holy Spirit is the soul of the Church. Just as a soul is the life of a body, so the Holy Spirit is the life of the Church. It is the Holy Spirit, the Third Person of the Blessed Trinity, Who teaches, sanctifies, and rules through her Popes, bishops, and priests.

What does it mean when we say that the Church *teaches*? What does the Church teach? Imagine for a moment that truth is a circle. A circle is complete without any breaks in the one line that reaches completely around. All religions contain some truths, some portion of the circle, but only the Catholic Church contains the full circle of divinely revealed truth. Only the Catholic Church was founded by the Son of God. God wants that truth, found only in the one true Catholic Church, to be spread to the whole world. In the Bible, we read the words of Jesus Christ. He tells us to teach "them to observe all things whatsoever that I have commanded you" (Matthew 28:20).

To whom did Jesus give the power to teach? He gave the power to teach to His Apostles, who were the first bishops of the Church. They in turn passed on their powers to teach to the bishops they ordained. The first Pope, St. Peter, was the chief Apostle whom Jesus Himself had chosen. Since the first Pope, there has been an unbroken line of Popes all the way to the present day. As we have seen, the Pope is the visible head of the Church. The bishops share the powers of the Pope, but only with the Pope and in subjection to him (not apart from him) to teach the members of the Church. The priests are given authority by the bishops to teach in their parishes.

What does it mean when we say that the Church *sanctifies* her members? Sanctify means to make holy. How does the Church make her members holy? The Church helps her children to be holy mainly through the seven Sacraments. Beginning with Baptism, the Sacraments infuse the souls of the members of the Church with Sanctifying Grace. When we study the Sacraments, we will see how each of the Sacraments helps people to be holy.

What does it mean when we say that the Church *rules*? We mean that the Pope and the bishops in union with him, govern the Catholic Church. How? The bishop's authority is exercised over his own diocese. The Pope's authority is exercised over the entire Church. There are hundreds of dioceses in the world, each one headed by a bishop.

As we have seen, the Church is composed of the Pope, bishops, priests, deacons, and religious, but also the lay people or laity. Who are the laity? The laity are all the members of the Church who are not ordained as priests or deacons or are not in a religious vocation. All of the members of the Church from the Pope to the least lay person are responsible to do some kind of work or Catholic action for the Church. Another name for Catholic action is *apostolate*.

Every Catholic should be involved in doing some work to spread the Gospel. There are many things we can do as members of the Catholic Faith. We must keep in mind that we received the Catholic Faith from someone else. That someone—probably our parents—passed their faith on to us. We, in turn, are obliged to pass on the gift of our faith to others. That is one form of Catholic action in which everyone should partake.

There are many other ways we can perform Catholic action. We can help the poor and the sick, we can teach others or write letters or stories. Even something as "small" as cleaning the Church is important Catholic action. The late Mother Teresa taught her sisters that whatever we do for God, no matter how small it may seem, if it is done for love of God and others, it is "something beautiful for God."

Holy Spirit, from all evil, deliver us.

Fill in the Blanks

1. The Church __teaches, sanctifies__ and __rules__ her faithful.

2. The Holy Spirit is the __life__ of the Church.

3. The supreme and visible head of the Catholic Church is the __Pope__.

4. The whole truth is found only in the __Catholic Church__.

5. Jesus Christ gave the power to teach to the __Pope__ and the __bishops__.

6. The first Pope was St. __Peter__.

7. The Church makes her members holy mainly through the __sacraments__.

8. Bishops have authority over their own __diocese__.

9. The Pope has authority over the entire __Church__.

10. Catholic action is the laity's __work__ in the apostolate.

If someone asks you, "How do I know which is the one true Church?" would you be able to answer? There are several ways we can recognize the one true Church.

There are four marks which identify the one true Church founded by Jesus Christ, the Son of God: the one true Church must be *one, holy, catholic,* and *apostolic.* The Catholic Church alone has the marks of the true Church.

What does it mean when we say the Catholic Church is "*one*"? It means that all Catholics the world over practice and profess the same faith, the same beliefs. What does that mean? It means that no matter where in the world we are, the very same Sacraments are received, the same Mass is celebrated, and the one Pope reigns supreme. It also means that even from the Church's very beginnings, and stretching all the way to the end of time, the one, holy, catholic, and apostolic Church essentially remains the same.

Bobby and Katie are thrilled to be going with their parents on vacation to Europe. They will visit England, France, Spain, Portugal, and Germany. They arrive in England on a Saturday evening. The next morning, they go to Mass and they are amazed to see that there is a Mass with a priest just like the Mass at home. A few days later, they fly to France and go to Mass with the same prayers as the Mass at home. It is the same in Spain, Portugal, and Germany. In every country they visit, it is the same Catholic Church except that the Masses are recited in the language of whatever country they are visiting. The Mass is the same all over the world, because the Catholic Church is one. That means all the members of the Church practice the same faith, have the same Sacraments, and are united under the one Pope.

Though there are different "rites" in the Church, such as the Byzantine Rite or the Melkite Rite, the Mass has the same parts, and many of the same prayers. Though the Eastern Rite Masses tend to be more elaborate and have longer prayers, and more singing is done by the priest and the people, the parts remain the same, especially the consecration. Of course, all the doctrines are exactly the same.

What does it mean when we say the Catholic Church is *holy*? Jesus Christ, the Son of God, is the Founder of the Church, and He is perfect holiness. The Holy Spirit makes the members holy through the Sacraments. In every age, the Catholic Church provides the means for her members to become holy through the Sacraments and through her teachings.

The Catholic Church has many thousands of organizations which promote holiness. There are hundreds of organizations of religious men and women, monks and sisters, who do all kinds of holy works in serving the needs of the poor, sick, and dying. Most of these were founded by saints, such as the Franciscans and the Dominicans, the Sisters of Charity and Little Sisters of the Poor. There are lay organizations which do the same. Many hundreds of organizations are dedicated to prayer, such as the cloistered Carmelite sisters.

What does the word "*catholic*" mean? It means universal or available to everyone in the world. The Church is everywhere in the world. Jesus Christ wants everyone in the world to belong to His Catholic Church, rich and poor, educated and uneducated, all peoples of all races and nationalities, in all times. Everyone is invited to belong to the true Church.

Finally, what does it mean when we say that the Church is *apostolic*? We mean that the history of the beginning of the Catholic Church goes all the way back to the *Apostles* Jesus chose and ordained as the first bishops. It means that the papacy or the history of the popes extends in an unbroken line from St. Peter, the first Pope, whom Jesus Christ appointed, all the way to the Pope of the present day.

From all sin, deliver us, O Jesus.

True (T) or false (F)

___F___ 1. Because there are so many different churches, we cannot know the one true Church founded by the Son of God.

___F___ 2. There are three marks of the one true Church.

___F___ 3. The Church is only for educated people.

___T___ 4. The Church is holy because Jesus Christ, her Founder, is holy.

___T___ 5. The word "catholic" means universal.

___F___ 6. The Church is apostolic. That means we should work hard to convert more people.

___T___ 7. Jesus appointed St. Peter to be the first Pope.

___T___ 8. Jesus Christ founded the one true Church.

___T___ 9. Except for the language used, Mass is the same in every country all over the world.

___T___ 10. The twelve Apostles were the first bishops of the Catholic Church.

Today we will learn three more ways we can identify the true church founded by Jesus Christ, the Son of God. They are the three *attributes* of the Catholic Church. What is an attribute? An attribute is a feature or quality of something. For example, Nicholas has blue eyes and brown hair, his brother Colin has brown eyes and blonde hair. Hair and eye color are features or attributes that describe and identify the two boys.

The Church also has identifying features. They are called her attributes. The chief attributes of the Catholic Church are *authority*, *infallibility,* and *indefectibility*.

What is *authority*? Authority is the power to command others. All authority comes from God. The person in charge, the person who makes final decisions, is the one who has authority. A father has authority over the important decisions in his family. An army general has authority because he makes decisions for the soldiers in his command.

In an even greater sense, the Catholic Church is the final authority and possessor of absolute truth because her authority is from God Himself. All the truths Jesus Christ has revealed to the Church is called the *deposit of faith*. The Church is the guardian of that deposit of faith or truth. In our last lesson, we learned about the Pope's authority and the bishops' authority when they are in

union with him. The Pope and the bishops are lawful successors of the Apostles, who were given authority from Jesus Christ Himself. They, therefore, have the power and authority from Jesus Christ Himself to teach, to sanctify, and to govern the faithful. They have the authority to protect the Faith, to explain the Faith, and to promote the Faith. No one else on earth has this final authority.

What is *infallibility*? Infallibility means freedom from error. We know that the Pope cannot make a mistake when he teaches about faith or morals to the whole Church in a document presented to the world. The Pope cannot make a mistake when he is speaking "ex cathedra" as the supreme teacher of the world. Why? The Holy Spirit guards the Pope from making errors in the areas of faith or doctrine, and morals. Does that mean the Pope does not make any mistakes? No. The Pope, like all human beings, can commit sin but it is impossible for him to *formally teach* to the members of the Church *anything that is opposed to the truth*. No other institution on earth can make that claim. No other institution on earth even attempts to make that claim.

We have a sacred duty to be loyal to the Pope in *all* that he teaches because God Himself has given him the sacred and awesome power to guide and direct the Church. When he issues encyclical letters, formal statements of doctrine and morals for the Church, we are required to accept them. Why? The Pope speaks with the help of the Holy Spirit when he speaks in a formal document. Even when the Pope is not speaking formally on Faith or Morals, we should study what he says with respect because he is aware of problems in the world, and sees a need to address particular problems. In the 1990's, Pope John Paul II issued a magnificent document on human life called *Evangelium Vitae* or "The Gospel of Life." The Holy Father recognized a need to remind the members of the Church about the sacredness of human life.

What is *indefectibility*? A defect means that something is lacking. If you purchase a defective clock, it means it is not keeping proper time, something is wrong with it. The only thing on earth which is perfect and has no defects is the Catholic Church. It has no defects which will allow it to pass away out of existence. The indefectibility of the Catholic Church means that the Church is now and will be in existence until the end of the world. Jesus said in the Gospel of Matthew (28:20): "I am with you all days, even to the consummation [the end] of the world." Since the Catholic Church was founded by the Son of God, it is the perfect institution of salvation. It will exist so that no matter when anyone lives, or where anyone lives, in the whole history of the human race, past, present and to come, a person can find the Catholic Church founded by Jesus Christ, the Son of God.

The indefectibility of the Catholic Church also means that her perfect teachings of doctrine and morals will never change. They are perfect teachings, and God will never allow them to become imperfect teachings. The Catholic Church will last until the end of time. Nothing on earth can destroy the Church founded by the Son of God!

While we say that the Catholic Church will last until the end of time on this earth, the *Mystical Body of Christ* will last forever in eternity. We remember that the Mystical Body of Christ consists of all her members, past, present and yet to come. All these members, these people, have eternal souls which can never die. They are here on earth, or in Heaven, or in Purgatory awaiting their release to Heaven. How blessed we are to be members of the one, holy, Catholic, and apostolic, as well as authoritative, infallible, and indefectible true Catholic Church. What a great treasure we have been given by our All-Loving God!

O Divine Infant Jesus, example of obedience, have mercy on us.

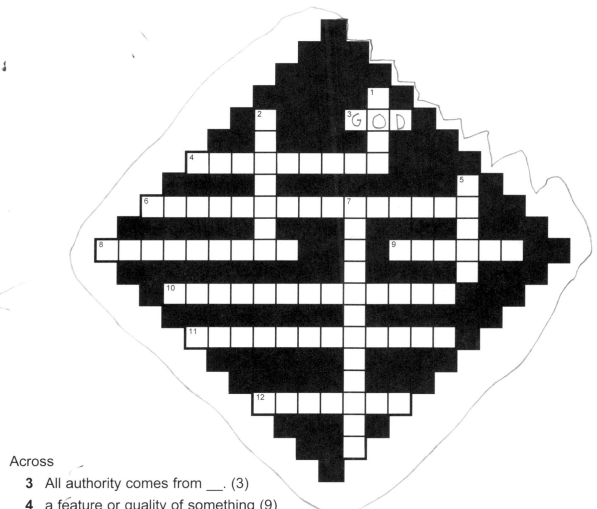

Across

3 All authority comes from __. (3)

4 a feature or quality of something (9)

6 The Latin name of the encyclical, "Gospel of Life." (10,5)

8 the power to command others (9)

9 The Pope and the bishps have the authority to teach, sanctify, and __. (6)

10 freedom from error (13)

11 "I am with you all days, even to the __ of the world." (12)

12 lawful successors of the Apostles (7)

Down

1 lawful successor of St. Peter (4)

2 The Catholic Church is the __ institution of salvation. (7)

5 Teachings of doctine and morals __ change. (5)

7 The __ __ of Christ will last forever. (8,4)

As we near the end of our study of the Apostles' Creed, we must keep in mind that we have been studying the basic doctrines of our Catholic Faith. We read in the Bible, "...faith is the assurance of things hoped for, the conviction of things not seen" (Hebrews 11:1). Everything in the Apostles' Creed is our Faith. The Creed contains the most important teachings revealed by Jesus Christ to His Church.

What is the *Communion of Saints*? We remember that the Communion of Saints is the Mystical Body of Christ on three levels: the Church Triumphant, or the souls in Heaven; the Church Militant, or the souls on earth; and the Church Suffering, or the souls in Purgatory.

Jesus Christ is Head of the Communion of Saints. We have seen that there is communication among the three levels in the form of prayer and good works. The saints in Heaven pray for us on earth and for the poor souls in Purgatory. We on earth call upon the saints in Heaven and pray for the souls in Purgatory. The souls in Purgatory beg for our prayers and sacrifices as well as for the intercession of the saints in Heaven for their release from the pains of Purgatory.

Purgatory is a place where the souls of the saved are purified. These are souls who still have guilt and punishment due for their venial sins and forgiven mortal sins. We know that the souls in Purgatory can no longer merit grace for themselves so they must rely on our prayers and sacrifices to shorten their time. We should pray for the poor souls in Purgatory every day, and to have Masses offered for them frequently. We should remember family members and friends who have died as well as souls who have no one to pray for them.

Here on earth, we, the Church Militant, show our love for each other by practicing the supernatural works of charity called the Corporal Works of Mercy which serve our neighbor's bodily needs. The Spiritual Works of Mercy serve the needs of our neighbors' souls.

Corporal Works of Mercy	**Spiritual Works of Mercy**
To feed the hungry	To admonish the sinner
To give drink to the thirsty	To instruct the ignorant
To clothe the naked	To counsel the doubtful
To visit the imprisoned	To comfort the sorrowful
To shelter the homeless	To bear wrongs patiently
To visit the sick	To forgive all injuries
To bury the dead	To pray for the living and the dead

All fourteen of the Works of Mercy spell out *how* we are to love and serve others. Our Lord gave us these specific instructions so no one should doubt what it means to be a practicing Christian: obey the Ten Commandments and practice these charitable Works of Mercy. When we practice charitable works, we are serving Jesus Christ Himself. How? We serve Jesus by loving others, especially those who do not like us or are mean to us. By practicing charitable works, we are loving and serving Jesus Christ, Who lives in the souls of those we are helping. Charity is serving God in others.

Infant Jesus, Treasure of Grace, have mercy on us.

Fill in the Blanks

1. Faith is the _assurance_ of things hoped for and the _conviction_ of things not seen.

2. The Communion of Saints is the _mystical_ Body of Christ.

3. The three levels of the Mystical Body are the Church _triumphant_, the Church _militant_, and the Church _suffering_.

4. The Church Triumphant are the souls in _heaven_.

5. The souls in Purgatory are the Church _suffering_.

6. We here on earth are called the Church _militant_.

7. The supernatural works of charity are called the _corporal_ and the _spiritual_ Works of Mercy.

8. The _creed_ contains the most important teachings revealed by Jesus Christ to His Church.

9. The corporal Works of Mercy serve the needs of our neighbor's _bodily_.

10. The spiritual Works of Mercy serve the needs of our neighbor's _souls_.

69

Today we will study the Resurrection of the body. Unlike any other creature in the universe, the human person is composed of a body and a rational soul. The body is material, something we can see and touch. The soul is spiritual, meaning it cannot be seen or touched. God created the body and the soul so closely connected, they were made to be together forever.

Bodily death is mankind's punishment for Original Sin, and also punishment for the sins that we ourselves commit. By obeying the Ten Commandments and practicing acts of charitable Works of Mercy here on earth, we will be rewarded in Heaven. At the end of time, our bodies will once again be reunited with our souls for all eternity. Both the bodies of the just and the damned will rise, but those who died in God's friendship will be happy with Him forever in Heaven. Those who die opposed to God will suffer eternal punishment in Hell.

We read in the Bible that when Martha called for Jesus to cure her brother Lazarus, Jesus came but He waited until He knew that Lazarus had already died. Why? Because He wanted to teach us about the Resurrection of the body. Martha said to Jesus, "If you had been here, my brother would not have died." Jesus told her, "Your brother will rise again." Then He said, "I am the Resurrection and the Life; he who believes in Me shall never die" (John 11: 21, 23, 25). What did Jesus mean? Among other things, He meant that our bodies are to be reunited with our souls. Later, when Jesus died on the Cross, His own precious Body and Soul were separated. However, on Easter Sunday morning, He rose from the dead, *Body and Soul once again reunited.* He showed us by His own Resurrection that, like Him, we too will rise again with our bodies and souls reunited!

Here on earth, we serve Our Lord with both our bodies and our souls. In our last lesson, we learned the spiritual and the corporal Works of Mercy. The spiritual works are works for the souls of others; and the corporal works are works we perform for the bodily needs of others. It is therefore logical that both soul and body will enjoy eternal reward (or punishment) for the love we show for God and for others.

Finally, we look to nature for a reminder of the cycle of life. We see how the sun rises and sets without fail, and how the trees lose their leaves in the fall only to regain them again in the springtime. It is as though God, the Creator of all things, is teaching us through the world He created that life goes on, and for us, even into the next world.

Because death is a punishment for sin, there is one person who did not die a bodily death because she never sinned: the Mother of God. The Church teaches that the Blessed Mother was assumed body and soul into Heaven as a reward for having so perfectly loved her Son and all men. Like her Son, she is in Heaven, body and soul. They await our arrival to our Heavenly home where we hope to be happy with them forever.

Infant Jesus, Head of the Angels, have mercy on us.

True (T) or False (F)

_F_ 1. Angels and men have bodies and souls.

_T_ 2. Death is a punishment for sin.

_T_ 3. Death is separation of the soul and the body.

_F_ 4. We would not have to die if Adam had not sinned.

_T_ 5. Martha called Jesus so He could heal her brother.

_T_ 6. Jesus healed Lazarus before he died.

_F_ 7. We do not really need our souls.

_T_ 8. Mary, the Mother of God, was assumed into Heaven, body and soul.

_T_ 9. The only body in Heaven right now is Mary's.

_T_ 10. We hope to live forever in Heaven with our bodies and our souls reunited.

The final article of the Apostles' Creed is, "I believe in the resurrection of the body, and life everlasting." In these two final days of the first quarter, we will learn about the four last things: death, judgment, Heaven and Hell.

Immediately after death, we are judged by Jesus Christ and our destiny is determined at that very moment. That happens the moment the soul leaves the body, and it is called the *Particular Judgment*. We will be judged on how well we have loved God and others during our lifetime.

Should we fear death? Absolutely not! If we live good lives loving and serving God and others, we should regard death as our birth to new life. We were not made for *this world*. God made us so that we might enjoy happiness with Him forever *in Heaven*. First, however, we must prove our love for Him by loving and serving Him.

There is a Particular Judgment for each person individually when he or she dies. However, there also will be a *General Judgment* or final judgment of all people who ever lived, at the end of time. What is the General Judgment? The General Judgment is a judgment of the whole human race together. It will be a *public judgment by Jesus Christ the King* of every person who ever lived.

Will the original sentence of the souls who were judged in their own Particular Judgment be changed? No, each judgment stands and will be confirmed at the General Judgment. The Particular Judgment is for the *souls* of men. The General Judgment, because it will take place after the resurrection of all bodies, will affect the bodies as well as the souls of all people.

The General Judgment will include a "social judgment."

No sin is really committed alone. Even the most secret sins affect others. At the end of time, the justice and mercy of God will be known to all, as sin affected all.

Every action has consequences. Everything we do or say *affects others* in ways we cannot know right now. If, for example, someone tells a lie, not only is the victim affected, but many others may be influenced who in any way knew the person about whom the lie was told.

In the Bible, the entire twenty-fifth chapter of the Gospel of St. Matthew describes the General Judgment. One of them, the story of the sheep and the goats, is a solemn explanation to us on how we will be judged. In the story, the Son of Man, Jesus Christ, will gather all peoples before Him. He will separate them into two groups: the sheep and the goats. He will tell the sheep they are blessed and that they will inherit the kingdom prepared for them from the beginning of the world. He tells them that they fed and clothed Him and visited Him when He was sick or in prison. They are puzzled. "When did we see Thee sick and in prison?" they will ask. He tells them, "Truly, I say to you, as you did it to one of the least of these My brethren, you did it to Me."

Then Our Lord will tell the goats: "Depart from me, you cursed, into the eternal fire prepared for the devil and his angels; for I was hungry and you gave Me no food; I was thirsty and you gave Me no drink; I was a stranger and you did not welcome Me, naked and you did not clothe Me; sick and in prison and you did not visit Me." They will ask the same question, "When did we see Thee hungry or thirsty or a stranger or naked or sick or in prison?" Then He will answer them, "Truly I say to you, as you did it *not* to one of the least of these, you did it not to Me." And they will go away into eternal punishment, but the righteous into eternal life" (Matthew 25: 31-46).

Divine Infant Jesus, Fountain of Love, have mercy on us.

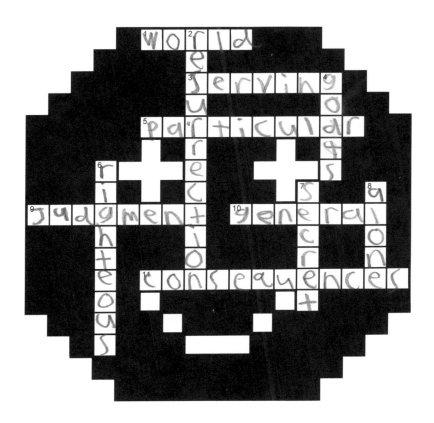

Across

1 We were not made for this __. (5)

3 We must prove our love for God by loving and __ Him. (7)

5 Immediately after death, we are judged by Christ at the __ Judgment. (10)

9 The four last things: death, __, Heaven, Hell (8)

10 the final judgment of all at the end of time (7)

11 Every action has __. (12)

Down

2 "I believe in the __ of the body and life everlasting." (12)

4 The story of the sheep and the __ in the Gospel explains how we will be judged. (5)

6 The __ will enter into eternal life. (9)

7 Even the most __ sins affect others. (6)

8 No sin is really committed __. (5)

Today, our last day on the Apostles' Creed, we will learn about the subject of greatest interest to every human being: life after death. There is much confusion and error about this topic in the world today. The Holy Spirit teaches us through His Church that, provided we have loved God and others according to His will, we will share happiness with Him forever.

We begin by reminding ourselves that we are naturally drawn to God. God made us for Himself. Anything or anyone that we allow to take us from Him makes us deeply unhappy. What could possibly have the power to do that? Sin! We recall that sin is breaking the union of our will with God's will. When that happens, we separate ourselves from God. You might ask why we are on the subject of sin instead of life after death? Because sin is what separates us from God, even from the very beginning of the human race.

At death, the soul separates from the body and, after the Particular Judgment, goes to one of three places: Heaven, Purgatory, or Hell. The souls whose wills have been perfectly conformed to God's holy will, go directly to Heaven. Heaven is reserved for those who love God above all people, above all things, and even above one's own self. Our love for God will take our souls to God. When we love someone here on earth, we want to be with that person as much as possible. Even more will we want to be with God. Our heavenly reward will be face to face vision, called the Beatific Vision, of the One we love, but could not see here on earth.

Those souls who have died loving God, but whose wills have not been perfectly conformed to God's will, must necessarily delay their entry into Heaven. Why? The Bible tells us that nothing unclean shall enter Heaven (Revelation 21:27). Heaven is the place or state of *perfect* love of God. Therefore, those souls who have loved God, but not completely, go to a place of purification called Purgatory.

We might think Purgatory is unfair. However, souls who did not completely love God over their own wills *beg to have their souls purified* once they have experienced God's perfection at the Particular Judgment. The moment the soul beholds its Creator, it will see its own weaknesses compared with the perfect holy purity of God. Therefore, when the soul leaves this life not having loved God as completely as He deserves, the soul goes to the place of purification called Purgatory. There the soul suffers, but in love and joy, because the person knows he has been saved, and will someday see God in Heaven.

Finally, we must mention that horrible place where souls go who die loving themselves above all things, all people, and especially God. When we speak about Hell, we are entering a great mystery. Jesus Christ Himself warned His followers many times about the reality of Hell. God is love and all love comes from God. Hell is a place of unspeakable hate, as well as pain and torment. Hell is a place of hatred where souls not only do not love, they despise God, they despise each other, and they despise souls on earth who are trying to love God. Hell means eternal separation from God.

We might ask, "Why would our good God send a soul to everlasting torment?" The reality is that God does *not* send souls to Hell. Souls who have lived their lives hating and rejecting God and others, *send themselves* to the only place where it is possible to exist in such hatred. We should desire and pray for the salvation of all men.

The children of Fatima had a vision of Hell, shown to them by the Blessed Mother. Lucia wrote: "She opened her hands again as she had done the two previous months. The light reflecting from them seemed to penetrate into the earth, and we saw as if into a sea of fire, and immersed in that fire were devils and souls of human form, as if they were transparent black or bronze embers floating in the fire and swayed by the flames that issued from them along with clouds of smoke, falling upon every side just like the falling of sparks in great fires, without weight or equilibrium, amidst wailing and cries of pain and despair that horrified and shook us with terror."

The existence of Hell should make us do everything possible to avoid mortal sin and to warn others of the unspeakable consequences of serious sin.

The final word in the Apostles' Creed is "Amen." The word "Amen" means "So be it!" By saying "Amen," I confirm my belief in what I have just prayed. I say "Amen" because every word of the Apostles' Creed is official Church doctrine, and we are seriously obliged to profess and believe what God has revealed to His Church.

How blessed we are to belong to the one true Catholic Church, where we find all truth.

Jesus, Who has loved us with an everlasting love, have mercy on us.

Matching

___7___ 1. God

___1___ 2. Sin

___10___ 3. Death

___2___ 4. Children of Fatima

___4___ 5. Heaven

___9___ 6. Purgatory

___5___ 7. Hell

___3___ 8. Amen

___6___ 9. Revelation 21:27

___8___ 10. The Creed

1. Not following God's will

2. Had a vision of Hell

3. "So be it!"

4. Face to face vision of God

5. Place of hatred and suffering

6. "Nothing unclean shall enter Heaven"

7. Made us for Himself

8. Our Faith

9. Place of purification

10. Separation of the soul from the body

Take this week to review the lessons from this quarter.

Day 1

Review lessons for weeks 1 and 2.

Day 2

Review lessons for weeks 3 and 4.

Day 3

Review lessons for weeks 5 and 6.

Day 4

Review lessons for weeks 7 and 8.

In our first quarter, we studied the Apostles' Creed. The Apostles' Creed is the first "pillar" of the Catholic Faith. The new *Catechism of the Catholic Church* states that the Catholic Faith is composed of four pillars: the Creed, the Commandments, the Sacraments, and Prayer. What is a pillar? When we go to a large church or cathedral, we usually see several large columns or pillars. Pillars are large strong support columns without which a building would collapse. It is the same with the four main foundations of the Catholic Faith. These four "pillars" are the foundation of our Catholic Faith.

We might ask, "Is faith in what God revealed enough for us to be saved?" You may be surprised at the answer. No, faith is not enough to be saved because we must *respond to our faith* in God. How? We must keep the Commandments. Today we begin our study of the second pillar of the Catholic Church: the Ten Commandments of God.

The Creed is our faith and tells us what we are to believe. The Commandments are God's laws, which were first given to Moses long, long ago, for all people for all time. The Commandments are the ways everyone is to live out or to respond to faith in God.

We begin our study with the *Two Great Commandments*. Jesus summed up the Ten Commandments in the *Two Great Commandments*. Even from the very beginning of time, long before Jesus was born, God's chosen people, the Jewish people, learned the *Two Great Commandments*. What are they?

The first Great Commandment is: "Thou shalt love the Lord thy God with thy whole heart, and with thy whole soul, and with thy whole mind, and with thy whole strength."

The second Great Commandment is: "Love thy neighbor as thyself."

These *Two Great Commandments* summarize the Ten Commandments.

What does it mean to love God? To love God means to want to do *His* will above our own will. To love God means to give ourselves to Him completely in all things. This means to obey Him completely. The first Great Commandment expresses the first three Commandments of the Ten Commandments given to Moses. The first three Commandments tell us our duties and responsibilities toward God.

I.   I am the Lord thy God; thou shalt not have strange gods before Me.

II.   Thou shalt not take the name of the Lord thy God in vain.

III. Remember thou keep holy the Lord's day.

If we love God the way He wants us to love Him, the second Great Commandment, "Love thy neighbor as thyself," follows easily. How do we love our neighbor as ourselves? By keeping all the Commandments and by performing the Corporal and the Spiritual Works of Mercy. By our expressions of love for one another, we give glory to God. The Works of Mercy are ways to show our love for God. How so? Because love is serving God in others.

When we perform the Works of Mercy, we are demonstrating our Catholicism and Catholic Faith. Our love and service for others makes our faith appealing to those who are not Catholic.

Multiple Choice

a   1. The Catholic religion is summed up in
    a) the four pillars of the Faith.
    b) the ten Commandments.
    c) the fourteen corporal Works of Mercy.

c   2. The pillars of the Catholic religion are
    a) faith, hope and charity.
    b) prudence, justice, fortitude and temperance.
    c) the Creed, Commandments, Sacraments, and Prayer.

a   3. In order to be saved we must
    a) keep the Commandments.
    b) have faith.
    c) have faith and keep the Commandments.

b   4. The two great Commandments are
    a) to love and to pray.
    b) to love God and to love one's neighbor.
    c) to pray and to serve others.

b   5. The Commandments are
    a) the will of Moses.   b) the will of God.   c) the will of the Chosen People.

b   6. The two great Commandments were given to us by
    a) Jesus Christ.
    b) God in the Old Testament.
    c) God and His Son, Jesus, in both the Old and the New Testaments.

b   7. To love God means
    a) doing the will of the state.
    b) doing the will of God.
    c) doing whatever I want.

b   8. The first three Commandments of God
    a) refer to how we treat each other.
    b) are about how we love and serve God.
    c) are the same as the First Great Commandment.
    d) b and c.

a   9. We love our neighbor by
    a) performing Works of Mercy for him.
    b) ignoring him when he is in need.
    c) not sharing our games with him.

d   10. The Commandments are
    a) given to us by the Church.   b) optional.
    c) suggestions.   d) none of the above.

Today we will see why the Works of Mercy or acts of charity are the best ways to show our love for God. We have seen that the two great Commandments are loving God first and then loving others. Charity is loving and serving God by loving and serving others because we are all children of God.

All the saints necessarily lived the fourteen Works of Mercy, what the Church calls the Spiritual and Corporal Works of Mercy. These Works of Mercy are the bodily and spiritual practices of charity. Aside from Jesus Christ Himself, the saints are our best examples of purest love. In our day, there may be no better example of selfless charity than Mother Teresa of Calcutta.

From the time she was eighteen years old, Mother had been a nun of the Congregation of Loretto where she lived comfortably in India in a religious community with the other sisters, teaching high school girls from wealthy families. She loved teaching, but she knew she wanted to do more, "Something beautiful for God," she said. On the feast of the Assumption in 1948, she made the very difficult decision to leave her comfortable religious community to serve the "poorest of the poor" in India.

"Mary, bodily assumed into Heaven, showed us Christians the importance of our bodies. The Church teaches that our bodies are temples of the Holy Spirit, and that they will be gloriously resurrected. Jesus redeemed *our bodies and souls* by His passion and death. Mother Teresa was about to begin serving the poorest of the poor in India. Many of these people had serious diseases. But even in these conditions, they were still children of God, whose bodies are destined to be resurrected" (*New Covenant*, August 1996, Renzo Allegri).

Not only was Mother Teresa to serve the poor of India, she knew she had to live among them to serve them properly. She knew God wanted nothing less of her. Someone asked her why she had given up her comfortable life to live among the poor where there were rats and roaches, filth, disease, and extreme heat. She told him, "… I had chosen that lifestyle in order to literally live out the Gospel, especially where it says, 'I was hungry and you gave Me to eat, I was naked and you clothed Me, I was in prison and you came to find Me.' Among the poorest of the poor of Calcutta, I loved Jesus. When I love like that, I don't feel suffering or fatigue" (Ibid.).

One day, while walking through the streets of Calcutta, Mother Teresa came across a woman lying in the street. She bent down and looked into her eyes. Why was she lying in the street? She could see that the woman was close to death. Here in Mother's own words is what happened. "…in a heap of rubbish, I found a woman who was half dead. Her body had been bitten by rats and by ants. I took her to a hospital, but they told me that they didn't want her because they couldn't do anything for her. I protested and said that I wouldn't leave unless they hospitalized her. They had a long meeting and they finally granted my request. That woman was saved. Afterwards, when thanking me for what I had done for her, she said, "And to think that it was my son who threw me in the garbage" (Ibid.).

Mother continued her works of charity among the poor of Calcutta, India. Soon a young woman came to her and asked her if she needed help. Mother smiled and answered, "Come and see." That young woman became the first of many sisters in the religious order known as the Missionaries of Charity. Today, there are nearly *five thousand* sisters feeding, clothing, sheltering, and serving in hundreds of houses in every country throughout the world. They dress simply, in a white habit and sandals.

What do the charitable religious orders do? They practice the Corporal and Spiritual Works of Mercy.

Corporal Works of Mercy	Spiritual Works of Mercy
To feed the hungry	To admonish the sinner
To give drink to the thirsty	To instruct the ignorant
To clothe the naked	To counsel the doubtful
To visit the imprisoned	To comfort the sorrowful
To shelter the homeless	To bear wrongs patiently
To visit the sick	To forgive all injuries
To bury the dead	To pray for the living and the dead

True (T) or false (F)

__T__ 1. Charity is loving and serving God in others.

__F__ 2. One of the corporal Works of Mercy is to admonish the sinner.

__F__ 3. One of the spiritual Works of Mercy is to feed the hungry.

__T__ 4. Mother Teresa founded the Missionaries of Charity.

__F__ 5. As a young nun, Mother Teresa taught wealthy children.

__F__ 6. Mother Teresa lived comfortably in Paris.

__F__ 7. Only sisters should practice the spiritual and corporal Works of Mercy.

__T__ 8. The corporal Works of Mercy serve the body.

__T__ 9. The spiritual Works of Mercy serve the soul.

__T__ 10. Mother Teresa knew she had to live among the poor to serve them.

Before we begin our study of the Ten Commandments, there are some words with which we should become more familiar: *law, freedom,* and *morality.* Why? Because in order to better understand God's laws and our responsibility, we should first look more closely at some words that are often misused in our world today.

What is *law*? A law is a rule or regulation for the common good passed and made public by a governing authority which a community recognizes as binding. A law is supposed to protect all members of the community. The authority of a law comes from God, not from agreement of a community. A law is a command of God and we will see that *all* laws come from God. If a law is not based on God's law, it is in fact no law at all. There are other laws that God made, such as the laws of nature. We are all familiar with the law of gravity. That is a law of nature that we learn very early in life. Once we learn the laws of nature we know what we can and what we cannot do.

It is the same with man's laws. When we drive a car, we are not allowed to go through a red light. Why? Because someone might get hurt. I cannot be free *from* the red light law because it is still there whether I believe in it or not. If I break it, I will either hurt myself or hurt someone else.

All laws come from God, the laws of nature and the laws of men. Just civil laws, the laws of men, are based upon the law of God. For example, the law in our society against taking someone else's property is based upon the Seventh Commandment. The laws against deliberately hurting others are based upon the Fifth Commandment.

Now we come to what is perhaps the most misunderstood word of all. What is *freedom*? Many people think that freedom is one's ability to do as one pleases, when they please. However, when we misunderstand freedom, we can hurt ourselves and others. Freedom is *always* linked to the laws of God. How so? First of all, God is the Author of the natural law, the civil law, and the moral law. All *just* laws come from God. Moreover, we have a natural instinct within us to keep God's laws. The Ten Commandments are, the Bible says, "written in our hearts."

There is no such thing as freedom *from* God's laws, but only freedom *within* God's laws. In fact, we are more free within God's laws because we can do so much more by obeying the Commandments than by doing what we please, when we please. Each new law that we learn gives us more freedom. If we break any of God's laws, our nature is as damaged as it would be if we ignore nature's law to nourish the body. Our body would soon die if we did not eat nourishing food. Our soul would be "damaged" by sin if we did not obey God's laws.

What is *morality*? Morality is living within the laws of God. There is a very real connection between what we do on earth and our final destiny in eternity. God made us for an eternal purpose. We recall that our purpose is to know, love, and serve God in this life so that we can be happy with Him in the next life, in eternity. Our human nature *was made* to be with God, and God made us with a built-in knowledge or natural revelation in our conscience of His laws. Our happiness in this life depends upon our willingness to love God by obeying His Ten Commandments.

Is it enough to follow God's laws and do no more? No, it is not enough. We experience an even deeper love of God if we do *more* than what is strictly necessary under the Ten Commandments. What does that mean? We certainly know that we must not steal, but is that enough? No, we must also give to the poor. Likewise, it is not enough to not hurt anyone. We must do more. We *must love* one another and treat others with the greatest respect.

Finally, God calls some people to a higher state in life. Sometimes "more" means giving ourselves completely to God in *a vocation* to the priesthood or religious life. No matter what our calling or vocation may be, however, our overall purpose in life is to love and serve God in this life out of love for Him, because He loves us so much.

Most Sacred Heart of Jesus, have mercy on us.

Fill in the Blanks

1. When we learn the Ten Commandments, we should know the meanings of ___law___; ___freedom___ and ___morality___.

2. A law is a ___command___ of God.

3. Gravity is a law of ___nature___.

4. The civil law is based upon ___God's___ law.

5. Freedom is always linked to the ___law___ of ___God___.

6. ___God___ is the Author of all laws.

7. Each law that we learn gives us more ___Freedom___

8. ___Morality___ means living within God's ___laws___.

9. We should do ___more___ than what is strictly necessary under God's laws.

10. God calls certain people to the ___priesthood___ or ___religious___ life.

This week we have been learning about the Two Great Commandments. They contain the whole Ten Commandments within them. The first Great Commandment is: Thou shalt love the Lord thy God with thy whole heart, with thy whole soul, with thy whole mind, and with thy whole strength; and second, thou shalt love thy neighbor as thyself.

Jesus gave us examples during His life of how we should be concerned about our neighbors' needs. The very first public miracle of Jesus took place at a wedding feast. This was a happy occasion and something went wrong because the hosts ran out of wine. Mary, the mother of Jesus, showed her compassion for their embarrassing situation, and asked her Son Jesus to help them.

Jesus knew the bride and groom would be ashamed before their guests. Mary told the servant, "Do whatever He tells you." Jesus then said quietly to him, "Fill the jars with water." The other servants quickly filled the water jars to the brim. When they had finished, Jesus told them to fill the table pitchers from the water jars, and carry them to the chief steward of the feast.

The waiters filled their pitchers and carried them to the chief steward. They filled the cup of the chief steward so he could taste the wine. When the chief steward tasted the wine, he paused, then took another sip. Suddenly he drank down the whole cup of wine!

Then the chief steward called out to the bridegroom and said, "Everyone puts out the best wine first, and after people have been drinking for a while, then the regular wine is served. But you have kept the best wine until the last!" [John 2:1-10]

We can look at this miracle as a foreshadowing of the miracle of the Holy Eucharist, but for the people at the wedding feast, Jesus gave an example of caring about His friends at the wedding feast. Sometimes when we think about being good and kind, we should think about the little things we can do for people around us and in our family. Loving our neighbor is not rescuing someone in a dramatic episode. It is caring about those people we live with every day.

Most of the people Jesus helped were little people, meaning people who were not big important leaders. One person Jesus helped was young Bartimeus. Bartimeus was blind. He would sit in the dust beside the road to Jericho, and ask people to give him food or money to buy food. Jericho was known as a beautiful city, but the poor blind beggar could not see it.

One day, Bartimeus was sitting beside the road as usual when he heard the sound of a crowd coming down the road. He could hear happiness and excitement, and even some singing!

"What is happening?" Bartimeus shouted. "What kind of procession is it? Why are people so excited?"

"It is Jesus, the Miracle Worker!" a man replied. "It is Jesus of Nazareth!"

Bartimeus suddenly became almost wild! He had heard of Jesus, the Miracle Worker. He had heard talk about His cures, and now He would be passing right down the road in front of him!

Suddenly, he used his walking cane to stand up and lifted his head as high as he could and shouted as loudly as he could: "Jesus, Son of David, have mercy on me!"

"Be quiet, you beggar!" the people nearby said. " We want to hear what Jesus is saying!"

But Bartimeus would not quit! In fact, he started yelling louder: "Jesus, Son of David, have mercy on me! Jesus, Son of David, have mercy on me! Jesus, Son of David, have mercy on me!"

"Hush, you beggar!" the people nearby said.

"Jesus, Son of David, have mercy on me!" Bartimeus yelled.

Then a strong gentle voice called out, "Who is calling Me?"

"A blind man named Bartimeus, Master!" said one of the disciples.

"Bring him to Me!" Jesus commanded.

Bartimeus became visibly shaken and could not move. A couple of men took the arms of young Bartimeus and started leading him as he carried his walking stick.

Jesus came forward to meet Bartimeus. He stopped directly in front of Bartimeus.

Bartimeus was filled with love and excitement. His heart was beating fast. He felt a strange warmth and power around him. Then he heard the most wonderful voice he had ever heard in his whole blind lifetime.

"What is it you wish Me to do for you, Bartimeus?"

Bartimeus suddenly remembered what some people were saying, that Jesus was the Messiah. At once he knew this voice belonged to the Messiah, the Son of God. He fell to His knees and worshiped Jesus. In a soft voice, in an emotional whisper, Bartimeus said slowly to His Lord, "Master, that I may see!" As he said those words, he realized that in fact he did "see," because he knew in his heart that Jesus was the Messiah. He had a tremendous peace in the realization that the Messiah had come to him, a poor beggar. Bartimeus was so happy he thought his heart would explode!

Then with great gentleness and love, Jesus said to Bartimeus, "Go your way, Bartimeus. Your faith has saved you."

Instantly Bartimeus could see! What he saw was the strong loving face of the Messiah. Instead of jumping around, he stayed on his knees worshiping the Messiah. Suddenly it did not seem as important to see the trees and the grass and the sky. Suddenly all he wanted to see for the rest of his life was the wonderful, gentle, loving face of Jesus. From that day forward, Bartimeus the beggar became Bartimeus, a disciple of Jesus.

God is the only Necessary Being Who exists in the entire universe. That is because without Him, nothing and no one would exist. He Himself did not *come* into existence because He *always was* and *always will be*. God is our Creator and our Destiny. When we think about that, we immediately see why the very First Commandment of God demands that we adore Him alone: "I am the Lord thy God; thou shalt not have strange gods before me."

God loves us so much that He brought us into existence. In return, He wants us to love Him with our complete affection. What does that mean? It means that nothing and no one should be given the reverence, adoration, and worship that only God deserves. God therefore forbids us to give our worship to anyone or anything but Himself.

In the Old Testament times, there were people who worshiped statues or worshiped their emperor. In our day, although we do not worship statues as they did in the Old Testament, some people today love things, like money, too much. Some people allow things, such as making money, to keep them from going to Church on Sunday. Anyone who does this is putting money before God.

We show our love for God by our worship or adoration of God. How do we adore God? We adore Him by discovering His will and then by doing His will. Once we know what God wants us to do, we should obey His will. How does God want us to adore Him? One of the most important ways we can adore God is by sacrifice. What is sacrifice? Sacrifice is giving something precious to God. The most precious thing we have is our own will. When we surrender our wills to God, when we obey God even when we would desire to do something else, we are giving Him a great gift. An even greater offering is the Holy Sacrifice of the Mass. There we can offer ourselves with Jesus Christ on the altar at every Mass.

Besides obeying and giving Him sacrifice, we worship God by praying, and by making acts of Faith, Hope, and Charity. These three theological virtues are directed towards God. We receive these three theological virtues when we receive the Sacrament of Baptism.

What is the virtue of faith? Faith enables us to believe all that God has revealed because He has revealed it. We cannot know what God has revealed unless we find out by studying the Catholic Faith. We do not stop learning about our Catholic Faith when we are finished with school. No. Our love for God should make us want to learn more about Him our entire lives. Once we know our Catholic Faith, we must share it with others.

God wants us to make Acts of Faith frequently. What is an Act of Faith? An Act of Faith is a prayer telling God that we believe in Him and that we believe all the truths He has revealed. We should say the following prayer every day: "O my God, I firmly believe that Thou art one God in three Divine Persons, Father, Son, and Holy Spirit. I believe that Thy divine Son became Man, and died for our sins, and that He will come to judge the living and the dead. I believe these and all the truths which the Holy Catholic Church teaches, because Thou has revealed them, Who can neither deceive nor be deceived."

By the virtue of hope, we confidently trust that, after we die, God will bring us to our final end, happiness with Him in Heaven. Hope is another theological virtue that is directed toward God. Along with the Act of Faith, we should daily pray an Act of Hope. What is an Act of Hope? An Act of Hope is a prayer stating that we trust in God to pardon our sins, for which we are sorry, and to give us the means to obtain eternal salvation. God is All-Merciful and we can trust Him to forgive us if we just ask for His forgiveness.

Say this Act of Hope at least once a day:

"O my God, relying on Thy almighty power and infinite mercy and promises, I hope to obtain pardon of my sins, the help of Thy grace, and life everlasting, through the merits of Jesus Christ, my Lord and Redeemer."

Matching

7	1. God	1. Were worshiped in Old Testament times
10	2. First Commandment	2. Performed by prayer and sacrifice
1	3. False gods	3. Belief in God
9	4. Theological virtues	4. Lifelong
3	5. Faith	5. The Perfect Sacrifice
8	6. Hope	6. Surrender of something precious to God
6	7. Sacrifice	7. The Only Necessary Being
2	8. Adoration of God	8. Trust in God
4	9. Study of Catholic Faith	9. Faith, Hope and Charity
5	10. Mass	10. "I am the Lord thy God…"

In our last lesson, we discussed the three theological virtues of Faith, Hope, and Charity. The greatest theological virtue of all, the one that will last for all eternity, is Charity. In the Bible, we read, "…faith, hope, and charity abide, these three; but the greatest of these is charity" (I Corinthians 13:13).

Why is Charity the greatest of the theological virtues? When God calls us from this life, we will no longer need Faith because we will see God face to face. Nor will we need the virtue of Hope, because what we have hoped for, the graces we needed to get to Heaven, we will have received. Charity, however, lasts for all eternity. We will love God and everyone else in Heaven forever. Actually, the kind of love to which we refer requires a special word: Charity.

We may say that we "love" certain foods, certain toys, or our pets. We say that we love our parents, our brothers, and our sisters. We use the same word for many different kinds of love. That is why we need a special word, Charity, for a higher and deeper love which expresses our love for God, and for our neighbor out of love for God.

We should say the Act of Charity every day: "O my God, I love Thee above all things, with my whole heart and soul, because Thou are all-good and worthy of all love. I love my neighbor as myself for the love of Thee. I forgive all who have injured me, and ask pardon of all whom I have injured." Notice that Charity is, first of all, love for God.

Let's return to the virtue of Faith. We have seen that learning our Catholic Faith should continue throughout our lives. If we study our Faith and pray daily for an increase in our Faith, we will go a long way toward cooperating with the graces God gives us to achieve our salvation. It is possible, however, to lose our Faith. How? By committing sins against Faith.

What are the sins against the virtue of Faith? There are four main sins against the virtue of Faith: apostasy, heresy, indifferentism, and taking part in non-Catholic worship.

What is apostasy? Apostasy is the total rejection of the Catholic Faith by a baptized person. If a baptized person rejects Christianity and goes to a non-Christian church (or no church at all), he has committed the very serious sin of apostasy. To be baptized into Christ and then to reject Christ, the Son of God, is very serious indeed.

Heresy is the rejection of one or more truths of the Catholic Faith by a baptized Catholic. If a Catholic decides he accepts all of the teachings of the Church except for one, he is committing a sin against the virtue of Faith. All the truths of the Catholic Church were given to His Church by the Son of God. If a person does not accept one of the teachings of Jesus Christ, he is guilty of heresy. Heresy is a serious sin. How can we reject a teaching of Jesus Christ and expect to attain eternal life in Heaven?

Pope John Paul II wrote a Church encyclical called *Veritatis Splendor.* In this encyclical, the Pope said that there is a terrible error which many people are accepting. Many people think that if they "fundamentally" accept the teachings of Jesus, but sin in one area, they will still be saved. The Pope said that is not true. The Pope said that if a person dies with just one mortal sin on his soul, he will not be received into Heaven.

Indifferentism is another sin against the virtue of Faith. Indifferentism means that a person denies that the worship of God is a *serious duty.* An indifferent person is one who says that it does not matter if a person prays or not, goes to church or not. God will save us all anyway! This kind of sin leads to a person lacking graces to avoid sin, and eventually this kind of person falls into practicing more serious sins.

Indifferentism also can mean that a person believes that one religion is as good as another. Indifferentism is a serious sin which deeply hurts Jesus Christ, because He founded the one holy Catholic Church. Although other religions, especially other Christian religions, contain *some* divinely revealed truths, only the one, true, holy Catholic Church contains *all* truths given us by God. While we should treat everyone, Catholics and non-Catholics alike, with love and respect, we must never take part in non-Catholic worship. We cannot be indifferent to the truth!

O Jesus, Whose delight is to be with children, have mercy on us.

Multiple Choice

_____c_____ 1. The greatest theological virtue is
    a) faith.   b) hope.   c) charity.

_____b_____ 2. The virtues of _____ will disappear in the next life.
    a) hope and charity.
    b) faith and hope.
    c) faith and charity.

_____a_____ 3. Charity is first of all
    a) love for God.
    b) love for self.
    c) love for everything.

_____c_____ 4. We should study our faith
    a) only through high school.
    b) through college.
    c) for our entire lives.

_____a_____ 5. It _____ possible to lose our faith.
    a) is   b) is not

_____c_____ 6. Apostasy is
    a) denying one or more truths of the faith.
    b) going to non-Catholic churches.
    c) completely leaving the Catholic faith.

_____b_____ 7. A heretic
    a) loves the Catholic faith.
    b) denies one or more truths of the faith.
    c) doesn't care what church he goes to.

_____a_____ 8. Indifferentism means believing that
    a) one religion is as good as another.
    b) Christ founded only one Church.
    c) worship of God is a serious duty.

_____a_____ 9. We should _____ non-Catholics.
    a) respect
    b) hate
    c) tolerate

_____c_____ 10. Love for God and love of neighbor is
    a) no different than love for people.
    b) no different than love for self.
    c) called the theological virtue of charity.

Today we will discuss the virtue of Hope.

We often say that we *hope* we will earn a good grade on a test, or we may *hope* to receive a puppy for Christmas. Those are natural feeling of hope, but there is a *supernatural hope* which is one of the theological virtues which we receive at Baptism. What is the theological virtue of Hope? The virtue of Hope encourages a person to desire eternal life and gives the confidence of receiving the grace necessary to reach Heaven. The virtue of Hope gives us confidence that we can attain eternal life as long as we are faithfully living our Catholic Faith. We have the virtue of Hope because we know how much God loves us, and we know God is All Merciful and wants us to be sorry for our sins. Once we reach Heaven, there will be no need for the virtue of Hope.

Just as there are sins against the virtue of Faith, there are sins against the virtue of Hope. There are two chief sins against the virtue of Hope: presumption and despair. What is presumption? Presumption means that a person believes he can save himself without God's help or without cooperating with God's grace. That is a grave sin. You might ask, "What is the difference between the virtue of Hope and the sin of presumption?" The virtue of Hope is confident assurance that we will be saved but *not* without our cooperation, and certainly not without God's grace. No one may *assume* he is saved. It is only through God's generous love and mercy that we can even hope to be saved, and not without our complete cooperation with the graces that He gives us, especially in the Sacraments and prayer.

The sin of despair is the opposite of presumption. A person despairs when he refuses to trust God. A person commits the sin of despair when he gives up all hope of salvation, or believes he no longer has the means necessary to reach Heaven. That is an offense against God's goodness, love, and mercy, because God alone has the power to save us. We have a duty to trust God, Who loves us so much that He made us.

Hope is complete trust and confidence in God; presumption and despair place trust in oneself. The *Catechism of the Catholic Church* tells us: "Hope is the theological virtue by which we desire the kingdom of Heaven and eternal life as our happiness, placing our trust in Christ's promises, and relying not on our own strength, but on the help of the grace of the Holy Spirit" (CCC 1817). God will save us if we do our part!

Pope John Paul II said "Hope is a gift of the Holy Spirit…even in the face of the difficulties of this life and the painful experiences of misconduct and failure in human history, hope is the source of Christian optimism" (General audience, May 27, 1992). St. Elizabeth Ann Seton faced many difficulties because of the illness and death of her husband. However, she continued to have hope and trust in God to help her and her children.

The spiritual Works of Mercy are especially important to help those who may have fallen into despair. *Counseling the doubtful* and *comforting the sorrowful* are important acts of charity, because despair can cause a person to lose hope in his own salvation.

Jesus, Son of the Blessed Mother, have mercy on us.

True (T) or False (F)

_____ F 1. Hoping I will get a good grade on a test is supernatural hope.

_____ T 2. Hope is a theological virtue.

_____ T 3. Theological virtues are received at Baptism.

_____ F 4. There are three chief sins against hope: pride, presumption and despair.

_____ F 5. Hope will last for all eternity.

_____ F 6. Despair and presumption are the same thing.

_____ F 7. We need not cooperate with the graces God gives us.

_____ T 8. Hope is trust that God will provide the means to save us.

_____ T 9. St. Elizabeth Ann Seton overcame great difficulty because of her trust in God.

_____ T 10. We should help people who despair, with counseling and comforting.

We have learned that the Church is more than just the faithful souls here on earth, whom we call the Church Militant. The Mystical Body of Christ also includes the souls in Heaven, that is, the Church Triumphant, and the souls in Purgatory, that is, the Church Suffering. Today we will see how the Church Triumphant shares with all the other souls in the Church.

The souls in Heaven were, of course, once here on earth. They fought the good fight and, with the help of divine grace, they are now in Heaven enjoying God face to face. They have what the Church calls the Beatific Vision of God. They are, therefore, God's special friends. The souls in Heaven know about our struggles and pains because they endured trials just like we do now. They are our special friends because they understand our sufferings and they pray for us. That is why it is good to honor the saints in Heaven and to ask for their prayers. Even as we say that, we immediately must see that only God can be adored. The saints, like our parents, receive our respect and love, but only God our Creator deserves to be adored.

The saints in Heaven practiced extraordinary virtue while here on earth. What does that mean? It means that they always chose to do the will of God over their own wills. The saints denied themselves bodily pleasures out of love for God and others. The saints gave God the first place, the most importance in their lives. What does that means to us? It means that we should honor and imitate the lives of the saints.

A good example of a saint for young people to imitate is Bernadette Soubirous. Bernadette was a simple, young teenage girl who lived in the middle of the nineteenth century. She was often sick because she suffered from asthma, a breathing disorder. She also had a difficult time learning her school lessons. One day, Bernadette and her sister went to look for firewood for their mother. Suddenly, a light breeze touched Bernadette's cheek and she found herself in the presence of a

beautiful Lady. The Lady later identified herself as the Immaculate Conception. The Mother of God appeared to this simple young girl! Bernadette suffered greatly after that, because many people did not believe her. However, many others did believe her and soon there were thousands of people coming to the Grotto where our Lady continued to appear. Many people were cured of illness. Today, millions of people have gone to Lourdes, France, to honor our Lady, and to pray and to ask for miracles.

Bernadette was declared a saint by the Church in the early part of the twentieth century. We can imitate her by living simply, praying often, and trusting completely in God's holy will. We know that she is in Heaven with God praying and interceding for us, especially when we ask her to intercede for us. Even on earth, we ask our family members and friends to pray for us. We should not hesitate to ask our heavenly friends to pray for us!

There are millions of saints in Heaven. A canonized saint is a person who has been officially raised to the honor of a saint of the altar by a Pope. These saints have special feast days and Masses in their honor, which offer us an opportunity to ask them for their prayers. There are biblical saints, saints we know from the Bible, such as St. Martha. There are traditional saints whom we know by their saintly lives or their martyrdom, such as St. Augustine who lived in the fourth century. There are multitudes of unknown saints whose feast day we celebrate every year on November first, called All Saints' Day. These are all the unknown souls enjoying the rewards of heavenly beatitude with God, the angels, and all the other saints.

Matching

___1___ 1. Church triumphant 1. Souls in Purgatory

___6___ 2. Church suffering 2. Raising souls to the honors of the altar

___9___ 3. Church militant 3. Practiced by all saints

___3___ 4. Extraordinary virtue 4. A saint for young people to imitate

___2___ 5. Canonization 5. Traditional saint

___4___ 6. St. Bernadette 6. Souls on earth

___8___ 7. St. Martha 7. France

___5___ 8. St. Augustine 8. Biblical saint

___10___ 9. All Saints' Day 9. Souls in Heaven

___7___ 10. Lourdes 10. November 1st

Today, we begin the study of the Second Commandment of God, "Thou shalt not take the name of the Lord thy God in vain." To better understand this Commandment, we must go back to the Old Testament times. From the beginning of time, names had important meanings to God. God surely named Adam and Eve. Remember that God asked Adam to name the animals.

When God gave special assignments or tasks for His people, He changed their names. For example, He chose Abram to be the father of the nation of Israel, changing his name to Abraham, which means "father of a multitude of people." Much later, Jesus changed Simon's name to Peter, which means "Rock," because Peter was to be the immovable rock foundation upon which Jesus Christ would build His Catholic Church.

If the names of certain people were special, how much more should the name of God be cherished? When God spoke to Moses from the burning bush, Moses asked God what was His name. God answered, "I Am Who Am" (Exodus 3:14). "I Am Who Am" expresses the very nature of God, Who always was and always will be.

So holy was God's Name to the Jewish people, they would not even pronounce His Name aloud. To Christians, the holy Name of the Son of God, *Jesus Christ*, must be spoken with great reverence and awe. In the Bible we read, "…at the Name of Jesus every knee should bow, in Heaven and on earth and under the earth" (Philippians 2:10). God's Name is so holy, we should speak it only in prayer or as we study our religion.

The Second Commandment could be considered one of the Commandments of speech (the other is the Eighth Commandment). The tongue is a very powerful means of expressing what is in our hearts. Jesus tells us, "…out of the abundance of the heart, the mouth speaks" (Matthew 12:34). It is a sin to deliberately and willfully use God's holy name in a way that is not reverent or prayerful. This would seem to indicate a heart which does not have reverence for God!

When we discuss the Second Commandment, keeping holy the name of the Lord, we often discuss oaths. This is because when we take an oath in court to tell the truth, we ask God to bear witness to the truth. We are asked if we promise to tell the truth "so help me, God." What a person is saying when he takes an oath is that he knows God is all-knowing, so the person is asking God to be a Witness to the truth of what he is saying. God is being called upon to witness the truth of his oath or promise to tell the truth. If a person knowingly tells a lie after asking God to be a witness to the truth of a statement, he commits the serious sin of perjury. People are put in jail for committing perjury. The Church tells us that oaths should be taken only for very serious reasons.

The Church teaches that when we take an oath, we must be completely convinced that what we are saying is absolutely true. We should use God's name to witness to some truth only in special circumstances, such as taking solemn oaths or witnessing to a truth in court. Otherwise, in daily conversation, when we say "yes," we should mean "yes;" and when we say "no," we should mean "no." In His Sermon on the Mount, Jesus tells us, "Let what you say be simply 'Yes' or 'No'" (Matthew 5: 37). Jesus wants us to give honest, simple answers when we speak.

The Church teaches also that we are committing a serious sin to take an oath to do something wrong. This is a very serious sin because we are asking God to be a Witness to our promise to do something against the law of God!

Most of the time when we hear someone take the name of the Lord God in vain, that is, without being in prayer or speaking in reverence, the person does not realize what he is doing. Some people may not think they are doing anything wrong when they say things like, "I swear to God," or "Honest to God." However, using God's Name carelessly, or for emphasis, or to use stronger language, is wrong!

If we hear someone take God's name in vain, we should silently adore God in prayer. "May the Name of Jesus be praised, reverenced, honored, and adored throughout the world, now and forever." If you cannot remember that prayer, simply say "Jesus, I love You." You could say, "Jesus, have mercy!"

When St. Maria Goretti was approached by the young man who spoke to her in a sinful way, she told him it was a sin to speak in such a way. She even warned him that he would go to Hell for his sins. Anytime we hear Our Lord's name used in a way that is not holy, let us first say a prayer to God to make up for the unholy speech, but then let us say a prayer for the person who is speaking, that he does not commit the sin again.

Jesus, Son of the Living God, have mercy on us.

True (T) or False (F)

____T____ 1. The Second Commandment forbids taking God's name in vain.

____F____ 2. God changed people's names because they did not like them.

____T____ 3. God told His Name to Abraham.

____T____ 4. Abraham was the father of a multitude of people.

____T____ 5. At the name of Jesus every knee shall bow.

____F____ 6. The First Commandment is a commandment of speech.

____T____ 7. When we take an oath, we ask God to bear witness to what we are saying.

____T____ 8. Jesus told us to say "yes" when we mean yes, and "no" when we mean no. That means we should say no more.

____T____ 9. If someone takes God's Name in vain, we should get angry.

____T____ 10. An oath should be taken only for serious reasons.

The Second Commandment of God is: "Thou shalt not take the name of the Lord thy God in vain." This commandment means we should not use the name of God in a disrespectful manner. However, as we learned about oaths and vows, we can see that this commandment applies to calling on God to be a witness to the truth.

There are two sins against the Second Commandment which we should know about. These are cursing, which is calling down evil on a person, and blasphemy, which is insulting God either directly or indirectly.

People may not realize that cursing is a sin against the Second Commandment. Cursing is calling down evil upon someone or something. It is a desire for someone to suffer harm. Here we will address the important subject of anger. John and Bill are playing in a soccer match. John runs into Bill purposely to keep him from kicking the ball. Bill becomes angry and begins to shout at John. He becomes so angry, that he begins to curse him, wishing harm on him. Anger can certainly lead to violence, but cursing is violence in use of language. Cursing is a terrible sin, since God told us we should love our neighbor as ourselves. Jesus said, "Everyone who grows angry with his brother shall be liable to judgment" (Matthew 5:21-22).

Another horrible sin is the sin of blasphemy. The holy Name of God should be used with the greatest reverence and awe because God has an infinite amount of love for us. For us to speak directly against God is a very, very serious sin. Blasphemy is speaking or acting against God, or religious people or religious things in a contemptuous, scornful, or abusive manner. Speaking against the Blessed Mother and the holy saints is also the sin of blasphemy. Drawings, paintings, movies, plays, and any other forms of communication which are used to show contempt toward God, God's Laws, the Blessed Mother, the Saints, the Catholic Church, priests and nuns, and any other sacred persons, places, or things, are examples of blasphemy.

The emotions can play a large part in the commission of any sin. Blasphemy can be committed by a person who is deeply troubled. If a person is going through a great trial and blasphemes God, he may not be as responsible for his sin, but it is up to the confessor to judge.

We should keep in mind what the Bible teaches about the tongue. "…the tongue is a fire…No human being can tame the tongue—a restless evil, full of deadly poison. With it, we bless the Lord and Father…From the same mouth come blessing and cursing" (James 3:6, 8-9).

Some people take God's holy Name in vain, but they do it carelessly, without thinking. We have seen that using God's Name carelessly is wrong, and it can even be a mortal sin. Whenever we hear someone taking God's Name in vain, we might bless ourselves or offer a silent prayer of reparation for the sin. We should pray for the person who is committing the sin. Returning to God the glory and honor due His name is a praiseworthy thing to do, and could even cause the person to change his behavior.

In the Old Testament, Job was visited by many, many terrible trials. He lost all of his children, all his land, and became very sick. However, Job would not become angry with God. His friends, thinking they were helping him, told him that he would feel better if he

became angry with God. Still, Job would not blame God. He trusted God through all the years of pain and sorrow. In the end, God lifted all of Job's afflictions, and he lived the remainder of his life in happiness and peace.

The virtue of Faith and the virtue of Hope or trust in God are key to meeting any trial in life. Nothing and no one should cause us to become so angry that we blaspheme God or God's holy Name, or curse anyone or anything. God is pure Holiness and Love. Praised be Jesus Christ, now and forever!

Jesus, Model of virtues, have mercy on us.

Matching

___3___ 1. Tongue

___10___ 2. Second Commandment

___1___ 3. Cursing

___6___ 4. Blasphemy

___2___ 5. Job

___9___ 6. Key to meeting trials in life

___4___ 7. Anger

___5___ 8. St. James

___7___ 9. We should treat God's name

___8___ 10. Internal pain

1. Calling down evil on someone

2. Would not complain to God about his sufferings

3. "Full of deadly poison"

4. Sometimes leads to cursing

5. "From the same mouth come blessing and cursing"

6. Speaking or acting against God in an unholy manner

7. With reverence and awe

8. Sometimes causes a person to blaspheme

9. Faith and Hope in God

10. "Thou shalt not take the Name of the Lord in vain."

As we begin the Third Commandment, we note that our very first obligation is to love and serve our Creator. That is why the first three Commandments summarize our responsibilities towards God. The Third Commandment, "Remember thou keep holy the Lord's Day," should be self-evident. What is God commanding? He is commanding that, because God is the Creator and we are the created, there should be no question of our love and service owed to our Creator.

We should think of it this way. We know how much we owe our parents. They have taken care of us by providing food and clothes and a home. They take us to the doctor when we are sick. They take us to ball games and provide us with ice cream and candy and toys. We owe our parents much because of all they do for us. Yet we love them deeply and truly *not* because we owe them our love, but because they love us so much. Their actions show what is in their hearts.

In the same way, while we know we *owe* God our love and respect for all the wonderful gifts He has given us, we really and truly love God because He loves us so much. He gave us His own Son to die on the cross for us so that we could enter eternal happiness in Heaven.

The Church teaches that we must attend Mass on Sunday. We might ask why do we go to Mass on Sunday and not another day of the week? In Old Testament times, the Jewish people worshiped God on Saturdays, not Sundays. In New Testament times, however, the Lord's Day, or the Sabbath, was changed to Sunday, the first day of the week. Why?

Sunday is the day of the week that Jesus Christ rose from the dead. We call it Easter Sunday.

Sunday is the day of the week on which the Holy Spirit descended upon the Apostles. We call this day Pentecost Sunday. Pentecost Sunday is the birthday of the Church.

In the *Catechism of the Catholic Church,* the Sabbath Day is stressed under the obligations of the Third Commandment. Quoting from Exodus 31:15, we read that the "Sabbath [is a day] of solemn rest, holy to the Lord."

"For in six days the Lord made Heaven and earth, the sea, and all that is in them, and rested the seventh day; therefore, the Lord blessed the Sabbath day and hallowed it" (Exodus 20:11).

Under the *Catechism* heading "Sunday – fulfillment of the Sabbath," we learn: "In Christ's Passover, Sunday fulfills the spiritual truth of the Jewish Sabbath and announces man's eternal rest in God."

In Section 2176 of the *Catechism*, the Church teaches "The celebration of Sunday observes the moral commandment inscribed by nature in the human heart to render to God an outward, visible, public, and regular worship 'as a sign of His universal beneficence to all.' Sunday worship fulfills the moral command of the Old Covenant, taking up its rhythm and spirit in the weekly celebration of the Creator and Redeemer of his people."

In Section 2177 of the *Catechism*, we read that "The Sunday celebration of the Lord's Day and His Eucharist is at the heart of the Church's life. Sunday is the day on which the paschal mystery is celebrated in light of the apostolic tradition and is to be observed as the foremost holy day of obligation in the universal Church."

The Church has always taught that we must fulfill our obligations towards God primarily by attending Mass on Sundays and Holy Days of Obligation. This is the minimum required by the Catholic Church to give to God the glory He deserves.

Why, we may ask, does the Church require that we go to Mass *every* Sunday? First, and most importantly, we go to Mass under the virtue of religion. What is the virtue of religion? It is a moral virtue which helps a person give to God the worship and service He deserves. We are mere creatures who need God at every moment of our lives. God created us and we need His help all throughout our lives.

When we attend Mass, we should not just be an observer. How should we be present at Mass? The Second Vatican Council wrote: "Christ's faithful, when present at this mystery of faith, should not be there as strangers or silent spectators. On the contrary, through a proper appreciation of the rites and prayers, they should participate knowingly, devoutly, and actively. (*Constitution on Sacred Liturgy*, n. 48).

The Church is telling us that when we go to Mass, we should present ourselves before God with the deepest reverence and gratitude to Him for all He is and for all He has given to us. We should try not to let our minds wander, and we should take part fully in the greatest mystery of our faith: the Holy Sacrifice of the Mass. We must not be silent spectators, but should join in saying our prayers and offering our fullest attention in giving reverence, respect, and worship to God.

Jesus, Infinite Goodness, have mercy on us.

Fill in the Blanks

1. Our first obligation is to love and serve **GOD**.

2. In Old Testament times, the Jewish people *worshiped* God on **Saturday**

3. Jesus Christ changed the Sabbath day to **Sunday**.

4. Sunday is the day we go to Mass because it is the day Jesus Christ **rose** from the dead.

5. Sunday is also the day the Holy Spirit descended on the **apostles** at Pentecost.

6. We are allowed to attend Mass on Saturday evening, but **Sunday** is the Lord's Day.

7. The virtue of religion is a **moral** virtue.

8. The Church teaches that we should **participate** at Mass knowingly, devoutly, and actively.

9. We must depend on God for **everything**

10. We should attend Mass with great **joy**.

Each of God's Ten Commandments instructs us to do what is God's will, but they also forbid us to do what is opposed to God's will. We have seen that the Third Commandment commands us to keep the Lord's Day holy. The Catholic Church tells us what we must do on Sundays and Holydays of Obligation to keep the day holy. We must attend Mass. To keep the Lord's Day holy, there are some things the Church says we must *not do* on Sundays.

Think about what we do six days a week. Six days a week, we are engaged in the activities of daily living. We go to work, we learn our lessons. We spend our time working and playing. Our thoughts are on whatever occupies us at the moment. On Sundays, however, God wants us to take time off from our usual daily labors. Why? He wants us to turn our *minds and hearts* to Him so that we may renew our souls and our bodies. The Church encourages us to take Sundays to reflect on our relationship with God and with others, especially with our family members.

So what does the Church teach we are forbidden to do on Sundays and holy days of obligation? The Church forbids us to do servile work on Sundays and holy days. What is servile work? Servile work is anything that requires us to use our bodies doing what was formerly "servants" work. We should avoid heavy unnecessary work or conducting regular business, unnecessary shopping, or housekeeping on Sundays.

The new *Catechism of the Catholic Church* emphasizes that our work must not keep us from attending Mass on Sunday. Our work must not keep us from celebrating the joy of the Sabbath or the special feast days on the Sabbath. At the heart of the matter is keeping the day holy. Aside from our attendance at Mass, we should spend extra time in prayer and spiritual reading on Sunday.

Pope John XXIII taught that "It is the right of God, and within His power, to order that man put aside a day each week for proper and due worship of the Divinity. He should direct his mind to Heavenly things, setting aside daily business. He should explore the depths of his conscience in order to know how necessary and inviolable are his relations with God" (*Mater et Magistra*, n. 249). What is the Pope telling us? He is telling us that our relationship with God should be so deep that nothing and no one should be placed before our duties towards God Who loves us beyond our imagination.

We are allowed to do what is necessary on Sundays and Holydays. Mother must prepare a meal, but she should not do what she is able to do any other day, such as housecleaning. Father may work only if his job requires it and he cannot find another job. Of course, policemen, firemen, doctors, nurses, and power plant workers must work on Sundays, but perhaps they can arrange to have some Sundays off.

Always keep in mind the basic reason why we abstain from unnecessary work on Sundays, and why we must attend Mass. All good gifts in this world come from God. We need to take one day a week to give God the worship, praise, and adoration we know He is due. Jesus told us "The Sabbath was made for man, not man for the Sabbath" (Mark 2:27). What does this mean? It means that man needs the Lord's Day as a way to express gratefulness to God. Most people *want* to take the time to thank God for all their blessings. It is because we love God above all things that we want to worship Him on Sundays.

O Jesus, Treasure of the Faithful, have mercy on us.

Fill in the Blanks

1. On Sundays, God wants us to rest from our __laber__.

2. __servile__ work is anything that requires us to use our bodies rather than our minds.

3. On Sundays, we avoid unnecessary work or unnecessary __conduct__ at the store.

4. Pope __John__ wrote an encyclical about keeping Sundays holy.

5. The name of the above encyclical is __mater et magistra__.

6. We must keep holy also the __holyday__ of __Obligation__

7. The Pope wrote that on Sundays, our minds should be on __holy__ things.

8. Our first duty is to attend __mass__ on Sundays.

9. We should not shop on __Sunday__

10. People who are allowed to work on some Sundays are __policemen__ and __firemen__.

We have seen that the first three Commandments are directed towards God. The last seven Commandments are directed towards others.

The first of the commandments of God which are directed towards others deals with our obligations towards the most important people in the world, our parents. The First Commandment of God commands that we must honor God above all others. That First Commandment is based on the fact that God is our loving Creator. He is the God Who made us and is responsible for keeping us in existence at every moment. So we owe Him adoration and worship as well as complete obedience to His laws.

Our parents also are responsible for our existence, and for keeping us alive at every moment until we are old enough to support ourselves. That is why God gave us the commandment to "Honor thy father and thy mother" as the very first commandment following our commands regarding God.

It is through our parents that we first discover God, learn our Catholic Faith, and become acquainted with our world. It is our parents who love us deeply. It is our parents who are our first teachers. For our homeschooling families, it is our parents who have dedicated their lives day-in and day-out to teaching us, by word and example, the ultimate truths of life.

We can look to Jesus and the Holy Family to see how to practice obedience, honor, and respect towards our parents. Jesus, the Son of God, obeyed Mary, His human mother, in everything she asked Him to do. Jesus, the Son of God, obeyed Joseph, His foster father on earth and a carpenter. Jesus, as the Son of God, wanted to obey the Fourth Commandment to show us the importance of obedience, even if we think we know better than our parents!

The virtue of obedience is so important in becoming holy, that Jesus wanted to show us by His example that we should be obedient to our parents. Obedience is a very important virtue because it means submitting one's own will to the will of someone else. Jesus knows that if children do not learn to be obedient and respectful to their own parents, especially to their own human father, they might never learn to be obedient to the Laws of God, especially to be obedient to God their Father in Heaven.

By the Fourth Commandment, God commands us to love and respect our parents, and to obey them in all that is not sinful, even when we do not understand the reason for their asking us to do something. It is easy to obey a command from our parents when we agree with them, or when we understand the command. It is when we do not agree or understand, but we are still obedient that we earn graces and learn to become holy. When God commands us to "Honor thy father and thy mother," He means for us to love, revere, be loyal to, respect, and be obedient to our parents. In addition, children are to care for their parents when they are in need. Parents need their children to help them when they become sick, disabled, or elderly.

When God gave the command, "Honor thy father and thy mother," He was also giving parents the right and responsibility to rule over their children. He thus gave parents the right and responsibility to give both the natural life as well as the supernatural life to their children. The parents are obliged to provide for the children's bodily needs as well as their supernatural needs. Because of our parents, we have the means, through the Catholic Faith they have given us, to attain everlasting life in Heaven.

Jesus, Strength of Martyrs, have mercy on us.

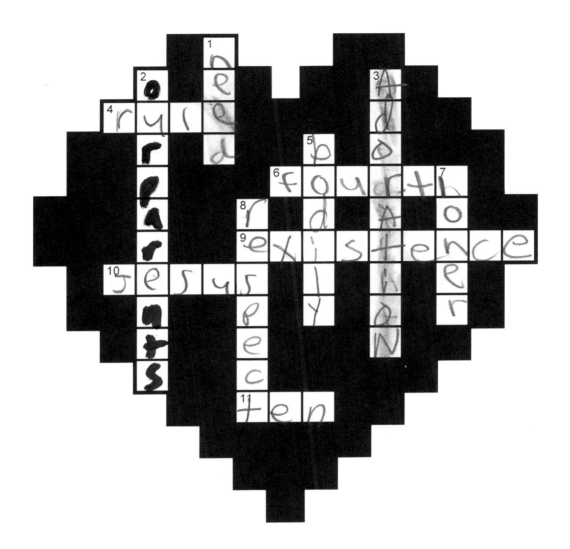

Across

4 God gave parents the right and responsibility to __ over their children. (4)

6 The __ Commandment commands us to obey our parents. (6)

9 God keeps us in __ at every moment. (9)

10 Children should follow the example of __ in obeying their parents. (5)

11 There are __ Commandments. (3)

Down

1 Children are to care for their parents when they are in __. (4)

2 the most important people in the world (3,7)

3 We owe God __ and worship. (9)

5 Parents are obliged to provide for their children's __ needs. (6)

7 "__ thy father and thy mother." (5)

8 God commands us to love and __ our parents. (7)

The Fourth Commandment of God is: Honor thy father and thy mother. This Commandment commands children to honor and respect their parents, and to obey them in all that is not sinful.

The Fourth Commandment is often called the "authority commandment." What does that mean? Everyone is under someone's authority, even the president of the United States. God reigns over us all. Our first contact with someone in authority is our parents. Who gives them that right? God Himself gives parents the right of authority over their children.

What can we give our parents in return for all the sacrifices they make for us? We can show them our respect and gratitude for all their sacrifices on our behalf by honoring and obeying them as God's instruments in our lives. We are always to honor and respect our parents in all that is not sinful. As they grow old, we are to care for them as they cared for us when we were children. Why? Because God put them in our lives and, like Him, they sacrifice for us and care for us by the graces God gives them.

As we have seen, all authority comes from God. Just before His death, Jesus Christ, Creator of the universe, stood before a human judge. Pontius Pilate had been waiting for Jesus to respond to his questions. When He did not respond, Pilate gazed into the suffering face of God Himself and said, "Do you not know that I have power to release you and power to crucify you?" Jesus answered, "You would have no power over Me whatever, unless it were given you from above" (John 19:10-11). With those words, Jesus forever made clear that all authority in Heaven and on earth comes from God.

Obedience is a very important virtue in the eyes of God. We are not sure exactly what the sin of Lucifer and the bad angels was, but we believe that the bad angels did not want to obey God or to recognize His authority to rule over them. We know that the one rule which God gave Adam and Eve was to obey Him by not eating of the fruit of the tree of knowledge of good and evil. Original sin was disobedience to God's single command.

Father D. Chisholm, in a book called *The Catechism in Examples,* tells the following story about the virtue of obedience, pp. 190 to 191.

"One of the ancient Fathers in the desert had a vision of Heaven. He saw there, as it were, four different companies of Saints, placed one above the other in glory.

"The lowest group was composed of those who, while on earth, had been afflicted with sickness and bodily infirmities, and had borne them patiently for God's sake. The second group consisted of those who had in this life been kind to strangers and the poor, and had spent their lives in acts of charity towards their neighbor.

"In the third group were those holy solitaries [hermits or monks] who for Christ's sake had left the world to seek only the kingdom of God by a life of prayer and penance. All these groups were enjoying great happiness in God's holy presence.

"But the fourth group was still more glorious; and those who composed it seemed to possess even a greater happiness than the others.

"The solitary [Father in the desert] asked the angel who showed him these things, who those were who formed that glorious company.

"'Those whom you see so high up and beautiful,' answered the angel, "are those who, when in the world, had been obedient.

"'The others served God well, therefore they are now enjoying the reward of their fidelity. But in their good works, there was much that was agreeable to themselves.

"'But those who were obedient renounced their own will to submit themselves to the will of others whom God had placed over them. And for this, God has bestowed on them a high degree of glory.'

Learn, then, from this example, how agreeable to God is an obedient child."

Jesus, Joy of Angels, have mercy on us.

Fill in the Blanks

1. The Fourth Commandment of God is: Honor thy _father_ and _mother_.

2. God gives parents the right of _authority_ over their children.

3. We must show our parents _honer_ and _respect_ for the sacrifices they make for us.

4. All authority comes from _GOD_.

5. The human judge of Jesus Christ was _Pontius Pilate_.

6. Jesus said, "You would have no power over Me whatever, unless it were given you from _above_."

7. Original Sin was _disobedience_ to God's command.

8. In the vision by one of the Fathers of the Church, the most blessed were those who renounced their own wills and were obedient to those whom _GOD_ had placed over them.

9. God finds greatly agreeable an _Obedint_ child.

10. As our parents grow older, we are to care for them as they _cared_ for us.

The Fourth Commandment of God is: Honor thy father and thy mother.

The Fourth Commandment obliges us to respect and obey others who are in authority over us. Sometimes when parents go out of the house, they hire a babysitter to take care of the children. Children are thus obliged to obey the babysitter in all that is not sinful. It would be a sin for children not to obey a babysitter or anyone else who is put in authority while parents are gone.

Sometimes parents take their children to swimming lessons or other sports activities. Sometimes parents take their children to art or dance classes. Parents are thus giving these teachers authority over their children for that period of time. Thus it would be a sin for children to be disobedient to these people whom parents have put in authority for a period of time.

As we have seen, the Fourth Commandment is directed primarily to our relationship with our parents. In addition, the Church teaches that we should honor, obey, and respect the Popes, the bishops, and the priests.

In addition to Church law, God wants us to respect the civil law, as well as all lawful authorities such as policemen, in all that is not sinful. Why? Because by breaking the law, we can be breaking God's law upon which the civil law is supposed to be based. The purpose of the law is to keep peace among the people. Most laws are good. They protect people and promote the general welfare. Some laws, however, are not good laws. When man's law disagrees with God's law, for example laws that promote the destruction of pre-born children, we must not only not obey them, we must do all that we can to stop them. St. Thomas Aquinas taught that, "A bad law is no law at all." In other words, laws or rules that are against the laws of God or the rules of Church are not binding as laws.

The Catholic Church encourages good citizenship and patriotism, which is love for one's country. How do we love our country? By obeying just laws, by paying taxes, by voting, and by defending one's country, especially by serving in the military service.

Public officials represent the people. They have a serious duty to promote the welfare of the citizens of their nation. Once they are elected, it is their responsibility to make good laws that protect the people. The laws should protect especially the weak, as well as those who are poor, sick, and disabled, the elderly and the unborn, the very young, and children. These are citizens who are not able to protect themselves.

For our part, we have a duty as citizens to vote. Our right to vote is a great privilege, and it should always be exercised with great care. What are we saying? We are saying that we have a serious responsibility to vote for moral people who stand for Christian principles, who are obedient to the Laws of God. It is a sin to vote for anyone who does not support and work for the just Laws of God. That is against the Church's teachings and against God's laws.

We should not end our study of the Fourth Commandment without remembering the holiest family of all: Jesus, Mary, and Joseph. They are our models of obedience, humility, patience, and charity. Should we not be obedient to our parents as Jesus was to His parents? Should we not humbly accept all that God allows to happen to us, as did the Holy Family when they were banished from their home and had to flee to Egypt? Should we not be uncomplaining as Jesus was when He patiently lived the first thirty years of His life in obscurity? Finally, should we not be charitable as Mary and Joseph were when they gave their Son to the world? They knew He would have to die to save us from our sins. What a glorious example we have in the Holy Family. We can best imitate them by our own loving obedience, humility, charity, and patience to our own parents.

Jesus, Eternal Wisdom, have mercy on us.

Matching

6 1. Fourth Commandment   1. Comes from God

1 2. All authority   2. Love of country

10 3. Duty as a citizen   3. Should promote the general welfare

2 4. Patriotism   4. "A bad law is no law at all"

8 5. Holy Family   5. A privilege and a duty

3 6. Public officials   6. Honor thy father and thy mother.

4 7. St. Thomas Aquinas   7. Lawful civil authority

5 8. Right to vote   8. Jesus, Mary and Joseph

7 9. Policemen   9. Our first teachers

9 10. Parents   10. Responsibility to vote

The Fourth Commandment of God is: Honor thy father and thy mother. By this Commandment, we are to respect and love our parents, to obey them in all that is not sinful, and to help them when they are in need.

Sometimes children forget what they are told to do. Parents often must repeat instructions, sometimes over and over again. Children should try to remember what they are told. Part of being obedient is trying to remember what parents have said to do. If you have a chore to do, ask Mother to write it down and tape it on the closet door or refrigerator so you can be reminded.

One time, a father told his son in the morning not to go outside that day. Later in the afternoon, when his friend came over, the boy forgot what his father had said. He went out to play. After he was outside for a while, he remembered what his father had said. He immediately came back in and told his father that he forgot that he was not to go out. Children not only should try to remember what they are told, but they should be instantly obedient when they do remember.

Some Catholic families have several children. In these families, the chores and the duties are many. Children need to help. Children should see their duties in the family as opportunities to earn graces. It is much easier to be a saint when there are many times to practice obedience and responsibility. The highest level of obedience is doing more than what you are told. The highest level of obedience is to honor and respect your parents by doing something which is needed without even being asked.

Mary was the oldest of seven children. From the beginning, she was needed by her mother to help with the babies and the toddlers, to help set the table, and even to do the laundry. Mary knew how much she was needed and was proud to be an important part of the family. Mary knew what was needed to be done around the house, and often took on chores when they needed to be done, even when she was not asked.

Mary came to love her work in the house, though she often loved to read books in the evening. Mother and Father were so grateful to Mary for being so obedient and helping, they would buy her books whenever they had an opportunity.

When Mary became old enough, the mothers in the neighborhood asked Mary to help them in the evenings. Mary would help take care of the children as she was asked. When the children were put in bed, she did not rest, but washed the dishes and cleaned up the kitchen for the mothers, just as she did at home. Mary became very popular in the neighborhood for her good attitude and good deeds for others. At the same time, she began to earn money to buy her own clothes. This helped out her family.

Larry had a few friends in the neighborhood. They often rode their bikes around the small lake and in the woods. At times, Larry's friends would complain about their mothers who would sometimes insist they stay at home and do a chore around the house. Larry would never complain about his mother because he knew that it was a sin not to show honor and respect for her. Larry was always careful to encourage his friends not to speak against their parents.

One day, Tommy's mother wanted him to paint the garage when he wanted to ride his bike with Larry. Larry said that instead of going bike riding, he would help Tommy with the painting. In this way, Larry was showing honor and respect for Tommy's mother, and was encouraging Tommy to be obedient. Larry was aware of the command to help parents when they are in need.

Sarah was only eleven when her mother became sick. The doctor said her mother needed to be in bed for three months. Mother asked Sarah if she would help take care of the two younger children by getting them dressed in the morning and giving them breakfast and lunch. Sarah knew that the Fourth Commandment means that she must help her mother when she is in need. Sarah not only did as she was asked, she also read stories to the younger children, took them for walks to the park, helped them with their prayers, and played with them in the backyard. Sarah was happy when her father came home, gave her a big hug, and asked her, "What did my little princess do today?"

The Fourth Commandment commands that we should show honor and respect for our parents. Peter's father worked long hours at the factory. He noticed that the fathers of his friends worked in offices and wore white shirts and ties. His friends did not want to come to his house. Peter loved his father very much and was proud that he spent his time and his money for the family.

One time, Peter was in the school play. All the parents came to watch the play. When Peter's parents came, he noticed they did not dress as well as the other parents. Inside himself, Peter was very proud of his parents for coming to watch him in the play. After the play, there was a reception. Peter made a point of introducing his parents to his friends and their parents. He was proud to show them that he honored and respected his parents for all they had done for him.

Monica had just received her First Holy Communion when her father became very ill. The doctor told her mother that he would not live much longer. Monica became very upset because she knew from her religion lessons that her father would not go to Heaven. He had not been going to church in a long time. Monica began crying. She climbed up on the big hospital bed with her father, and put her arms around him. She could not stop crying.

"Why are you crying, Monica?" he asked.

"Because the doctor said you would not get better! And I know you have not been going to church and Holy Communion. You will not be going to Heaven, and I will never see you again."

The little girl's tears and her words shook the father. He suddenly realized how much his daughter loved him, and how much he wanted to be in Heaven with her and with God. He realized he had been lazy all his life. Suddenly, tears came to his eyes as he said, "Monica, go call your mother and have her call the priest. I want to say my Confession and receive Jesus in Holy Communion."

After the priest came and the father was received back into the Church, he told the story to his friends before he died. He said, "My sweet little Monica saved me from eternity in Hell."

Little Monica knew her father was in spiritual need, and did not hesitate to show her love for her father and to help him when he was in need.

The Fifth Commandment of God is: Thou shalt not kill.

By the Fifth Commandment, we are commanded to take care of our own spiritual and bodily well-being, and that of our neighbor. This commandment means not only that we are not allowed to kill anyone, but it also means we are not to injure other people by fighting or taking revenge, by hating people, or by being reckless or by endangering the welfare of others.

The human race had hardly begun when one human being took the life of another. One of the sons of Adam and Eve, Cain, killed his brother Abel. The root cause of that tragedy was Cain's envy of his brother's sacrifice to God. Not much has changed in the years of mankind that have followed. People still get angry, become envious and hateful, injure others, and even kill others. In our own time, we find parents hurting children, children hurting parents, children hurting brothers and sisters. Why? Because people do not have Faith in God, do not trust God to solve their problems, are not living in God's grace, and thus easily fall into serious sin from their weakened and fallen human nature.

As with all the Commandments, the Fifth Commandment both forbids and commands. Life is a gift of God. By the Fifth Commandment, we are commanded first, to take care of our own bodies. We are to get enough sleep, eat proper meals, and not to deliberately or carelessly mistreat our bodies by eating junk food all day long! We must not abuse our bodies with alcohol or drugs; we must not overeat or neglect our health. When we are sick, we should obey our parents when they advise us about how to get well again. We should drink plenty of water to keep our bodies healthy. Our bodies are the temples of the Holy Spirit, and they will take us to the edge of eternity where we hope to live with God forever. Later, on the last day of the world, as we have seen, our souls will be reunited with our bodies.

What does the Fifth Commandment forbid? We are forbidden to take our own life or the life of another human being. The Church always has taught that human life is sacred from the first moment of existence until natural death. No one has a right to interfere in God's divine plan for the life of another. Human life belongs to God. No one may take the life of another.

When God became Man, He elevated all the Commandments. What does that mean? It means that the Catholic Church now includes *much more* than what is absolutely minimal in each commandment. What are we saying? We are saying that while the Fifth Commandment forbids killing or even being angry at another human being, that is not enough. We are not only to avoid anger; we are to love others, especially our enemies. This means we should be praying for the salvation of not only those we love and who love us, but also for those who do not love us.

In His Sermon on the Mount, Jesus told us, "You have heard that it was said to the men of old, 'You shall not kill; and whoever kills shall be liable to judgment.' But I say to you that everyone who is angry with his brother shall be liable to judgment…" (Matthew 5:21-22). Love bids us to do good and avoid evil. Love also should make us go the extra mile for others. We should try to be patient and forgive others lest we fall into sin.

O Jesus, true God and true Man, have mercy on us.

Fill in the Blanks

1. Cain killed his brother ___abel___.

2. We have a weak and ___fallen___ human nature.

3. The Fifth Commandment tells us we must take care of our ___Welfare___.

4. We should not ___neglect___ our health.

5. Human life is ___sacred___ from the moment of existence to natural death.

6. No one may take the ___life___ of another.

7. Jesus told us that anyone who is ___angry___ with his brother is liable to judgment.

8. No one has the right to interfere with ___God's___ Divine Plan.

9. We have an obligation to ___Pray___ for the salvation of others.

10. Suicide is the taking of one's own ___life___.

The Fifth Commandment of God is "Thou shalt not kill."

Sometimes students quickly go past this Fifth Commandment because they feel it is not something for them to worry about. They are not tempted to kill anyone. However, the Fifth Commandment forbids sins which young people are often tempted to commit.

The Fifth Commandment forbids fighting. Even in homeschooling families, sometimes children get into fights. This is a sin against the Fifth Commandment, and should be told in Confession.

The Fifth Commandment forbids anger. Sometimes it is difficult to control anger when something suddenly happens. Someone might break something you own, or someone takes something of yours without your permission. However, we must try not to become angry even in a quick response. It we become angry about something, we need to quickly dispense with it and not carry it around in our hearts. Once we realize we have "lost our temper," we should do our best to get rid of it, and then there is no sin.

The Fifth Commandment forbids hatred of another person. Most young people do not hate other people, but nevertheless, young people must keep in mind that it is important to separate the sin from the sinner. We can hate the sin someone commits, but we must continue to pray for and care about the welfare of the sinner. Thus if someone is responsible for beating up someone in the family, we can hate the deed, but we must pray that the sinner will repent and make some sort of restitution, for the sake of his own soul.

The Fifth Commandment forbids revenge. Revenge means a desire to hurt someone for what a person did. If John's bicycle was damaged on purpose by the boy next door, John cannot seek revenge, looking for opportunities to hurt the boy next door. Revenge is a sin that can easily lead to other sins, such as hatred and violence. One of the horrible sins we see today is a person going to seek revenge because of a family member being hurt. When people are seeking revenge, many others live in fear and terror. In the Bible, we read "'*Revenge is mine, I will repay,*' saith the Lord." It is up to God, not up to us, to punish someone for his sins.

Drunkenness is forbidden by the Fifth Commandment mainly because people lose the use of their reason. They become like animals because they cannot think straight. This is an offense against God Who gave us the use of reason to make good decisions.

When people are drunk, they don't realize what they are doing. While drunk, people are more likely to hurt other people. Many young people die because of being drunk and hurting themselves. Innocent people are often killed because someone is drunk while driving. Mothers Against Drunk Driving and the police are making sure that drunken drivers are put in jail before they kill someone.

Reckless driving is a sin that many young people commit as they try to show off for their friends. This can result not only in the person driving being hurt or killed, but often results in other innocent people being killed.

Bad example is against the Fifth Commandment because it leads others into sin, which causes them bodily and spiritual injury. It is very sad when older brothers and sisters give bad example to their younger brothers and sisters. Younger children look up to their older siblings as role models. Giving bad example can be a serious sin especially if it leads a young person into serious sin. Our Lord was especially angry with people who gave bad example to children. Jesus said it would be better that a person have a heavy stone around his neck and be drowned in the sea than to give bad example to a child (Matt. 18:6). Jesus considers injuring the soul of a child an especially serious sin!

O Jesus, Father of the Poor, have mercy on us.

Fill in the Blanks

1. The Fifth Commandment of God is: thou shalt not kill .

List seven sins against the Fifth Commandment:

2. fighting

3. anger

4. hatred

5. reveng

6. drunkness

7. reckless driving

8. bad example

9. "injuring souls is mine, I will repay," saith the Lord.

10. It would be better to be drowned in the sea than to give bad example to a child.

The Fifth Commandment of God is: Thou shalt not kill.

We have learned that by this Commandment, we are commanded to take care of our own bodies and souls, and to take care not to injure the bodies and souls of other people.

There are times when someone may be called upon to risk injury or even his life to save another. Because the object is to save or help another, this kind of risk is allowed. Priests and missionaries who expose themselves to diseases and dangers in order to help others are heroes, and often martyrs. We think of the Blackrobes, the priests who came and lived and suffered among the Indians, as heroes and martyrs who sacrificed their lives to save the souls of the American Indians.

It is a work of mercy to help those who are sick, to work in a hospital or in a foreign country where perhaps help or medicine is not easily available. Father Damien, who worked with the lepers to try to help them save their souls, is an example of a saintly man who gave his life to save the souls of the sick and abandoned.

There are times when killing someone is lawful. It is allowed in self-defense. If the only way we can save our life is by killing an attacker, this is justified. However, if an attacker can be stopped by wounding him, then that is what must be done. Sometimes policemen in the line of duty are forced to shoot someone who attacks them. St. Francis de Sales one time was forced to defend himself with a sword when he was attacked by a band of young men.

It is lawful to fight in a war in defense of one's own country. This is called a just war. There are many Catholics who fought, killed, and died fighting for their lives and their homes in many countries of the world. St. Ignatius of Loyola fought for his country; eventually, he realized that becoming a soldier for Christ and saving souls was more important. St. Francis of Assisi became a knight and fought for his country; after spending time in prayer and meditation, he realized he should spend his time building up Christ's Church. St. George was a brave Roman soldier, but spoke out against the persecution of Christians, and was eventually killed by the Roman emperor.

A government is allowed to execute criminals who endanger the lives of others, "if this is the only possible way of…defending human lives against an unjust aggressor" (*Catechism of the Catholic Church*, 2nd ed., no. 2267). A government has the responsibility to stop criminals from killing citizens again and again.

"Mercy killing" or euthansia is a term used to mean killing a person who is sick, elderly, or dying. "Mercy killing" is murder and forbidden by the Fifth Commandment.

Priests often warn children that they should stay close to their parents and their family members who love them. They tell children to stay away from those who are living sinful lives, who talk about sinful deeds, who look at sinful pictures or watch sinful movies, or play video games which show evil actions as good. If we want to be saints, we need to read about saints, learn about saints, see movies about saints, look at holy cards of saints, carry medals of saints. The saints will then become our friends and help to protect us against sins.

O Jesus, true Light, have mercy on us.

Fill in the Blanks

1. The Fifth Commandment of God is: _thou shall not kill_.

2. By this Commandment, we are commanded not to _injure_ the bodies and souls of others.

3. We may risk injury or even death to _save_ the life or soul of another.

4. The _____ were the missionary priests who sacrificed their lives for the American Indians.

5. It is a work of _mercy_ to help those who are sick.

6. _father damien_ worked with the lepers to help them save their souls.

7. Killing is allowed in _self defense_.

8. It is lawful to fight in a _war_ to defend one's own country.

9. St. _ignatius_ of Loyola, St. _francis_ of Assisi, and St. _george_ were all brave soldiers.

10. A government is allowed to _stop_ criminals who endanger the lives of others.

The Sixth Commandment of God is: Thou shalt not commit adultery. Adultery is a sin which only adults can commit. The Sixth Commandment does mean, however, that children should be pure and modest in their behavior and dress. It means children should avoid pictures, movies, and games which promote bad language or indecent behavior or dress.

One practical way to keep pure and modest is to avoid temptations. Temptations frequently come about because we have allowed ourselves to be exposed to a *near occasion of sin*. A near occasion of sin is anything or anyone that could easily lead us into temptation and then into committing sin, such as impure books and magazines, bad movies, or bad companions. For instance, if we go to a movie and we see that it is a bad movie, we should leave the theatre, thus avoiding a near occasion of sin and possibly temptations to sin.

What does God want us to do with regard to these temptations? Clearly, He wants us to avoid them. A good practice is to substitute something good for something bad. For example, if we are tempted by our friends to go to play a bad video game, we should persuade them to play a game of soccer or baseball. Doing something for someone else, such as helping an elderly person, is an excellent way to spend our time and energy. There are many constructive and healthy things to do to keep busy. The greatest weapon against temptation is prayer, especially to the Blessed Mother.

In our world today, there are many different styles of dress. Fashions change over the years, but the standards for decency do not change. In 1917, the Blessed Mother appeared to three children in Fatima, Portugal. Among the many things she told them, she warned them about fashions in the future. She said, "Certain fashions will be introduced that will offend Our Lord very much." She knew that people would dress in disgraceful clothing such as scanty clothing and revealing summer clothing. The Blessed Mother asked the children of Fatima to pray and make sacrifices for poor sinners.

Pope Pius XI was concerned about lack of modest dress. He said "… Furthermore, dresses of transparent materials are improper…." That statement was written many years ago, but it gives us a practical example of what it means to dress modestly. Dresses without sleeves and without backs are not allowed in the churches of Rome, and should serve as a standard for Catholic girls and women. Tight jeans or pants, and shorts at mid-thigh or higher for boys and girls are inappropriate.

Our power of speech is a privilege which can be abused. It is a mistake to assume that just because some people use bad language or tell dirty jokes, it must be all right for me to do so. The influence of the television on everyone is overwhelming. Modern television and the movies are not good indicators of what is right.

As a rule, the television reflects pagan behavior, talk, and dress. If it is on television, you can almost be positive that it is not the way to act, speak, or dress. No child should watch anything on television without the explicit permission of his (or her) parents.

The most important thing we can do to preserve purity and modesty is to frequent the Sacraments. The very source of divine grace is Jesus Christ. The Sacraments of Penance and Holy Eucharist, when properly received, fill the soul with grace and strength to help us to resist temptations. The Sacrament of the Holy Eucharist gives us strength for the will and light for the mind so that we can know immediately what God wants of us, and what is opposed to His holy will. Prayer, especially to the Blessed Mother, helps us to be strong when we are tempted. A silent "Hail Mary" will bring our Heavenly Mother quickly to our aid in times of temptation.

Finally, good intentions are not enough. We must actively choose what is good and actively reject what is bad. We meet daily challenges that make it difficult to stay in the state of grace, but with God's help and the help of His holy Mother, we can and will remain in His grace and be good examples to others.

Holy Mary, Mother of God, pray for us.

Fill in the Blanks

1. The Sixth Commandment of God is: _thou shall not adultery_

2. The Sixth Commandment means that children should be _Pure_ and _modest_ .

3. Children should avoid pictures, movies, and games which promote _____ behavior or _____ dress.

4. We should avoid places which are _near_ occasions of sin.

5. There are many constructive and _healthy_ things to do to keep busy.

6. Pope _Pius XI_ was concerned about the lack of modest dress.

7. Dresses or shirts or blouses without sleeves or backs are not _allowed_ in the churches and shrines in the city of Rome.

8. Modern television behavior, talk, and dress reflects the _____ values.

9. No child should watch television without the permission of his _Parents_ .

10. The most important thing to do to preserve purity and modesty is to

_____ .

The Seventh Commandment of God is: Thou shalt not steal.

Most children understand this Commandment because they do not like it when someone takes their things! Children inherently know when something belongs to them. They naturally know it is an injustice for someone to take or to destroy what belongs to them.

In spite of children knowing that others should not take what belongs to them, some people, especially older children or adults, often take what does not belong to them. They think that there is so much injustice in the world, particularly toward them, that they excuse themselves when they steal from others. They "rationalize," that is, falsely reason, that if others take from them, then they will take from others.

It is against the law of God to steal. We are not allowed to take or damage what belongs to another. The right to one's property is so basic that the Church teaches that a person can defend his property, especially his home. Families have the right to defend themselves against those who attack them and their homes.

One afternoon, Bill and Jeff entered a music store. Bill had ten dollars he wanted to spend on a new CD. As they looked through all the selections, they found several they liked but they especially liked one. They noticed, however, that the price was fourteen dollars. Pooling their money together, they were still two dollars short. Bill put the CD back. He decided to return the next day to purchase the CD. Before Bill realized what was happening, Jeff was already out the door frantically signaling to his friend. Bill joined his friend outside the store. When they were a distance away, Bill watched in horror as Jeff gleefully reached into his pocket and drew out the stolen CD. Bill immediately grabbed the CD from Jeff, and ran back to the store to return it. He decided that Jeff was not a good friend.

The Seventh Commandment is "Thou shalt not steal." The Seventh and Tenth Commandments forbid sins against justice. What does that mean? Justice is the virtue that disposes us to give everyone his or her rightful due. In our example above, Jeff committed an injustice against the storeowner. He claimed as his own what belonged to another.

The Seventh Commandment commands us not to steal; it commands us to respect the property of others. We are forbidden to take what belongs to another. It is a terrible sin to steal. If people in a society cannot trust each other, if everyone is afraid that someone will take their property, no one will feel safe or trust anyone around them.

In our current society, many people are stealing. In public places, everything must be locked up because so much is stolen. In government offices, money and things worth million of dollars are stolen every year. Offices must hire security guards to protect the office property. Stores are often forced to raise their prices to include their losses because so much is stolen.

We must obey the Laws of God, the Ten Commandments. Only by giving good example to those around us can we hope to change our fellow citizens to realize that, for our own salvation, we all must obey the Laws of God.

Blood of Christ, Price of our salvation, have mercy on us.

Fill in the Blanks

1. The Seventh Commandment of God is:
   Thou shalt not steal

2. It is an _Injustice_ to take something that belongs to someone else.

3. There is no reason to justify the taking or _destroy_ of things which belong to others.

4. Justice is the virtue that disposes us to give everyone his or her rightful _due_.

5. A person has the right to _defend_ himself against someone trying to take his home property.

6. The Seventh Commandment commands us to _respect_ the property of others.

7. We are _forbidden_ to take what belongs to another.

8. A society suffers when citizens cannot feel safe or believe they cannot _____ those around them.

9. We must obey the _laws_ of God.

10. We must give _____ _____ to our fellow citizens.

The Seventh Commandment of God is: Thou shalt not steal. This is a very simple and understandable Law of God. We are not to take what belongs to another. We must not damage or destroy what belongs to another.

The Seventh Commandment also commands people to keep their business agreements. If a person agrees to work for someone for a certain amount of money, the employer is bound to pay what was agreed. Many salesmen are not paid a just wage because some employers do not pay the agreed-upon commission. This is a sin against the Seventh Commandment because the employers are stealing the commission from the salesmen.

The Seventh Commandment also commands employees to work the hours they have agreed to work, and to do a good job. It is stealing if a person agrees to work a certain number of hours, but does not work those hours, or does not do an honest day's work. When a boy is hired to cut the grass, he is stealing if he does a sloppy job or does not cut all the grass, yet takes the money from the homeowner.

The Seventh Commandment also commands that people pay their just debts. If a child keeps a library book for several weeks past the due date, the library charges a fine. Refusing to pay this just debt is a sin against the Seventh Commandment.

What are some other sins against the Seventh Commandment? Cheating on an exam is against the Seventh Commandment. If someone cheats on a test, he is stealing the information from someone else rather than answering the questions from his own knowledge.

Public officials are stealing if they accept bribes. Public officials are working for those who elected them or who are paying for the official to represent them. If a public official makes decisions against the public for the sake of taking money from a criminal, he is stealing from the public by not giving them what they are paying for, namely to represent the taxpayers' best interests. The public official who takes bribes has allowed his decisions to be stolen for money.

Not returning what we have borrowed is another sin against the Seventh Commandment. What underlies all sins against the Seventh Commandment is a lack of respect for others and for their property. Stealing includes robbery and theft. *Robbery* is taking something against the owner's will by the use of violence or intimidation. *Theft* is the *secret* taking of something against the owner's will.

People do not like being around someone who steals. People want to hide their money and their things. The thief gets a reputation and no one wants to trust him. The thief will find he will not have friends, and people will keep their possessions carefully guarded. A thief will find that it is not easy to change his bad reputation.

We may be thinking, "I could never steal," but when we cheat in games, we are taking what we did not earn or what does not belong to us. We are sinning against the Seventh Commandment. Cheating in small things when we are young, leads to cheating in bigger things when we are older. Jesus said we are to do unto others as we would like them to do unto us. We need to practice this when we are young.

The Seventh Commandment also requires that we must restore to others what we have taken unjustly. If we damage something, we are required to repair it or to replace it. Justice demands returning stolen property, and the repair or replacement of damaged property.

A good priest once said that we should be careful not to borrow things from others unless it is necessary. That way there is less chance of something being lost or damaged which does not belong to you. When we must borrow from someone, we should treat the borrowed things more carefully than we treat our own things. Many a friendship has been lost due to damaged or lost borrowed things.

As with all the Commandments, Jesus Christ elevated the Seventh Commandment to a high standard. In other words, to be holy, to be the saint we are called to be, we need to not simply *avoid* sin but we need to do something positive in regards to each Commandment. In regards to the Seventh Commandment, Jesus said we should give to the poor. The poor usually want only what they need to live. Sharing with those less fortunate is very pleasing to God. We should not keep money and buy extra things just because it is fun. We must continually do things to help others.

Mother Catherine Drexel was a very wealthy lady because she inherited money from her family. Instead of purchasing a nice home and expensive clothes, she gave her money to the poor and needy. She helped to build schools and hospitals. Because of her lifetime of generosity, she was recently declared a saint by the Church.

Blood of Christ, River of Mercy, have mercy on us.

Matching

10 1. Seventh Commandment

6 2. Catherine Drexel

1 3. Cheating on tests

2 4. Stealing

8 5. Robbery

4 6. Theft

3 7. Giving to the poor

7 8. Restoration

5 9. People should pay

9 10. Justice

1. Stealing information

2. Taking property without permission

3. Pleasing to God

4. Secret stealing

5. Just debts

6. Gave her money to the poor

7. Virtue at the root of the seventh Commandment

8. Stealing with the use of force

9. Giving back stolen property

10. "Thou shalt not steal."

By the Seventh Commandment we are commanded to respect what belongs to others, to live up to our business agreements, and to pay our just debts.

The Seventh Commandment forbids cheating, keeping what belongs to someone else, damaging the property of others, and the accepting of bribes by public officials.

We are obliged, in justice, to restore whatever we have stolen, or to pay the value of it. If we have damaged someone's property, we are obliged to repair it or to replace it.

One time Jerry borrowed his friend's bicycle. He had an accident and the bike was severely damaged. Jerry's father told him that he must fix or replace the bicycle. Jerry's father purchased a new bike for his friend, and Jerry had to work on Saturdays to pay back his father for the cost of the bike. Jerry learned the hard way that first, it is best not to borrow from others unless it is necessary. He also learned that if he damages someone's property, he is responsible for fixing it.

Joseph has a big heart. He was always generous in loaning people his football and his baseball bat, his videos and his fancy jacket. He was not selfish at all. Joseph purchased a motorcycle with his hard-earned money. He was very careful to ride it just in the neighborhood and did not take it out on the main roads. One day, one of Joseph's friends said that he needed to go somewhere, and asked to borrow the motorcycle. Joseph, who could never say no to his friends, agreed to loan his motorcycle.

The next day, his friend did not return the motorcycle. Joseph asked, "Where is my motorcycle?" His friend said that it broke down on the highway, and was still sitting out on the road. Joseph went to a great deal of trouble to go out on the highway to find his motorcycle. He brought it back. He asked his friend to pay for it to be fixed. His friend refused to pay for it, saying that the motorcycle was defective when he rode it, and it was not his responsibility. Joseph was not able to pay to fix his own bike, and never rode it again. Joseph learned that many people in this world do not obey the Seventh Commandment.

God is the owner of all things. He has given us the right to own things, but we are to be generous, considerate, kind, and charitable. Those who have things have a responsibility to do good with their possessions. Those who are poor should not steal, not be unjust, not be envious.

An Irish family of eight children did not have an abundance, but they shared what they had with others. When a poor Hungarian family moved to town, they could not afford very much for housing and food. The Irish family invited the Hungarian family to dinner as often as possible, sharing their food and home. The families became good friends, and eventually the Hungarian family was able to do better after the father found a good job.

In the years to follow, the Hungarian family showed their thanks by bringing Hungarian pastries to the Irish family during Christmas and Easter holidays. Both families showed Christian charity, justice, kindness, and responsibility. They understood the high standard that Christ is calling us all to attain. The Seventh Commandment does not simply mean we should not steal. It also means we should give to others.

Martha borrowed a watch from Jennifer so she could watch the time while she took her math test. When Martha came to visit Jennifer the next day, she told Jennifer that she had lost the watch. When Jennifer asked her to buy her another one, Martha said that she felt she did not owe it to Jennifer. Martha said that since her friend had borrowed her pretty skirt so many times, Martha felt she did not owe anything to Jennifer. Jennifer went to Father Williams and asked if Martha owed her the watch. The priest said, "Yes. Martha must purchase another watch for you." The Seventh Commandment teaches us that we must pay our just debts. We cannot argue that because we have done other things for the person, we do not owe the lost or damaged item.

The ice cream shop sold their ice cream in little cups. It was very fine home-made ice cream, and many tourists in the area purchased the ice cream. The owner of the shop knew that his customers would never return since they were tourists. So when he sold his ice cream, he put it in a cup that appeared to be so big. However, the bottom was raised inside the cup, so the customer purchased less ice cream than the appearance of the size of the container. This owner was stealing from his customers by giving them less ice cream than appeared to be in the cup.

It is easy to memorize a Commandment. It is easy to say "Thou shalt not steal." What is not so easy is to realize that each and every day, we should be thinking about respecting what belongs to others, not cheating others, and being kind and generous to others. Being a good Catholic is important. In the days of the early Church, when St. Peter and St. Paul were teaching people about Jesus, the pagans were surprised to see the kindness and generosity of the Christians. The pagans would often say "See how they love one another."

The Seventh Commandment is "Thou shalt not steal."

Sometimes children do not think about it very much when they take things from their parents or their brothers and sisters. One day, Mother saw a poor man standing on the sidewalk near the store. He was selling apples as a way to make money for himself. Mother took one of the big red apples, and looked in her purse to give the poor man a dollar bill. She was surprised and disappointed to discover that money was missing from her wallet. She suspected that her eleven-year-old son Johnny had "borrowed" the money. Now she could not give it to the poor man.

Children should not take money or other things from their parents without permission. While this may be a venial sin because it is usually a small amount of money, still it can lead to discomfort for Mother or Father. Perhaps the biggest danger is that if children are taking things so freely within the family, a habit forms which might develop in a child taking things freely outside the family. What started as a venial sin in youth can turn into a mortal sin in adulthood.

Probably the most famous thief in the Bible was Judas. He held the moneybag for the Apostles, but he stole some for himself. He was "concerned" when money was spent on expensive ointment which was used by Mary Magdalen to wipe the feet of Jesus. Eventually, his disloyalty led to being a traitor, to despair, and to suicide.

Another famous thief in the Bible was the Repentant Thief. Remember the thief who was hung on the cross next to Jesus? He was sorry for his sins of thievery, and recognized that Jesus is the Son of God. He asked Jesus, "Remember me when You come into Your Kingdom." Jesus told him, "This day thou shalt be with Me in Paradise!"

St. Paul, in his letter to the Ephesians, wrote "He that stole, now let him steal no more; but rather let him labor, working with his hands the thing which is good, that he may have something to give to him that is suffering in need." St. Paul is teaching us that not only should we not steal from others, we have a responsibility to work so we can give to those in need.

In the early days of the Church, a Roman official heard that St. Lawrence was in charge of the treasures of the Church. The Roman official wanted to steal the treasures. He called St. Lawrence to come to his court, then asked St. Lawrence for the Church treasures. "Show us the treasures of the Church!" he demanded. St. Lawrence said he did not have them with him, but would bring them back the next day. The Roman official let him go, expecting to see gold and precious jewels the next day. When St. Lawrence returned the next day, he brought a huge crowd of poor people into the court. "Here are the treasures of the Church!" Lawrence cried. Lawrence knew that the poor and the needy are great treasures of the Church. They give those of us who have things the opportunity to earn graces by helping those who have few possessions.

One time, three boys found a wallet along the road. They looked inside the wallet and found a few hundred dollars. Instead of reporting it to their parents, they decided to share the money equally. The three friends divided up the money and threw the wallet in the trash can. The boys began to spend their ill-gotten gain, buying video games and expensive shirts. One bought a CD player, another bought a guitar. The parents began to ask their sons where they obtained the money they were spending. Each of the boys began to lie to their parents about where they got the money. A few of their friends asked them questions, but they lied to their friends. Then the three boys began to distrust each other, each afraid one of the others may tell the truth. Each boy began to be nervous and irritated. Pretty soon their consciences were not letting them sleep at night, and they became frightened that someone would tell.

Finally, one of the boys became so unhappy, he met with the other two and said, "We were so happy when we found this money. But it was not ours and we stole it and spent it, and I have never been so unhappy and frightened in my whole life. I think we need to tell our parents and give the rest of the money to them. Otherwise, I think I will die of unhappiness." The other two boys admitted they were avoiding their parents and friends, and were very unhappy. That evening, each of the boys met with his parents and told the whole story. The parents returned the money to the police, and made the boys work to earn the money they had spent. The boys went to Confession, had a clean conscience again, and were once again happy boys. They learned a hard lesson that committing the sin of stealing can lead to other sins and to deep unhappiness.

The Eighth Commandment of God is: Thou shalt not bear false witness against thy neighbor.

God gave us these Ten Commandments because they are necessary to achieve holiness, and they are also necessary for living peaceably with our neighbors.

This Commandment forbids lying, and commands us to speak the truth in all things, but especially in matters concerning other people, their good name, and their honor.

Lying is a terrible sin. Lying about someone else is truly terrible. There is a famous story about a woman who went to Confession and told the priest she had told untrue stories about her friend. The woman now was very sorry for what she had done. She went to Confession and for her penance, the priest told the woman she must take a pillow from her bed, go outdoors, and throw all the feathers from inside into the wind. She paused, confused at the priest's suggestion. He then told her that she must then pick up every single feather and put it back into the pillow. "That would be impossible, Father!" she exclaimed. "Yes," said the priest, "as impossible as it would be to take back what you have said about your friend to all the people who have now heard the untrue stories!"

When someone steals something, it can be replaced or the value can be paid. When someone tells a lie, the truth cannot always be replaced in the minds of all the people who heard the lie in the first place. Lying can be much more damaging than damaging property!

The Eighth Commandment is "Thou shalt not bear false witness against thy neighbor." "False witness" means we are witnessing to the truth of something when we know it is false. If I say something which I know is *not* true, I have told a lie. What are we commanded by Eighth Commandment? We are to speak the truth in all things. We must speak the truth especially when it concerns the good name of another person. To harm someone in speech is far more lasting and harmful than to harm someone with our fists.

What are some sins which the Eighth Commandment forbids? The Eighth Commandment forbids *rash judgment*, *detraction*, *calumny*, and *telling secrets* we are bound to keep.

What is *rash judgment*? Rash judgment is jumping to conclusions about someone's behavior. This is an interior sin in that it is a mental judgment.

Terri and Diana are taking tests. Terri glances over at Diana and sees her reach into her pocket. She pulls out something white. Terri concludes that Diana is cheating. That is an example of rash judgment.

What is *detraction*? Detraction is revealing something about another person that is true, but not necessary to reveal, and is harmful to that person's reputation. Jay wants to play soccer. Bobby knows that Jay, who just moved into town, once stole things from his neighbors. Bobby tells the coach about Jay's thievery. Bobby has committed the sin of detraction. Bobby should not say anything about Jay because Jay may have repented.

Sometimes we *must* tell the truth to someone who has a right to know. If someone is stealing from the local grocery store, you need to tell your parents so they can tell the grocer. The grocer has a right to know who is stealing his groceries.

What is *calumny*? Calumny is injuring another person's good name by lying. Another name for calumny is *slander*. Many newspapers print information without checking if it is true because they want to destroy someone's good name. It is a very serious sin. The writer or the newspaper is promoting a falsehood because either they are too lazy to check it, or they purposely are destroying the good name of another person. Calumny is also a sin against justice.

The Eighth Commandment also forbids the *telling of secrets* we are bound to keep. A good policy is to tell your friends or family *not* to tell you secrets in the first place. That way you cannot accidentally reveal something you should not.

We are required by the Eighth Commandment to repair any damage that was done by our telling a lie, or by committing any of the sins against this Commandment. The damage can never be fully repaired, but we should try our best.

The virtue we should practice in regards to the Eighth Commandment is to spread the Truth about Jesus Christ and His Catholic Church.

O Jesus, True God and True Man, have mercy on us.

Fill in the Blanks

1. The Eighth Commandment is "Thou shalt not bear false _Witness_ against thy neighbor.

2. The Eighth Commandment tells us to love _truth_ and not lies.

3. We must speak the _truth_ in all things.

4. We must always tell the truth to those who have a _need_ to know the truth.

5. Rash judgment is _jumping_ to conclusions about someone's behavior.

6. _Slander_ is saying something false about someone else.

7. Detraction is _harming_ another person's good name by revealing something true but harmful to that person's reputation.

8. We may never tell a _lie_.

9. A virtue we can practice in regards to the Eighth Commandment is to spread the _truth_ about Jesus Christ.

10. Calumny is a sin against the good _name_ of another.

The Eighth Commandment of God is: Thou shalt not bear false witness against thy neighbor.

A priest was teaching the children about the Eighth Commandment. He told them that God gave us the gift of speech to use for good, and to give knowledge of the truth to each other. We were given a mind to know the truth, and we were given a tongue to spread the truth to others.

We must use our tongue for justice, kindness, and love, Father said. Lying causes terrible evils, even violence. Peace and happiness for each of us is dependent on our trusting each other and telling the truth at all times. Children need to be truthful to their parents as well as to their brothers and sisters. Parents need to be truthful with their children. Parents need to be truthful to each other. People doing business must be truthful and honest with their customers. Workers must be honest with their employers, and employers must be honest with their employees.

In our last lesson, we touched on some of the sins against the Eighth Commandment. Today we will take a closer look at some of the ways we sometimes misuse our speech and hurt other people. We may not realize how quickly we may say something hurtful without even thinking about the harm we can cause.

Rash judgment can lead to terrible hurt even if nothing is said to anyone else. This is because an attitude comes over the person who has made the rash judgment. This attitude is reflected whenever the person meets the victim, or the victim's name is mentioned.

Rash judgment is a sin usually committed by someone when they think someone else is lying. Sometimes a thing appears to be one way, when in fact it is not that way at all. Tommy was driving by the movie theatre and saw Barbara's car parked outside the theatre. A bad movie was showing, and Tommy immediately judged that Barbara was inside watching. Tommy was judging the character of Barbara based on her car being parked there. When Tommy next saw Barbara, he said, "Oh, I see you like to watch movies with that famous actor!"

"Oh, no!" said Barbara. "He is in very bad movies and I don't go to bad movies like that!" Tommy kept quiet but he judged that Barbara not only watched bad movies but also was a liar. Tommy committed the sin of rash judgment a second time, and he must go to Confession.

We cannot know all the details about a situation. It is important to trust that people usually tell the truth. If anyone is telling a lie, it is between him and God. It is not for us to judge anyone. Our responsibility to God and to others is to always tell the truth ourselves!

Jesus taught, "Judge not, that you not be judged" (Matthew 7:1). What is the judgment about which Jesus is speaking? Does it mean that when we see someone committing a crime, such as stealing, we should not view that as wrong? No. In fact, we *must* see sin as sin, otherwise why would God have given us the Ten Commandments? In other words, we may judge the *sin*, but not the sinner. What Jesus is telling us is not to judge a person's intentions or *motives*. The sin of rash judgment means jumping to conclusions without definite proof. Only God knows what is in a person's heart. Rash judgment is when we believe, without just cause, that a person is guilty of something.

Blood of Christ, courage of martyrs, have mercy on us.

True (T) or False (F)

___T___ 1. We were given a mind to know the truth.

___T___ 2. We were given a tongue to spread the truth.

___T___ 3. Jesus said, "Judge not that you not be judged."

___T___ 4. We may judge sin but not the sinner.

___T___ 5. Rash judgment can lead to terrible hurt.

___T___ 6. Rash judgment often occurs when someone thinks someone else is lying.

___F___ 7. The sin of rash judgment need not be told in Confession.

___T___ 8. It is important to trust that people usually tell the truth.

___T___ 9. It is not for us to judge people's motives.

___T___ 10. We must always tell the truth ourselves.

The Eighth Commandment of God is: Thou shalt not bear false witness against thy neighbor. By this Commandment, we are commanded to speak the truth in all things, but especially in what concerns the good name and honor of others. This Commandment forbids lies, rash judgment, detraction, calumny, and the telling of secrets we are bound to keep.

What is the sin of *detraction*? Detraction is making known the true but hidden faults of others.

Telling the truth about someone could be harmful to a person's name. What should we do when we are asked to reveal something about a person that could be harmful to that person's reputation? We may use mental reservation. *Mental reservation* is using careful language to hold back giving information which another person has no right to know about. We may never lie. Mental reservation is not lying, but holding back information which is not necessary to reveal.

Someone you met in the store may ask you how your cousin is doing. You know that in fact he is in trouble with his job and is losing his home because he does not have enough money to pay the bills. However, the person in the store does not need to know about your cousin's personal problems. You should simply answer, "He seems to be fine, thank you."

Many people carelessly slip into the sin of detraction because they are always anxious to talk about other people. It is usually a venial sin among children because children's faults are

usually very minor. But it can be a dangerous habit to talk too much about other people. Good Catholic adults try to focus on telling the good points about people, and encourage people to pray for others.

The sin of *calumny* or slander is a greater sin because it *purposefully* aims to injure the good name of another by lying about him. The one who tells the lie is guilty of a great sin. One who listens to stories which harm another also can commit a sin, especially if he rejoices in the information, or if he passes on the information. If we hear a story about someone and realize that it is dangerous to someone's good name, we must try to change the subject, or, if that fails, simply walk away.

If we love our neighbor as God has asked us to do, we should not commit sins of lying, detraction, calumny, or slander. We should do positive things to promote our neighbor. We should talk about the good qualities of a person and overlook their faults. After all, is that not what we wish people would do for us? It is best to use our tongue to help and to encourage people, to cheer them up, to help them to persevere on their path to holiness. Jesus said, "Blessed are the clean of heart, for they shall see God." Let's keep a clean heart in our thinking about other people!

The end does not justify the means. This means that even though someone is doing something which is supposed to help people, but is in itself morally wrong, it is still a sin. The lady at the bank knew that Mr. Miller was beating his wife. When the investigator was asking who stole the money from the bank, the lady figured that she would accuse Mr. Miller so that Mrs. Miller would be rid of him. Although the intention to have Mr. Miller stop beating Mrs. Miller was a good intention,

the lady was not justified in telling a lie about Mr. Miller. As one priest told the children in his class, we should respect the good name of a person more than we respect his possessions. The poorest person values his good name, perhaps even more than the rich person. A good name is a precious thing. Shakespeare wrote in a play that "He who steals my purse, steals trash, but he that steals from me my good name" steals a treasure that cannot be replaced very easily.

It is said that St. Francis de Sales was very careful to always tell the truth. He revealed to his friends what his mother told him when he was very young: "Never tell a lie, my child, for a lie dishonors us in the sight of God and before men. A lie comes from the devil, and the child that tells a lie becomes a child of Satan."

The devil is known as the Father of Lies because of the lies He spoke to Eve in the Garden of Paradise.

The Ninth Commandment is: Thou shalt not covet thy neighbor's wife. The word "covet" means to desire greatly, almost to the point of taking something if one has the chance to "get away with it" without being caught! This is a Commandment mostly for adults. However, for children, the Ninth Commandment means that they should be pure in their thoughts and in their desires.

The Tenth Commandment is like the Ninth Commandment, in that it commands us not to have bad *thoughts* and *desires*. People are not to strongly desire taking what belongs to another. The Tenth Commandment is: Thou shalt not covet thy neighbor's goods.

We want to have good and holy thoughts and desires. The way to do that is to pray, receive the Sacraments, read good books about the lives of the saints, read the Bible, look at holy pictures, and stay close to Our Lord and the Blessed Mother. If I look at an impure book, I will most likely have impure thoughts and desires. We can control our thoughts if we stay away from *near occasions of sin*, that is, people, places, or things which draw us into temptation.

Usually thoughts are not sins. Thoughts come and go without any planning. However, if we have a bad thought, we should be trying to find something else to think about or to do. We can turn to a book and start reading, or we can start saying a prayer, or we can think about something we did last weekend, or we can start doing a chore.

If a person knows that when he sees certain movies or pictures, or plays violent or ugly video games that bad thoughts arise, these are called the *near occasions of sin,* which can bring about temptations. A person must avoid those things which lead him to bad thoughts. The Church says we must avoid all occasions of sin if at all possible. If a person has a job and everyone at the place is promoting evil ideas and ways of life, a person must look for another job.

Think of it this way. You want to be a racer. You love to run and feel the wind as you run. You want to try out for the racing team. You know that to be faster, you need to lose ten pounds. On the way home from racing practice, there is an ice cream shop. Every time you go by the ice cream shop, you are tempted to go in and buy an ice cream cone. Some days you even do buy a cone. If you walk on the other side of the street, you can resist buying the ice cream. To be the racer you want to be, you need to avoid that ice cream shop!

In the same way, if we want to be holy, if we want to be good and avoid committing sins, we must keep away from those things which tempt us to have bad thoughts which lead to sin.

One of the saints complained to Our Lord that she was tempted by impure and dangerous thoughts. Our Lord told her that her heart and soul were not soiled by sin because she actually hated the thoughts. "Where there is hatred of sinful thoughts, there is no guilt."

Sometimes children associate with people who lead them into sin. This is wrong. If that kind of person comes to the door, and wants you to play with him, you need to tell your mother or father, or a big brother or sister to go to the door and say you cannot go out with him. If you let the person in, or if you go out with that person, it is dangerous and sinful because you have chosen not to avoid an occasion of sin! It could even be a serious sin if you are happy to see that person who usually leads you into sin, such as stealing or lying.

At times of temptation, read a good book! Say the Rosary! Watch a good video. Wash the floor! Take out the trash! Help Mom and Dad! Toss the basketball! Help your little sister!

The Tenth Commandment is: Thou shalt not covet thy neighbor's goods. This Commandment commands us to be happy with what we have and not be jealous or envious of what others have. The Holy Family was good and happy, though poor. They did not have many material things. Jesus chose to live in a poor family to teach us that material things do not make a person happy. *Being good* makes a person happy. *Helping others* makes a person happy.

God wishes for us to use the gifts and talents He gave us to provide sufficiently for our family and to give help to those in need. God gives different gifts to different people. Those with gifts to make money should be generous to those who do not have what they need for clothes, food, or a home.

Heart of Jesus, Source of all consolation, have mercy on us.

Fill in the Blanks

1. The Ninth Commandment is: Thou shalt not covet thy neighbor's __wife__.

2. The Tenth Commandment is: Thou shalt not covet thy neighbor's __goods__.

3. For children, the Ninth Commandment means they should be __pure__ in their thoughts.

4. We must avoid persons, places, or things which lead us into __temptation__.

5. The Church calls these persons, places, or things __near occasions__ __of__ __sin__.

6. The Ninth and Tenth Commandments are concerned about sins of __things__ and __places__ rather than actions.

7. Where there is hatred of sinful thoughts, there is no __guilt__.

8. Write one thing I might do to avoid persons, places, or things which lead into sin: __pray__.

9. God wants us to be happy with what we have and not be __jealous__ of what others have.

10. __Being good__ makes a person happy.

This week we will study the Six Commandments of the Church. These Six Commandments are given to us by the Catholic Church in order for us to better fulfill our responsibilities of obeying the Ten Commandments given to us by God.

The First Commandment of the Church is: "To assist at Mass on all Sundays and Holy Days of Obligation." We can see that this relates to the First Commandment of God. By attending Mass on Sundays and Holy Days, we are fulfilling the First Commandment, which is to honor God above all things.

Why does the Church command us to attend Mass? First of all, the Mass is *holy*. No activity on the earth is as holy as the Mass. Nothing you can do in a day can be anywhere close to being as holy as attending Mass. Jesus Christ, the Son of God, comes to be with us, truly present, at the Holy Mass.

The Mass is also a *sacrifice*. What is a sacrifice? A sacrifice to God is an act of divine worship by which a victim is offered to God by a priest. The Sacrifice of the Mass is the greatest sacrifice of all.

The Mass is the sacrifice of Jesus Christ Himself as Victim to God His Father in Heaven. It is the highest form of adoration in which a priest, representing Jesus Christ, in the name of the people, offers the Victim, Jesus Christ, to God our Heavenly Father. Our attendance at Mass truly fulfills the First Commandment of God to honor and adore Him. The Mass is the only *perfect* worship of God.

This sacrifice of the Mass gives to God the highest honor and worship it is possible to offer on the part of a human being on this earth. The Mass is a re-presentation of what happened on Calvary. What does that mean? It means that it is the same sacrifice as the Sacrifice of the Cross on Calvary. On the Cross, Jesus sacrificed His Body and Blood and died for our sins.

The Church sets as a bare minimum for our duty to worship God to attend Mass on Sundays and Holy Days of Obligation. We must never miss Mass on Sundays or Holy Days without a very good reason! Illness, impossible weather conditions, or a very great distance would be serious reasons why we might be allowed to miss Mass. It is a mortal sin for a Catholic to deliberately miss Mass on Sundays or Holy Days without a very good reason. As we have seen, the Mass is not just something we must do on Sundays, but something very special and good for the soul. It is an opportunity to love, adore, and honor God in the greatest way possible.

Aside from our Sunday Mass duty, we must also attend Mass on holy days of obligation. In the United States there are six days in the Church year when we must attend Mass under pain of sin:

Christmas Day (December 25)

Solemnity of Mary [also known as the Octave of the Nativity] (January 1)

Ascension Thursday (40 days after Easter)

The Assumption (August 15)

All Saints' Day (November 1)

The Immaculate Conception (December 8)

The Church year officially begins with the first Sunday of Advent, four weeks before Christmas. There are two holy days of obligation in December: the Immaculate Conception and Christmas Day. The Feast of the Immaculate Conception celebrates Mary's own pure beginning. She was kept free from sin by God because she was to be the mother of God's Son! Mary was without sin from the first moment of her existence. The words "Hail Mary, full of grace," first said by the Angel Gabriel, mean that Mary was always totally free of Original Sin. The Church teaches that she remained free of sin throughout her life.

Christmas Day, more properly called the Feast of the Nativity, should be regarded primarily as a holy day on which we honor the birth of Jesus Christ, Our Savior, into the world. Jesus was born as a tiny Baby in a stable in order to redeem the human race. How fortunate we are to be living after Jesus became Man so we can receive Him in Holy Communion!

January First is the Feast of the Solemnity of Mary, Mother of God. How appropriate to begin a new year paying homage to Our Blessed Mother and our protectress in Heaven. While the Blessed Mother has many titles, none has more significance than *Mother of God*. With His dying breath from the Cross, Jesus Christ gave us His Mother to be our Mother as well.

Forty days after Easter, Ascension Thursday, is the commemoration of the day on which our Blessed Lord, having completed His mission of our salvation on earth, returned to Heaven. From Heaven, our Lord sends us the graces we need for us to reach Heaven too.

On August Fifteenth, we celebrate Our Blessed Mother's Assumption into Heaven. At the end of her time on earth, Mary was assumed into Heaven, body and soul. Her body was preserved incorrupt because she was free from all sin. "You were a Mother and yet remained the Blessed Virgin Mary. You went up to Heaven, and yet you did not forsake us." She is always ready to intercede for us. "Your glory, shining forth with the radiance of divine grace, surpasses every splendor! Behold, all the heavenly angels sing a hymn of glory. All human races rejoice at your glory. Kings, together with the angels, sing out to you: Hail, Mary, full of grace!

All Saints' Day, November First, commemorates all the saints in Heaven. There is a saint's feast day for every day of the Church year, but there are many more saints in Heaven about whom we are not aware. We honor them all on November First every year. As we have seen, there are canonized saints, Biblical saints, and traditional saints. All the saints in Heaven deserve our veneration, and they are happy to intercede for us when we ask them for their prayers.

Blood of Christ, freeing souls from Purgatory, pray for us.

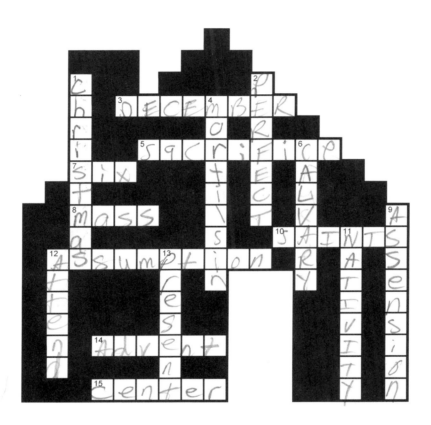

Across

3 The Feast of the Immaculate Conception occurs in this month. (8)

5 The Mass is a ___. (9)

7 There are ___ Commandments of the Church. (3)

8 No activity is as holy as the ___. (4)

10 On November 1 we honor all the ___ in Heaven, known and unknown. (6)

12 August 15 (10)

14 The Church year begins on the first Sunday of ___. (6)

15 Jesus Christ is the ___ at each Sacrifice of the Mass. (6)

Down

1 December 25 (9)

2 The Mass is the only ___ worship of God. (7)

4 It is a ___ ___ to deliberately miss Mass on Sundays and Holy Days of Obligation. (6,3)

6 The Mass is a re-presentation of what happened on Calvary. (7)

9 40 days after Easter (9)

11 Another name for Christmas (8)

12 "To ___ at Mass on all Sundays and Holy Days of Obligation" (6)

13 Jesus Christ is truly ___ at each Mass. (7)

Today we will learn about the Second Commandment of the Church: To fast and abstain on the days appointed. Fasting and abstaining are Sacramentals of the Church. What is a Sacramental? It is a special prayer, action, or object that reminds us of God and supplies Actual Grace. Sacramentals include holy things such as medals, holy water, and holy actions. Fasting and abstaining remind us of God because they make more room in our souls for God.

Fasting means limiting our intake of food. Why, we might ask, would we want to limit our food? Fasting is a form of penance. Our Lord Himself fasted to show us that He wants us to practice fasting. Fasting was a penance practiced by the Hebrews in the Old Testament, and the early Christians in the New Testament, and in the early days of the Church until the present time.

Penance is a virtue of the heart by which we are sorry for our sins and turn back to God. Penance is a form of self-denial in which we make our bodies do what they do not like, and what we do not like. There is probably nothing more that people of all ages in all places like more than eating. By controlling this great desire to eat, we are teaching our bodies to obey our souls. We are training or disciplining our wills to control our bodily desires.

When does the Church want us to fast? There are only two days in the year when fasting is required: Ash Wednesday and Good Friday. Who must fast? All adults between the ages of eighteen and fifty-nine must fast at least on those two days of the year, although they may choose to fast additional days of the year. In the past, Catholics would fast three days of the week during Lent and Advent. Some people would fast all days of Lent and Advent. Some people still do as a special sacrifice or penance.

The Church teaches that fasting is a special means to obtain remission of our sins, spiritual favors from God, and a good way to gain self-control. Everyone loves to eat. Eating is pleasurable and if it were not for food, we would soon die. That is what makes fasting a very special way to do penance. Giving up some of the food we eat makes it easier for our souls to respond to the graces that God wants to give us.

Abstinence is another Sacramental. To abstain means to not do something, or not eat something. When we speak about abstinence, we mean not eating meat. Days of Abstinence are days in which we are not allowed to eat meat or meat products. All Fridays of the year are days of penance and everyone has a serious obligation to do some form of penance on these days. Abstinence from meat is still the main way we do penance as Catholics. It is still the universal law of the Church that we abstain from meat on all Fridays of the year. In recent years, however, the Church has allowed in the United Sates the substitution of some other penance on Fridays. People must be sure that if they eat meat on Fridays, they do some other form of penance. Particularly recommended are the corporal Works of Mercy as a means of doing penance. On all Fridays of *Lent,* however, we *must* abstain from meat.

Who must abstain? All persons fourteen years of age and older must practice Friday abstinence. Once again we note that fasting and abstinence help us to grow in holiness by helping us to control our desires, by making us better able to raise our minds to God in prayer, and by making satisfaction for our sins. We may not realize how important it is for us to cooperate in the graces God wants to give us. Fasting and abstaining are important ways for us to cooperate with God in making our souls His sanctuary.

Why does the Church choose Fridays as days of fasting and abstinence? Good Friday is the day on which Jesus Christ died for our sins. We remember the dear cost of our redemption. The Son of God Himself went to the Cross for our sins on that first Good Friday. When we treat Fridays as special days, we are commemorating His suffering and death, and our own spirit of penance and self-denial helps us to become more like Him Who loves us so much! Jesus Christ gave up His life in a very painful way so that we might live with Him forever.

Blood of Christ, Most Worthy of all honor and glory, have mercy on us.

Matching

__9__	1. Sacramental	1.	Limiting food intake
__1__	2. Fasting	2.	Self-denial
__5__	3. Days of Abstinence	3.	Adults must fast, and abstain from meat
__2__	4. Penance	4.	Days of penance
__3__	5. Ash Wednesday and Good Friday	5.	Abstain from meat
__6__	6. Up to age fourteen	6.	Need not abstain
__10__	7. Up to age eighteen	7.	Being sorry for our sins
__4__	8. All Fridays of the year	8.	The day Jesus Christ died for our sins
__8__	9. Good Friday	9.	A holy thing or action
__7__	10. Repentance	10.	Need not fast

The Third Commandment of the Church is: To confess our sins at least once a year. We are strictly obliged by the Church to confess our sins at least once a year if we have a mortal sin to confess.

Obviously, if we are conscious of having committed serious sin, we must go to confession as soon as possible. We immediately add that the Church considers *once a year* confession the bare minimum to remain a Catholic. Our souls are weak and are in need of frequent healing by divine grace just as our bodies are in need of medicine when we are sick. Imagine if when we are sick, we do not take the medicine the doctor prescribed. We would soon succumb to our illness, and could even die.

Down through the centuries, the Popes and Church Fathers always encouraged frequent confession. In fact, the popes have a habit of going to confession every day! What does the Church mean by frequent confession? The Church means confessing our sins to a priest in confession much more often than just once a year. Keep in mind that confession is not just for mortal sins. The Sacrament of Penance helps us to grow in holiness.

The Sacrament of Confession gives us special divine Sacramental grace *without fail* if our hearts are truly open to God's grace. We have seen how essential is divine grace in helping us stay away from mortal sin. We also need the help of divine grace to stay away from venial sins, which can lead to more serious sins.

What does frequent confession mean? Once a month is often recommended as a way to keep our souls ready to receive Holy Communion every week. Many families make it a practice to go together to confession on the first Saturday of each month. Some families go to Confession twice a month, the first and third Saturdays of the month.

Another recommendation comes from the Church's granting of indulgences. When we learn about indulgences, we will see that one of the requirements to gain an indulgence is to have been to confession within eight days. If we therefore form the habit of going to confession once a week, we will be able to gain indulgences on a regular basis.

The Fourth Commandment of the Church tells us: To receive Holy Communion during the Easter time. A Catholic who neglects to receive Holy Communion worthily during the Easter time commits a mortal sin. Easter time is between the first Sunday of Lent to Trinity Sunday.

We should want to go to Holy Communion with eager anticipation because we receive the Son of God, Our Lord Jesus Christ. Holy Communion, Jesus Christ Himself, keeps our souls alive in grace.

Of all the effects of the Sacrament of the Holy Eucharist, the most important is *union with Jesus Christ.* Holy Communion "preserves, increases, and renews the life of grace received at Baptism" (*Catechism of the Catholic Church*, n. 1392).

During World War II, the Nazis, a group of wicked people, held many Jews and Catholics in horrible prison camps, where they were starved to death. Of all the tortures they had to endure, Catholics were most distressed that they could not receive Jesus Christ in the Sacrament of the Holy Eucharist. In one of the camps, one day a quiet cry of joy rang out throughout the camp: "We have a priest!" From that time until the end of the war, Catholics in that camp had the blessing of a secret Sacrifice of the Mass, during which they were able to receive Holy Communion. Later, many Catholic prisoners reported that life in that horrible camp was endurable only because of the peace and consolation they received from Jesus Christ in Holy Communion.

Fill in the Blanks

1. We *must* go to confession if we have committed a _mortal_ sin.

2. We should go to confession even if we have only _venial_ sins.

3. The Third Commandment of the Church is: _to confes our sins at least once a year._

4. We are strictly obliged to go to Confession if we have a _mortal_ sin to confess.

5. The Popes have always encouraged _frequent_ Confession.

6. The Sacrament of Penance helps us to grow in _holiness_.

7. The Fourth Commandment of the Church is to receive Holy Communion during the _Easter_ time.

8. Easter time is from the first Sunday of Lent to _trinity_ Sunday.

9. Holy Communion keeps the soul alive in divine _grace_.

10. The most important effect of Holy Communion is union with _Jesus Christ_.

The Fifth Commandment or Precept of the Church is: to contribute to the support of the Church.

What does that really mean? We must support the Church on several levels: the local parish, our diocese, the missions, and the Holy See in Rome.

God gave us the Precepts or Commandments of the Church through His Church which the Holy Spirit is constantly directing. As early as the sixteenth century, the Precepts of the Church were in place. In 1555, St. Peter Canisius wrote that (the Commandments of the Church) "foster a sense of personal responsibility by reminding the faithful of their minimal responsibilities toward the Church." St. Peter Canisius was telling us that we are members of the Mystical Body of Christ. This means we are not alone in our struggle toward a happy eternity; we must help one another by means of our time, our talent, and our treasure. The Fifth Commandment of the Church refers to our treasure.

On the local level, we should contribute to the support of our parish. Our own parish owns the church building, a rectory, perhaps a school and a social hall. There are bills that must be paid, such as electricity, heating, and telephone expenses. Our local parish helps those in need, in both spiritual and bodily ways. We are responsible for one another as members of the Body of Christ. Jesus told us, "…as you did it to one of the least of these My brethren, you did it to Me" (Matthew 25:40). The pastor and priests of our parish are, in turn, responsible for seeing to our spiritual care by giving us the Sacraments and teaching us the Faith.

We know without being told that there are poor people, but did you know that most people in the world go to bed hungry? That is very hard for us to understand because we can eat whenever we wish. Most of us have seldom gone without food for more than a few hours. Even more important is the need to tend to those who suffer spiritual starvation. There are people even in your own neighborhood who do not know Jesus Christ. The money we give to the Church goes towards helping the poor to eat, to live, and to know God.

We must also support our diocese. Our contributions toward the diocese help to educate new priests and seminarians. Our donations to Catholic organizations help to feed the poor in the diocese, place children for adoption and build new churches. These are just a few of the many things our dioceses do to help those in need.

Finally, the Holy See needs support for Catholic missionary efforts throughout the world. There are still parts of the world where people do not know about God and Jesus Christ. Missionaries are sent to every corner of the world to bring the good news of salvation to people who would otherwise be in danger of losing their souls.

The *Catechism of the Catholic Church* tells us "The faithful also have the duty of providing for the material needs of the Church, each according to his abilities" (n. 2043). This means we should contribute to the support of our parish, from which we receive the Sacraments. No matter how rich or poor we are, we should give not from our spare or extra money, but we should budget our contribution as we budget money for all bills.

Pastors and priests take care of people in each individual parish, bishops head each diocese throughout the world, and the Pope is the visible head of the entire Catholic Church. At all three levels, we have the dedication of priests, bishops, and the Pope all devoting their lives for our salvation. When we contribute to the support of the Church, we help them in their work of saving souls by providing the material means they need.

The Sixth Commandment of the Church is: To observe the laws of the Church concerning marriage.

Catholics must be married in the presence of a priest or deacon and two witnesses. The priest or deacon and the witnesses represent the Church, which publicly acknowledges the couple's union.

The Sacrament of Matrimony is ideally performed during a Nuptial Mass, where the Rite of Christian Marriage takes place. There the sacredness of the marriage is assured, and the graces are poured out onto the couple. Like any Sacrament, there are special graces for Matrimony.

St. Joseph, ruler of the family of Jesus, pray for us.
St. Joseph, foster father of the Son of God, pray for us.

Fill in the Blanks

1. The Fifth Commandment of the Church is: *contribute to the support of the church*

2. St. *Peter canisius* wrote that the Commandments of the Church foster a sense of personal *risponsibility* toward the Church.

3. We should contribute to the support of the local *parish* .

4. Our contributions to the diocese helps to educate new *priests* and seminarians.

5. The Holy See needs support for Catholic *missionary* efforts throughout the world.

6. "The faithful also have the duty of providing for the *material* needs of the Church, each according to his abilities."

7. The Sixth Commandment of the Church is *to observe the law of the church concerning marriage*

Take this week to review the lessons from this quarter.

Day 1

Review lessons for weeks 10 and 11.

Day 2

Review lessons for weeks 12 and 13.

Day 3

Review lessons for weeks 14 and 15.

Day 4

Review lessons for weeks 16 and 17.

Day 5

Take the Second Quarter Test.

As we begin our lessons on the Sacraments, we need to start by answering the question "What is a Sacrament?" The Church teaches that a Sacrament is an outward *sign* instituted *by Christ* to give *grace*.

What is a *sign*? There are two meanings or connotations for the word "sign." First, a sign is something meant to get our attention. Sometimes when we are out driving in a car, we see two large flashing red lights in the distance. The lights are a sign that there is a possibility of danger. Secondly, a sign is also a symbol. A symbol is something that stands for something else. An octagonal red sign on a street corner is a symbol for us to stop. A sign is a symbol we can see or hear, but tells us about something we cannot see or hear at the moment.

Why do we need signs and symbols? We need signs and symbols because we are creatures composed of both a body and a soul, both the physical and the spiritual. Our bodies have five senses with which we come to know the physical world around us. For example, although we seldom think about it, our sight gives us information every moment of every day. That information helps us to make decisions with our intellects, and then to act upon our decisions with our wills, both of which are invisible and spiritual.

As we study the Sacraments, we will see how each has a unique sign that symbolizes something spiritual. In Baptism, for example, water symbolizes cleansing. Cleansing from what? Cleansing from Original Sin and re-birth to new life. In the Sacrament of Confirmation, the oil the Bishop uses symbolizes strength and the very presence of the Holy Spirit. We need the special help of the graces of the Sacrament of Confirmation to grow stronger in our faith and to resist temptation.

Our souls, which are composed of our intellect and our will, are capable of communicating with God. The Sacramental signs we see with our eyes, such as water or oil, contain a much deeper meaning that we cannot see with our eyes, but which we can understand with our intellect.

A Sacrament is a sign of Grace and a sign of Jesus Christ.

Jesus Christ instituted each one of the Sacraments personally and immediately. What does this mean? It means that Jesus Christ Himself established each one of the Sacraments, which were immediately in effect. Each of the Sacraments were instituted not by the Church but by Jesus Christ Himself, directly.

Why did Jesus Christ institute the Sacraments? Jesus instituted the Sacraments in order to give us the *grace* we so desperately need to know Him, to love Him, and to serve Him. As human persons, we are not completely spiritual, nor are we completely material. Because we are both spiritual (we have a soul) and material (we have a body), God uses something material that we can see to give us something spiritual that we cannot see. What is that spiritual reality? Divine grace is the spiritual reality that we receive from the Sacraments. Divine grace is the free and undeserved gift that God gives us, a share in God's own divine life.

The main Divine grace we receive from the Sacraments is Sanctifying Grace.

The Sacraments receive the power to give grace from God through the merits of Jesus Christ. The grace given by the Sacraments is Sanctifying Grace. A Sacrament is a channel of grace. The Sacraments are God's plan for us to obtain Grace, that is a share in divine life, in our souls. Grace is divine life in our souls. The seven Sacraments given us by Jesus Christ help us to share in His divine life.

As Catholics, we are able to receive all the seven Sacraments given to us by Jesus Christ! It is impossible to fully appreciate this terrific, fantastic gift we have received from Jesus Christ to help us to save our souls and to reach eternal life in Heaven with Him.

Most Sacred Heart of Jesus, I implore that I might love You more and more.

Fill in the Blanks

1. A sign is something we can see or hear, but which represents something we cannot see or ___hear___.

2. A Sacrament is an outward ___sign___ instituted by Jesus Christ to give ___grace___.

3. Another word for sign is ___symbol___.

4. We are creatures composed of ___physical___ bodies as well as spiritual souls.

5. The seven Sacraments were given to us by ___Christ___.

6. The Sacraments give us ___spiritual___ Grace.

7. We need grace to ___know___, ___love___, and serve God.

8. Sanctifying Grace is ___Divine___ life in our souls.

9. In the Sacrament of Confirmation, ___oil___ symbolizes strength.

10. In the Sacrament of Baptism, ___water___ symbolizes cleansing.

A Sacrament is an outward sign instituted by Jesus Christ to give grace. The seven Sacraments are Baptism, Confirmation, Penance, Holy Eucharist, Matrimony, Holy Orders, and Anointing of the Sick.

Jesus Christ instituted the seven Sacraments. How do we know Jesus Christ instituted the Sacraments? We know from the Bible, Sacred Tradition, and the teaching of the Church Jesus founded. Jesus Christ instituted the Sacraments for the new way He wants us to live, the Christian way of selfless love of God and neighbor.

Jesus is asking us for a special love of God and neighbor that requires special graces, graces only the Sacraments can give. The purpose of the seven Sacraments is to give us grace. It is God's plan for us to receive grace through receiving the Sacraments. The main grace is Sanctifying Grace.

We can better understand the Sacraments if we compare them with human life. Consider that we are born into the world, but we are also "born" in a different sense, spiritually or sacramentally, when we are born into the new life of grace by the Sacrament of *Baptism*. As we grow physically from infancy to adulthood, we also grow and are strengthened spiritually by the Sacrament of *Confirmation*. As we must nourish our bodies in order to live, we also must nourish ourselves spiritually through the reception of the Sacrament of the *Holy Eucharist*.

When we are physically sick, we need medicine to heal us; when we are sick spiritually (when we have sinned), we are healed by the Sacrament of *Penance*. As our parents guide us spiritually and physically, the Pope, bishops, and priests, after receiving the Sacrament of *Holy Orders*, guide us spiritually by administering the Sacraments to us.

As a society reproduces itself, the Church gains new members through the Sacrament of *Matrimony*. Finally, as we prepare for death by making our peace with loved ones, with the Sacrament of *Anointing of the Sick*, we prepare for eternity and make our final peace with God. We can see how our natural life has corresponding Sacraments for our spiritual life.

We can think of the Sacraments as our connection with God in eternity. How so? All of the Sacraments are channels of grace, graces which come to us directly from God when we receive them. When Jesus Christ died on the Cross, He won for us, He merited for us the graces we would need to obtain Heaven. The main channels through which we receive those graces are the Sacraments. Jesus instituted the Sacraments for the purpose of giving us the graces we need to obtain Heaven.

In addition to Sanctifying Grace, each Sacrament also gives a special Sacramental Grace, to carry out the particular purpose of each Sacrament. As long as we have the right dispositions, as long as we want these graces and have the intention of the Church for these Sacraments, we will receive the Graces which God gives through the reception of these Sacraments.

The power of these Sacramental Graces comes *directly* from Jesus Christ. Just before He died, Jesus told us, "I am the vine, you are the branches. He who abides in Me, and I in him, he it is that bears much fruit, for apart from Me, you can do nothing" (John 15:5).

Some of the Sacraments may be received only once. Baptism, Confirmation, and Holy Orders may be received only once. However, the Sacraments of Penance and the Holy Eucharist should be received frequently. The Church encourages us to receive the Sacrament of Penance at least once a month, and even once a week if possible. This is because we often sin, even every day, in some way. The Sacrament of Penance gives us an opportunity in a special way to tell God we are sorry for our sins and to receive forgiveness.

The Church encourages us to receive Jesus Christ in the Sacrament of the Holy Eucharist at least at Sunday Mass. However, we also are encouraged to attend Mass during the week and to receive Jesus Christ every day if possible. How blessed and privileged we are as Catholics to be able to receive the seven Sacraments that enable us to live in Christ's love and divine life with Sanctifying Grace.

*Heart of Jesus, of infinite majesty,
have mercy on us.*

True (T) or False (F)

_____ T 1. We know from the Bible, Sacred Tradition, and the teaching of the Church that Jesus Christ instituted the seven Sacraments.

_____ T 2. A Sacrament is an outward sign instituted by Jesus Christ to give grace.

_____ T 3. We are born into the life of grace through the Sacrament of Baptism.

_____ T 4. The Sacrament of Confirmation strengthens us spiritually.

_____ T 5. The Sacrament of Holy Eucharist nourishes our souls as food nourishes our bodies.

_____ T 6. All of the Sacraments are channels of grace.

_____ T 7. When Jesus Christ died on the Cross He won for us the graces we would need to obtain Heaven.

_____ T 8. Baptism, Confirmation, and Holy Orders may be received only once.

_____ T 9. The power of the Sacramental graces comes directly from Jesus Christ.

_____ T 10. Jesus Christ told us, "I am the vine, and you are the branches."

A Sacrament is an outward sign instituted by Jesus Christ to give grace. The seven Sacraments are Baptism, Confirmation, Penance, Holy Eucharist, Matrimony, Holy Orders, and Anointing of the Sick.

The Sacraments receive their power to give grace from God through the merits of Jesus Christ as a result of His Passion and Death on the Cross. The Sacraments give mainly Sanctifying Grace, but they also give Sacramental Grace, which helps us to fulfill the purpose of the particular Sacrament.

The Sacraments always give grace if we have the right disposition and want to receive help.

We know that there are different categories of flowers. We can organize them according to their color, whether or not they have a scent, whether they bloom in the summer or fall, and whether they are wild or can grow indoors. There are also different categories of the Sacraments. They can be organized according to whether they are Sacraments of the living or dead, and whether they are Sacraments of initiation, healing, or vocation.

Five of the Sacraments are known as Sacraments of the Living; two are known as Sacraments of the Dead. What does that mean? The purpose of the Sacraments of the Living is to give more grace to souls already spiritually alive through Sanctifying Grace. The purpose of the Sacraments of the Dead are to give the supernatural life of Sanctifying Grace to souls spiritually dead through sin.

 Using our flower example, suppose a little girl finds a beautiful flower growing in a field. It is a bright yellow wild flower with radiant golden petals. It is so lovely she decides to pick it. She takes it home and puts it in a jar filled with water. Soon the flower begins to wilt and the petals begin to fall off. Because she wants to keep the flower, she takes it out of the water and plants it in soil. As she transfers the flower from the water to the soil, more petals fall off. Sadly, she watches the dying flower, hoping it will once again bloom into the same full loveliness. As you might expect, the flower leans over, turns brown, and dies. The little girl tried to give life to something that was dead.

Something like that happens when we are dead in sin. As we have seen, when we commit serious sin which we call mortal sin, there is no life in the soul. The life of Christ cannot live in a soul that is dead. The person in mortal sin, therefore, may not receive the Sacraments of the living any more than the little girl could bring the flower back to life. Why? Because something lifeless cannot receive what is living. In our flower example above, no matter what the little girl did, she could not bring the flower back to life. But unlike the dead flower, the person in mortal sin *can* have his soul brought back to life by going to the Sacrament of Penance.

There are two Sacraments of the dead, Sacraments for souls which are dead in sin: Baptism and Penance. Before a baby is baptized, the baby is sweet and innocent, but living a merely natural life with Original Sin on the soul. The supernatural life of grace enters into the soul only at Baptism. At that time the new Christian—whether an infant or adult—receives the new life of Sanctifying Grace into the soul. Not only is Original Sin removed, but the guilt and punishment due to any actual sins are also removed. If a person were to die immediately after receiving the Sacrament of Baptism, he or she would go directly to Heaven.

The Sacrament of Penance enables the soul that is dead in Actual Sin to become once again alive in Sanctifying Grace. The words of absolution from the priest remove the guilt and some punishment due to sin as soon as the priest says the words of absolution. The Sacraments of the Dead bring life to souls that are spiritually dead in sin.

Whether there is Original Sin or mortal sin in the soul, the soul is, supernaturally speaking, without the life of grace. The Sacraments awaken the soul to the new or renewed life of divine grace.

Anyone who knowingly receives a Sacrament of the Living while his soul is dead, that is, the person is still in mortal sin, commits a mortal sin of sacrilege. That is because the person has treated a sacred Sacrament with grave irreverence.

Heart of Jesus, Holy Temple of God, have mercy on us.

Matching

_8_	1. Sacraments of the Dead	1.	Original Sin in the soul
_1_	2. Before Baptism	2.	Actual sins removed
_9_	3. Categories of Sacraments	3.	Instituted by Christ to give grace
_7_	4. Mortal sin	4.	Original Sin and any actual sins removed
_10_	5. Before Sacrament of Penance	5.	Only through Sacraments
_3_	6. Sacraments	6.	Received when no mortal sin in soul
_6_	7. Sacraments of the Living	7.	No life of Christ in the soul
_4_	8. After Baptism	8.	Baptism and Penance
_5_	9. Supernatural life	9.	Organization according to what they do
_2_	10. After Sacrament of Penance	10.	Actual sin on the soul

A Sacrament is an outward sign instituted by Jesus Christ to give grace. The seven Sacraments are Baptism, Confirmation, Penance, Holy Eucharist, Matrimony, Holy Orders, and Anointing of the Sick.

There are five Sacraments of the Living: the Holy Eucharist, Confirmation, Matrimony, Holy Orders, and the Anointing of the Sick. The Sacraments of the Living may be received only while a person is in the state of grace. This means the soul must be alive with the life of Jesus Christ. The Sacraments of the Living give the soul—already alive in grace—more grace, an increase in grace. Anyone in mortal sin may not receive a Sacrament of the Living.

Sanctifying Grace enables us to live more closely to Jesus Christ. Why do we need grace? So that we might discover God's holy will and, once we know His will, we need divine grace to carry out his holy will. In short, we need grace to do absolutely everything that God wants us to do. We need grace even to pray.

Divine grace inspired St. Paul to become one of the greatest saints and Scripture writers. Divine grace inspired St. Cecilia to answer the call to consecrate herself to God at the age of fourteen and later to die a martyr. Divine grace inspired St. Monica to pray for more than 20 years for her son Augustine to abandon his life of sin and become a Catholic. It was Divine grace which helped St. Augustine to become one of the greatest saints and Doctors of the Church.

Divine grace prompted St. Brigid of Ireland to inspire holiness among young Irish women who in turn answered the call to become religious and then to build convents all over Ireland. By the time of Brigid's death, all of Ireland was Catholic. Divine grace inspired St. Francis of Assisi to love poverty so much that he gave himself completely to working for the poor and founded a religious order which is one of the largest in the world today. Divine grace inspired the French Jesuits to enter the North American wilderness in order to convert hundreds of pagan American Indians.

Lest we think that divine grace is only for heroic people whose courageous deeds changed the world, we must immediately note that no one, not a single person, can do anything that is good, virtuous, or noble without divine grace. Not a single good thought, good word, or good deed for the right reason, the sake of loving our neighbor for the love of God, can enter our minds without grace. In other words, we must avail ourselves of the means of grace, namely the Sacraments and prayer. Grace is necessary for everyone, even for infants, to reach Heaven and the eternal vision of God.

By means of the Sacraments, we receive Sanctifying Grace. By means of the Sacraments, we grow in holiness according to our state in life. This is God's plan for people to receive divine grace.

A person must be in the state of grace to receive Holy Communion, the most important Sacrament of the living. The state of grace is the normal disposition required for a person to fruitfully receive any of the Sacraments of the living. If, however, a person knowingly receives any of the Sacraments of the living while in mortal sin, he commits the serious sin of sacrilege. Why? Because he profanes, or defiles something that is sacred.

Some Sacraments can be received only once: Baptism, Confirmation, and Holy Orders. This is because these Sacraments leave an indelible seal on the soul, a spiritual mark which lasts forever.

Our Blessed Lady, Queen of Divine Grace, pray for us.

Fill in the Blanks

1. In order to receive a Sacrament of the ___living___, a person must be in the state of grace.

2. We need the graces of the Sacraments in order to ___do___ God's will.

3. We need divine ___grace___ even to pray.

4. St. Monica prayed for her son, ___augustine___, for 20 years to become a Catholic.

5. St. Francis of Assisi founded the largest ___religious___ order in the world.

6. The Sacraments of the living are ___comfort___, Holy ___eucharist___, the Anointing of the ___sick___, Holy ___orders___ and _____.

7. We must not receive any of the Sacraments of the living if we are in ___motel___ sin.

8. We commit the sin of ___s_____ if we receive Holy Communion in mortal sin.

9. Without divine grace, we cannot do a single good ___deed___.

10. All the Sacraments help us to grow in ___grace___.

Baptism is the Sacrament that gives our souls the new life of Sanctifying Grace, by which we become children of God and heirs of heaven.

Why do we begin our study of the Sacraments with Baptism? Because Baptism is the first Sacrament we receive. In fact, without Baptism, no other Sacrament can or may be received. Known as the "door to the Church," Baptism is our entrance into the new life of divine grace. Baptism is the Sacrament of spiritual rebirth. Baptism gives us new spiritual life through Sanctifying Grace. When we are baptized, we receive a permanent indelible mark on our souls. This mark makes us members of the Church. As members, we are now eligible to receive the other sacraments.

In the Gospels, we read about a man named Nicodemus. He was a good man and a ruler of the Jews who had been following Jesus. He was an important leader and did not want his friends to know he was following the teachings of Jesus. He visited Jesus only at night when it was dark. One night, Nicodemus approached Jesus with a question about the signs and wonders He was performing. Jesus answered, "Truly, truly, I say to you, unless one is born anew, he cannot see the kingdom of God." Nicodemus was puzzled. He then asked Jesus, "How can a man be born when he is old?" Jesus answered, "Truly, truly, I say to you, unless one is born of *water and the Spirit*, he cannot enter the kingdom of God" (John 3:1-5).

It is very clear from the words of Jesus that a person cannot enter Heaven unless he is baptized. Later, Jesus told His followers a story about a Marriage Feast, which represented Heaven. He said that the guests must wear a wedding garment to attend the Marriage Feast. Jesus was teaching that just as a person must be properly dressed to attend a wedding, so our souls must be properly adorned in God's Sanctifying Grace in order to enter Heaven.

Jesus wanted to show us how important Baptism is, so He asked John the Baptist to baptize Him. Of course, Jesus did not need to be baptized, because He is the Son of God. But Jesus wanted to show us what we should do. By doing so, Jesus instituted the Sacrament of Baptism for all of us.

There was a second reason Jesus told John the Baptist to baptize Him in the River Jordan. According to the Council of Trent and according to the famous Doctor of the Church, St. Augustine, Jesus had another reason for being baptized. The Church Council declared that "He gave to water the power of sanctifying." Thus water is used in Baptism to sanctify us. St. Augustine, great saint of the Church, said it was necessary for Jesus to be baptized so that "by the contact of His pure flesh, He might purify the waters and impart to them the power of cleansing." Thus all the waters of the world have been blessed mainly for the purpose of using them in the Sacrament of Baptism!

When Jesus was baptized in the Jordan River, God the Father, in the form of His voice, and God the Holy Spirit, in the form of a dove, were present. God the Father declared, "This is my Beloved Son in Whom I am well pleased." How great this Sacrament of Baptism must be for all three Persons of the Blessed Trinity to be present!

When we were baptized, we became children of God and heirs of Heaven because God gave us a spiritual rebirth! God is now our spiritual Father! What an astounding event! You became a child of God when you were baptized. God is your Father in Heaven because of your baptism. God wants you to be with Him forever in Heaven when He calls you from this life. He wants you to inherit Heaven! In return, we strive to behave as good children of God. How? We can be good children of God by living our lives as a truly loving and obedient child of a loving and generous Heavenly Father. We must also exercise the virtues of faith, hope, and charity which we receive in the Sacrament of Baptism.

The most important effect of the Sacrament of Baptism is the removal of Original Sin. Original Sin is what we inherited from the sin of Adam and Eve. We recall that we are born with Original Sin. It is difficult to imagine that a beautiful, sweet, tiny baby has any sin at all. He or she certainly has no actual sins but Original Sin is part of each person's human nature when he or she is born.

Baptism removes Original Sin, which we inherited from the sin of our first parents, Adam and Eve. With Baptism, we now are going to inherit Heaven.

If an older person is baptized, not only Original Sin is removed, but also any Actual sins for which the person is truly sorry. Baptism removes all sins. Baptism removes also all the *punishment* due to sin. This means if a person were to die immediately after receiving the Sacrament of Baptism, the person would not need to suffer any punishment in Purgatory, but would go directly to Heaven!

What a wonderful gift from God! Before Jesus, the Son of God, came into the world, all the people born could not receive the Sacrament of Baptism. What a blessing that we have the opportunity to be baptized into Christ.

Heart of Jesus, House of God and Gate of Heaven, have mercy on us.

Multiple Choice

_____C____ 1. Without the Sacrament of Baptism, no other Sacrament _____ be received.
         a) can   b) may   c) can or may

_____a____ 2. Baptism is the Sacrament of
         a) spiritual rebirth.
         b) spiritual renewal.
         c) spiritual growth.

_____C____ 3. Nicodemus was
         a) not a good friend of Jesus.
         b) afraid.
         c) looking for the truth.

_____C____ 4. Jesus told Nicodemus
         a) that he should see Him during the day.
         b) that he was a sinner.
         c) that he must be born again.

_____a____ 5. When we are baptized, we become
         a) children of God.   b) heirs of Heaven.   c) a and b.

_____a____ 6. The Sacrament of Baptism removes
         a) Original Sin.
         b) actual sin.
         c) all the punishment due to sin.
         d) a, b and c.

_____C____ 7. The Sacrament of Baptism is the first Sacrament because
         a) it was the first one instituted by Jesus.
         b) it is the door to the Church.
         c) no other Sacrament can be received without it.
         d) b and c.

_____a____ 8. The most important effect of the Sacrament of Baptism is
         a) the removal of Original Sin.
         b) families come together for a celebration.
         c) babies become members of the Church.

_____C____ 9. Present at John's baptism of Jesus in the River Jordan was
         a) God the Father.   b) God the Son.   c) the Blessed Trinity.

_____C____ 10. For the Sacrament of Baptism to be valid
         a) the correct words must be used.
         b) water must be used.
         c) the correct words must be used while pouring the water on the forehead.

Baptism is the Sacrament that gives our souls the new life of Sanctifying Grace by which we become children of God and heirs of Heaven. Baptism takes away Original Sin. For an older person, Baptism takes away Actual sins, and the punishment due for sins.

A permanent indelible mark, a character, is imprinted on the soul at Baptism. The effects of this mark imprinted on the soul at Baptism makes the person a member of the Church, and able to receive the other Sacraments.

During His visible stay on earth, Jesus Christ taught us about the Kingdom of God. One of His most important teachings was how we are saved. Jesus said, "He that believes and is baptized will be saved; but he that believes not shall be damned" (Mark 16:16).

St. Peter, the first Pope, made the following statement "Baptism now saves you" (1 Peter 3:21). It is clear that only the baptized may enter a happy eternity in Heaven

We enter the Church by way of the Sacrament of Baptism. When we enter a building, we must use a door. That is why Baptism is called the "door of the Church." All baptized Catholics bear a indelible special mark or character on their souls. That mark identifies us as members of the Church, as coming through the door of the Church. Thus as members, we are able to receive any other Sacrament. As members of the Church, we are also bound, of course, to obey the laws of the Church.

The priest or deacon is the usual minister of Baptism. Most families go to the parish church for the very special event of baptizing the new baby in the family. The priest uses ordinary water, but water, according to St. Augustine, once blessed by Jesus. The priest pours the water over the forehead of the person to be baptized. At the same time the priest pours the water, he says the words: "I baptize you in the Name of the Father and of the Son and of the Holy Spirit. Amen." These words must be spoken while the water is poured over the forehead for the Sacrament to be valid.

Because Baptism is essential for entering Heaven, the Church allows anyone to baptize in case of an emergency! Even though the usual minister of Baptism is a priest or a deacon, under emergency circumstances, anyone may validly baptize.

Fifteen-year-old Joan has a new baby sister, only three days old. Joan is alone in the house with her mother when her baby sister begins to have trouble breathing. Mother calls the doctor, who tells her what she must do while waiting for the ambulance. Suddenly, Joan's mother tells Joan to hurry into the kitchen to get some water. Joan's mother takes the cup of water, and while pouring it over the baby's tiny head, speaks the words, "I baptize you in the Name of the Father and of the Son and of the Holy Spirit." The mother has spoken the beautiful, powerful, and awesome words of Baptism. The tiny baby is now a child of God and an heir to Heaven.

How blessed we are to have been born into the Catholic Church! When we were just a few days old, our parents took us to a Catholic Church. There we were received into the Church. Our souls were filled with the Holy Spirit. Original Sin was taken away, and we received the virtues of Faith, Hope and Charity. We thank our dear Lord for giving us the Sanctifying Grace that we need to someday enter a happy eternity in Heaven.

Heart of Jesus, full of goodness and love, have mercy on us.

Matching

_8_	1. Sanctifying Grace	~~1~~	Able to receive the other Sacraments
_5_	2. Priest or deacon	~~2~~	"Baptism now saves you"
_1_	3. Effect of Baptism	3.	Baptism removes Actual Sin as well
_10_	4. Baptism	4.	Permanent mark on the soul
_4_	5. Character	5.	Ordinary minister of Baptism
_9_	6. Anyone	6.	"He that believes and is baptized will be saved."
_2_	7. St. Peter said	7.	Makes us children of God
_6_	8. Jesus Christ said	8.	Infused at Baptism
_3_	9. For older people	9.	May baptize in an emergency
_____	10. Faith, hope and charity	10.	Gateway of the Church

Baptism is the Sacrament that gives our souls the new life of Sanctifying Grace by which we become children of God and heirs of Heaven. Baptism removes Original Sin from our souls. For older people, Baptism also removes actual sin as well as the punishment due to sin.

The effect of the permanent mark or character imprinted on the soul in Baptism is that the person becomes a member of the Catholic Church and may receive the other Sacraments. Being a member of the Church also means that the person is bound by the laws of the Church.

We know that Baptism is necessary to enter Heaven because Jesus said, "...unless a man be born again of water and the Spirit, he cannot enter into the kingdom of God." (John 3:5)

What about those who, through no fault of their own, do not *know* about Baptism? You might think it does not seem fair that someone who does not know what the Church teaches is denied Heaven. While no one may enter the Kingdom of God without Baptism, God has provided for those who sincerely do not know they should be baptized.

The Church teaches that Jesus died for every man, woman, and child, and provided the means, the Sacraments, for everyone to obtain Heaven. "Greater love than this no man has, that a Man lay down His life for His friends" (John 15:13).

How then is someone saved who is not a baptized Catholic? Those who through no fault of their own have not received the Sacrament of Baptism, can be saved by Baptism of Blood or Baptism of Desire.

The Church explains Baptism of Blood by stating that "those who suffer death for the sake of the faith without having received Baptism are baptized by their death for and with Christ. This *Baptism of blood*...brings about the fruits of Baptism without being a Sacrament" (*Catechism of the Catholic Church*, n. 1258). Another name for Baptism of blood is martyrdom. Someone who has died as a martyr for the Christian faith before he or she could receive the Sacrament of Baptism, has received Baptism of Blood. In the first century, many people who were awaiting the Sacrament of Baptism died for their Faith before they could receive the Sacrament. They are now enjoying Heaven for their faithful act of perfect love of God.

"For he who would save his life will lose it; but he who loses his life for My sake and for the Gospel's sake, will save it" (Mark 8:35). "And I say to you, everyone who acknowledges Me before men, him will the Son of Man also acknowledge before the angels of God" (Luke 12:8).

God is infinitely merciful and He has provided for the salvation of those who sincerely love Him and serve Him to the end. We cannot understand all the ways of God. The Church teaches, "…since Christ died for all, and since all men are in fact called to one and the same destiny, which is divine, we must hold that the Holy Spirit *offers to all* the possibility of being made partners, in a way known to God, in the paschal mystery" (*The Church in the Modern World*, 22, 5).

The Second Vatican Council, from which the foregoing passage was taken, was declaring that, "Every man who is ignorant of the Gospel of Christ and of His Church, but seeks the truth and does the will of God in accordance with his understanding of it, can be saved. It may be supposed that such persons [who do not know about the Gospel of Christ] would have *desired Baptism explicitly* if they had known its necessity" (*Catechism of the Catholic Church*, 1260). What is the Church telling us? That by the Baptism of Desire, and because of God's infinite mercy, certain men can be saved. St. Paul said in his letter to the Romans that someone can be saved if he has the law of God written on his heart.

Is Baptism of Desire a Sacrament? No, Baptism of Desire is not a Sacrament. Only Baptism with water imprints the permanent seal or character on the soul. A person cannot receive the other Sacraments unless he has received the Sacrament of Baptism by the pouring of water on the forehead, and the words, "I baptize you in the Name of the Father, and of the Son, and of the Holy Spirit. Amen."

We know that some American Indians wanted to join the Church, but were not able to find the missionary priests to baptize them. Some may have been killed in the Indians wars or by their own tribe. Some may have died before finding a priest to baptize them. Kateri Tekakwitha waited several years before she was able to escape her Indian tribe which persecuted her. She was finally baptized in a Catholic Indian community.

On December 28th, we celebrate the Feast of the Holy Innocents. At about the time of Jesus' birth, little boys, two years old and under, became martyrs when they were killed by the soldiers of the wicked King Herod who was trying to kill the Baby Jesus. The Church recognizes these babies as saints in Heaven, not by the Sacrament of Baptism by water, but by their likeness to Christ by their baptism in their own blood. Only God knows how many Sacramentally un-baptized souls have loved God to the point of the shedding of their blood.

From the very beginning, the Church has taught that the Church was to be a society for the salvation of all men on earth. In the Acts of the Apostles, we read about a God-fearing man named Cornelius who was a pagan. Although he had not been baptized, all knew him to be a very good and charitable man. Through no fault of his own, however, he had not been baptized. When St. Peter came to him, he recognized Cornelius' goodness and desire to become a member of the new Christian community, and baptized him.

Infant Son of the Virgin Mary, have mercy on us.

Fill in the Blanks

1. Baptism is the Sacrament that
   _removes original sin_____.

2. Baptism removes _original sin_____ from our souls.

3. Cornelius was baptized by _St. Peter_____.

4. Everyone has been redeemed through the _death_____ of Jesus Christ.

5. Greater _love_____ than this no man has, that a Man lay down his life for His friends.

6. Those who suffer death for the sake of the Faith receive Baptism of _blood____.

7. …but he who loses his life for My sake, and for the Gospel's sake, will _save_____ it.

8. Everyone who acknowledges Me before men, him will the Son of Man also
   acknowledge before the _angels_____ of God.

9. God is infinitely merciful, and has provided for the _slavation_____ of all who
   sincerely love Him and serve Him to the end.

10. A person cannot receive the other Sacraments unless he has received the Sacrament of
    _baptism_____.

Baptism is the Sacrament that gives our souls the new life of Sanctifying Grace by which we become children of God and heirs of heaven. Baptism is necessary for the salvation of all men. Baptism removes Original sin and any actual sins which the person may have committed. The priest or deacon is the usual minister of Baptism, but anyone may baptize in case of an emergency.

The Church emphasizes the importance of parents having their new-born babies baptized as soon as possible after birth. It can be a sin for parents to delay having their baby baptized because delay puts the eternal salvation of the baby in jeopardy.

In infant baptism, the promises are made on behalf of the infant by the parents and godparents who are promising to raise the child in the Catholic Faith. During the Baptism, the priest speaks the following words: "You have asked to have your child baptized. In doing so, you are accepting the responsibility of training your child in the practice of the faith. It will be your duty to bring him up to keep God's Commandments as Christ taught us, by loving God and our neighbor. Do you clearly understand what you are undertaking?"

What are some of the baptismal promises? On behalf of their children, the parents:

Renounce Satan and all his works. This means rejecting all thoughts, words, desires, and deeds that are opposed to God's laws.

Renounce all that the world loves because Satan uses them to take people away from God.

Promise to live according to the teachings of Christ and to follow His example.

The name of a saint is given to the person being baptized. This is done so that the person being baptized may imitate the virtues of the saint. This saint will be a lifelong protector for the baptized person.

The Church encourages parents to choose names of saints for their children. The saints in Heaven are those faithful Catholics who gave themselves to Jesus Christ. They are now enjoying perfect happiness with God in Heaven. They are, therefore, our models of virtue. We honor especially our own patron saint and pray to him (or her) for protection and guidance throughout our lives. What are some popular saints' names?

Perhaps the most significant and popular name is "Mary." To name a girl—either her first or middle name—after the Mother of God, is to give special honor to our Lady in Heaven who followed the will of God perfectly. The young lady who bears the name "Mary" should strive throughout her life to imitate the virtues of her Mother in Heaven. There are many variations of the name Mary. Marie, Marilyn and Muriel are variations.

A popular boy's name is "Joseph," after the foster father of Jesus. The name means "God will increase." Joseph was the strong, gentle, humble protector of the Holy Family. God chose Joseph and Mary to be the privileged parents of Jesus.

There are many other beautiful Catholic names parents may choose for their children which can be found in many books about the lives of the saints. Children should study the lives of their patron saint, and reflect on the virtues of that saint which they themselves should consider imitating.

For the Sacrament of Baptism, parents must choose godparents who are good, practicing Catholics and who believe in the Faith of the Mystical Body of Christ. The parents should choose godparents very carefully. A godparent should never be chosen merely because of friendship. Why? The godparent takes on a serious responsibility to see to it that the godchild is brought up in the Catholic faith. If anything happens to the parents, the godparent(s) would make sure the child continues the practice of the Catholic Faith. Godparents must be at least sixteen years old. They must have been confirmed and regularly receive the Sacrament of Holy Eucharist. The godparents' names are noted on the Baptismal certificate and in the Baptismal registry in the Church.

The world in which we live is a wonderful place, but it has many temptations. We have only to look at television and the movies to discover how opposed is the world to what is sacred. Sin is made to look appealing and fascinating. At the same time, goodness and decency are ridiculed. Without the Sacraments and prayer, we would have no hope of overcoming the strong temptations that surround us every day.

Most Sacred Heart of Jesus, worthy of all praise, have mercy on us.

Matching

_7_	1. Removes Original Sin	1. Necessary for salvation
_1_	2. Baptism	2. Must be practicing Catholics
_10_	3. First weeks of life	3. To raise their children in Catholic Faith
_9_	4. Name of a saint	4. To renounce Satan and his works
_3_	5. Parents' duty	5. Usual minister of Baptism
_4_	6. Baptismal promise	6. Most popular Baptismal Name
_8_	7. Joseph	7. Baptism
_6_	8. Mary	8. God will increase
_2_	9. Godparents	9. For child to imitate virtues
_5_	10. Priest	10. Parents must have their babies baptized

Today we begin our studies on the Sacrament of Confirmation. Confirmation is the Sacrament through which the Holy Spirit comes to us in a special way. Through Confirmation, the Holy Spirit enables us to profess our faith as strong and perfect Christians and soldiers of Jesus Christ.

In a sense, Baptism and Confirmation go together as introduction and fulfillment. Baptism *introduces* us into the life of the Holy Spirit and gives us Sanctifying Grace, a share in divine life. Confirmation strengthens us in the life of the Holy Spirit, in the divine life of grace, and helps us to *fulfill* our baptismal promises.

Confirmation is a Sacrament of the Living. This means our souls must be alive in Sanctifying Grace when we receive Confirmation. The Sacrament of Confirmation enables us to grow from the infancy of the supernatural life in Baptism into spiritual maturity. A person who is spiritually mature is a real soldier of Jesus Christ.

The Sacrament of Confirmation was given to us by God when He sent the Holy Spirit upon the Apostles on Pentecost Sunday. Recall that the Apostles had been so frightened when Jesus was crucified that they ran and hid in the Upper Room. After Jesus had risen from the dead, He visited with them for forty days. During that time, He commanded them not to leave Jerusalem, but to wait "for the promise of the Father."

Just before Jesus ascended into Heaven, He told them that they would "be baptized with the Holy Spirit not many days hence." He told them that "You shall receive the power of the Holy Spirit coming upon you, and you shall be witnesses for Me in Jerusalem, and in all Judea, and Samaria, and even to the uttermost part of the earth."

The Apostles stayed in the Upper Room with the Blessed Mother, praying with some other followers, numbering about a hundred and twenty people. In the Acts of the Apostles, we read that after nine days, "Suddenly there came a sound from Heaven, as of a mighty wind coming, and it filled the whole house where they were sitting. And there appeared to them parted tongues as it were of fire, and it sat upon every one of them;

"And they were all filled with the Holy Spirit. And they began to speak in various tongues according as the Holy Spirit gave them to speak.

"Now there were dwelling at Jerusalem Jews, devout men, out of every nation under Heaven. And when the noise [of the mighty wind] was heard, the multitude came together, and were confused because every man heard them speak in his own tongue. And they were amazed, and wondered, saying: Behold, are not all these that speak Galileans? And how have we heard every man our own tongue wherein we were born?…..We have heard them speak in our own tongues the wonderful works of God. And they were all astonished, and wondered, saying one to another: What does this mean?"

Peter, filled with the Holy Spirit, gave a sermon to thousands of people in the streets of Jerusalem, explaining the Old Testament prophecies about Jesus, as well as about the Resurrection of Jesus and that He is the promised Messiah for whom they had been waiting.

The rest of the Acts of the Apostles tells us about the brave deeds and heroic charity of the newly transformed Apostles. They were no longer frightened. They became warriors for their Savior, making new converts, healing the sick, and casting out demons just as Jesus did during His visible stay on earth. The Sacrament of Confirmation is *our* Pentecost. Just as the disciples were transformed into soldiers for Jesus Christ, so we too acquire the same graces of the Sacrament, enabling us to be brave warriors for Jesus Christ.

The Holy Spirit helps us to become loyal witnesses and soldiers for Jesus Christ and His Kingdom here on earth. St. Thomas Aquinas wrote, "…the Sacrament by which spiritual strength is conferred on the one born again [in Baptism] makes him in some sense a front-line fighter for the faith of Christ" (St. Thomas, IV *Contra Gentiles*, c. 60). For every soldier of Christ, there are many thousands of souls who do not know the Good News of the Gospels. It is our special mission as soldiers to spread the Faith here on earth.

We should not forget to pray to the Holy Spirit, the Third Person of the Blessed Trinity, Who comes to us in a special way in the Sacrament of Confirmation. Pope John Paul II's beautiful letter on the Holy Spirit in the life of the Church and in the world is a clear explanation of the Holy Spirit. The Pope wrote, "…[we should fix our eyes] on Him Who *is* the love of the Father and the Son" and Who is also "the Spirit of peace" who "does not cease to be present in our human world, on the horizon of minds and hearts, in order to 'fill the universe' with love and peace" (*Dominum et Vivificantem*, n. 67).

We received the greatest treasure on earth, our Catholic Faith, most likely from our parents. Our Catholic Faith is the greatest gift we shall ever receive. But there are countless people in the world who do not know Jesus Christ. We need to pass on this wonderful gift we have received. By the graces of Confirmation, we must tell others about the Catholic Faith. Confirmation gives us boldness and bravery to be real warriors for Christ in His Kingdom here on earth.

Holy Spirit, Source of all holiness, have mercy on us.

True (T) or False (F)

_____ 1. In a sense, Baptism and Confirmation go together as introduction and fulfillment.

_____ 2. Confirmation is a Sacrament of the living.

_____ 3. In some Catholic rites and countries, the Sacrament of Confirmation is received in infancy.

_____ 4. Baptism, Confirmation, and Penance are the Sacraments of initiation.

_____ 5. At the first Pentecost, the Apostles received the grace of the Holy Spirit.

_____ 6. Confirmation is the Sacrament in which the Holy Spirit comes to us in a special way.

_____ 7. Baptism must be given before Confirmation.

_____ 8. St. Thomas Aquinas wrote *Dominum et Vivificantem.*

_____ 9. Pope John Paul II wrote *Contra Gentiles.*

_____ 10. The Sacrament of Confirmation enables us to become soldiers for Jesus Christ.

Confirmation is the Sacrament through which the Holy Spirit comes to us in a special way, and enables us to profess our faith as strong and perfect Christians and soldiers of Jesus Christ.

The bishop is the ordinary minister of the Sacrament of Confirmation. The original Apostles were the first bishops of the Catholic Church. It was upon these first bishops that the Holy Spirit descended on Pentecost Sunday. These first bishops and Apostles were the first ministers of Confirmation to others. The bishops of today are the direct successors of the first bishops, and continue to be the proper ministers of the Sacrament of Confirmation.

Does that mean that *only* a bishop may confer the Sacrament of Confirmation? No. However, it is only in certain circumstances that a priest is permitted to administer Confirmation. If a person is in danger of death, a priest may confirm him. When a person is being admitted to the Church, a priest may confirm a new Catholic at the time of his reception into the Catholic Church. We see these Confirmations on Holy Saturday.

How is the Sacrament of Confirmation conferred? Just as the matter of the Sacrament of Baptism is water, which signifies the washing away of sin, the matter of the Sacrament of Confirmation is chrism, a mixture of holy oil and balm.

What is signified by the chrism composed of oil? Oil signifies strengthening. Oil has been used to condition and strengthen the muscles of athletes. In the Old Testament times, new kings were anointed with oil to signify they had been specially chosen by God and to give them strength in their new position of leadership. Perhaps you recall the story of the prophet Samuel, who anointed David as King, at the express command of God Himself. Fragrant balm which is mixed with the oil to make the chrism signifies the sweetness of virtue and freedom from the stain of sin.

As with all Sacraments, signs and symbols are used because of their special meanings. The laying on of hands is very significant and has special meaning. When the bishop lays his hands upon the head of each young person to be confirmed, the person receives the Holy Spirit at that instant. This also indicates the person's role in the Mystical Body of Christ as future healer or converter of souls. The bishop is encouraging the newly-confirmed to be inspired to labor in the kingdom of God as soldiers and missionaries for Jesus Christ.

The bishop draws a Sign of the Cross with chrism on the foreheads of those being confirmed. It is the most popular way we have of expressing our Catholic faith. When we make the Sign of the Cross, we are professing our belief that Jesus Christ died for our sins and that we are Catholics. The Sign of the Cross is a Sacramental, which, as we have seen, gives grace.

The Apostles and first Christians frequently made the Sign of the Cross. In the Sacrament of Confirmation, the Sign of the Cross indicates an invitation to imitate Jesus Christ by being His special witness and a willingness to suffer and carry the cross which might be sent. Just as Jesus died for our sins, so we are to give ourselves to others for the greater glory of God.

The bishop makes the Sign of the Cross on the forehead of the young people being confirmed. Our faith resides in our intellect or mind. Thus the Sign of the Cross on our forehead symbolizes our faith being *strengthened in our minds* so that we may *exercise our wills* to carry out God's holy will. With the gifts of the Holy Spirit for our minds and wills, we will then be able to love God more, and to willingly make the necessary sacrifices to convert others.

Confirmation is meant to remind us that the saints and martyrs of all times were imitators of Jesus Christ as they won souls for the Kingdom of God, sometimes even at the cost of their own lives. To remind us, in the old rite of Confirmation, the bishop gave the young person he confirmed a slight blow on the cheek, to remind him that he must be ready to suffer everything, even death, for the sake of Jesus Christ.

Holy Spirit, Divine Guardian of our Virtue, have mercy on us.

Multiple Choice

_C_ 1. The _____ is the ordinary minister of Confirmation.
    a) priest   b) deacon   c) bishop

_C_ 2. The twelve Apostles were
    a) deacons.   b) priests.   c) bishops.

_d_ 3. A priest may confer the Sacrament of Confirmation
    a) when someone is in danger of death.
    b) when he is receiving someone into the Church.
    c) never.
    d) a and b.

_a_ 4. The matter of the Sacrament of Confirmation is
    a) water.   b) oil.   c) bread.

_b_ 5. In the Sacrament of Confirmation, holy oil signifies
    a) washing.   b) strengthening.   c) happiness.

_a_ 6. Confirmation is the Sacrament through which _____ comes to us in a special way
    a) the Holy Spirit   b) God the Father   c) God the Son

_b_ 7. The Sign of the Cross began
    a) in apostolic times.   b) in modern times.   c) in the fifteenth century.

_a_ 8. The Sign of the Cross is
    a) a Sacramental.   b) a Sacrament.   c) a greeting for Christians.

_b_ 9. The Sign of the Cross is made _____ by the bishop at the Sacrament of Confirmation
    a) on the wrists   b) on the forehead   c) on the lips

_C_ 10. Confirmation strengthens
    a) our faith.   b) our wills.   c) a and b.

Confirmation is the Sacrament through which the Holy Spirit comes to us in a special way, and enables us to profess our faith as strong and perfect Christians and soldiers of Jesus Christ.

The bishop is the usual minister of Confirmation. When the bishop confirms, he extends his hands over those who are to be confirmed, and prays that they may receive the Holy Spirit. In the new rite of Confirmation, the bishop says, "Be sealed with the Gift of the Holy Spirit." While laying his hand on the head of each person, the bishop anoints the forehead with holy chrism in the form of a Cross. Holy Chrism is a mixture of olive oil and balm. The anointing on the forehead with chrism in the form of a Cross signifies that the young Catholic who is confirmed must always be ready to profess his Catholic Faith openly, and to practice it fearlessly.

What are the effects of the Sacrament of Confirmation? The first effect is an increase in Sanctifying Grace. Remember that Sanctifying Grace confers on our souls a new life, that is, a sharing in the life of God Himself. Sanctifying Grace makes us holy and pleasing to God. We receive Sanctifying Grace from each Sacrament, each time we receive a Sacrament.

Confirmation increases Sanctifying Grace which we received originally in Baptism. St. Augustine taught, "Our hearts are made for Thee, O Lord and they are restless until they rest in Thee." God made us to know, love, and serve Him in this world, but we were made primarily to be with God forever in the world to come. Our hearts cannot be happy until we go to our true home in Heaven with God. Confirmation increases Sanctifying Grace, that is, divine life in our soul, thus helping us to go to Heaven. Confirmation thus prepares our soul to receive more and more special graces so that we can live our faith, profess our faith, practice our faith, defend our faith, and spread our faith to others.

The second effect of Confirmation is that it gives us Sacramental Grace. We recall that each Sacrament has its own special Sacramental Grace. The Sacramental Grace of each Sacrament helps the person to carry out the particular purpose of that Sacrament. The Sacramental Graces of Confirmation make us brave followers and soldiers of Jesus Christ, ready to profess our Catholic Faith even when our lives may be in danger for doing so.

It has never been easy to be a Catholic. Even in our own beloved United States, in our early history, Catholics were not allowed to vote or to hold public office in several states. While at the present time Catholics may hold office in our country, nevertheless, pro-life Catholics find it very difficult to be elected to office. Why? Because we stand for the value of life, from the first instant of life to the last dying breath. We follow God's laws and do not make compromises. However, we need the Sacramental Grace from Confirmation to be strong in upholding the Ten Commandments.

One of the problems we all have is a desire for human respect. Everyone wants to be liked. There are times when, if we stand up for our faith, we may be laughed at, mocked, or ridiculed by our friends or important people. That is unpleasant because we naturally want to be liked. The Sacramental Graces from Confirmation help us to overcome these natural instincts and help us to speak out bravely for the truth.

The third effect of the Sacrament of Confirmation is the imprinting on our soul of a permanent mark, an indelible or lasting character. The Church expresses it this way: "The

Sacrament of Confirmation impresses a character [on the soul], and by it, the baptized … are enriched by the gift of the Holy Spirit and bound more perfectly to the Church; it strengthens them and obliges them more firmly to be witnesses to Christ by word and deed, and to spread and defend the faith" (Canon 879).

Confirmation is the Sacrament which helps us to be the saints and martyrs we are called to be. Do you know who was the very first martyr? After Jesus Christ ascended into Heaven, the Jewish authorities began to persecute the new Christians! A young Christian man named Stephen was stoned for his love of Jesus Christ. Just before he died, Stephen forgave his murderers. Kneeling, he cried out, "Lord, do not hold this sin against them" (Acts 7: 59-60).

From the time of St. Stephen to the present day, there have been countless Christians, many young people, who have given their lives for Jesus Christ. A few of the young martyrs of the Church are Saints Cecilia, Joan of Arc, Maria Goretti, Bernadette, Francisco, Jacinta, Joseph of Cupertino, Tarcisius, and many others. Throughout the centuries, saints received the graces of the Sacrament of Confirmation to help them be faithful and strong Christian soldiers for Jesus Christ.

We may not be called to such a dramatic calling, but we receive the same Holy Spirit in the Sacrament of Confirmation. The Holy Spirit guides us throughout our lives and gives us all the powerful graces we need to know and perform God's will as perfectly as each of Christ's saints and martyrs.

Holy Spirit, Who made me a soldier of Christ, have mercy on me.

Matching

_____	1. Code of Canon Law	1.	Perfects baptism
_____	2. Confirmation	2.	Means openness to suffering
___9___	3. Makes us soldiers for Jesus	3.	Holy Thursday
_____	4. Consecration of holy chrism	4.	Persecuted Christians
_____	5. Slight blow to the cheek	5.	Became powerful witness to Jesus Christ
___8___	6. St. Stephen	6.	Collection of Church laws
___4___	7. Saul	7.	Comes to us in Confirmation
_____	8. St. Paul	8.	First martyr
___7___	9. Holy Spirit	9.	Confirmation
_____	10. Martyrs	10.	Give their lives for Jesus Christ

173

Confirmation is the Sacrament through which the Holy Spirit comes to us in a special way and enables us to profess our faith as strong and perfect Christians and soldiers of Jesus Christ.

When the bishop gives the Sacrament of Confirmation, he extends his hand over those to be confirmed. This is called the "laying on of hands." While laying his hand on the head of each person, he anoints the forehead with holy chrism in the form of a cross. At the same time, the bishop says, "Be sealed with the Gift of the Holy Spirit."

The effects of the Sacrament of Confirmation are an increase in Sanctifying Grace, the Sacramental Grace of Confirmation, and a lasting permanent mark or "character" on the soul, marking the newly-confirmed as a soldier in the army of Jesus Christ.

Remember that Confirmation is a Sacrament of the living. This means we must be in the state of grace in order to receive it properly. In the Roman Rite, the bishops have required that the young person being confirmed know the chief truths and duties of our religion. The bishop often calls on the young people to be confirmed to answer catechism questions.

In the Eastern Rite Catholic Churches, it is traditional for the new baby to be baptized, confirmed, and receive the Holy Eucharist, all at the same time.

After we have been confirmed, it is important to continue to study our Catholic religion. We should be able to understand it better, to explain it better, and to defend it better. We should be more willing to be soldiers for Jesus Christ, and stand up to those who try to promote lifestyles which are against the teachings of Jesus.

Confirmation makes the virtue of faith clearer and the truths of the faith understandable. Confirmation makes us more certain that what we believe is the truth. That is one reason why those who are confirmed must have been receiving the Sacraments of Penance and Holy Eucharist for some time. We are very thankful to our dear Lord for giving us the great gift of the Sacrament of Confirmation, also known as the Sacrament of Martyrdom.

The Church teaches that all Catholics should be confirmed in order to be strengthened against the dangers to salvation, and to be better prepared to defend our Catholic Faith. This is a Sacrament given to us by God on Pentecost Sunday when the Holy Spirit came down upon the Apostles in the form of tongues of fire. The Holy Spirit came in such a powerful way, that the Apostles were able to convert thousands of people immediately. Certainly such a dramatic Sacrament as this is not to be ignored, or to be considered optional.

Some of the prayers for the Feast of Pentecost remind us of the great occasion of the coming of the Holy Spirit for the first time. We should consider these prayers when we are confirmed.

"Blessed are You, Christ our God, Who have filled the fishermen with wisdom by sending down the Holy Spirit upon them."

"When the Most High came down and confused the tongues of the people in Babel, He divided the nations; but when He distributed the tongues of fire at Pentecost, He called all men to unity. Therefore we glorify the Holy Spirit as with one voice."

"You renewed Your disciples, O Christ, by giving them a variety of tongues with which to proclaim that You are the Immortal God."

"We have seen the true Light, we have received the Heavenly Spirit, we have found the true Faith! Wherefore we worship the undivided Trinity for having saved us!"

"O Lord, when You sent down Your Spirit upon the assembled Apostles, the Hebrews were struck with awe as they heard them speak in many tongues, as the Spirit inspired them. They knew them [the Apostles] to be illiterate and now saw them wise, speaking divine truths, and bringing Gentiles to believe. We also cry out to You: O Lord, Who have appeared on earth and saved us from error, glory be to You."

Holy Spirit, Strength of my will, have mercy on me.

Fill in the Blanks

1. St. _____ said, "Our hearts . . . are restless till they rest in Thee."

2. The Sacramental graces of Confirmation make us brave _____ of Jesus Christ.

3. Human respect makes us _____ of being ridiculed.

4. The divine life of the _____ is increased in Confirmation.

5. The graces of the Sacrament of Confirmation make us want to learn _____ about our Faith.

6. Confirmation makes us _____ what we believe.

7. Those who are to be confirmed should have been receiving the Sacraments of

    _____ _____ and _____ for some time.

8. The seal of the Sacrament of Confirmation is a permanent _____ on the soul.

9. Confirmation makes us better able to endure _____ just like Jesus Christ.

10. Confirmation is the Sacrament through which the Holy Spirit comes to us in a special

    way and enables us to _____ as strong and perfect Christians, and soldiers of Jesus Christ.

Today we begin the study of the Sacrament of the Holy Eucharist. The Holy Eucharist is a Sacrament and a Sacrifice. In the Holy Eucharist, under the appearances of bread and wine, the Lord Jesus Christ is contained, offered, and received.

We go back momentarily to our Baptism when we became supernaturally alive. Our new supernatural life, like any living thing, needs food in order to survive. Our natural life needs food in order to survive and our supernatural life needs food. This food for our supernatural life is the living Bread, the Holy Eucharist, Which comes down from Heaven, Jesus Christ Himself!

Like the other Sacraments, the Holy Eucharist is a Sacrament containing a sign. But unlike the other Sacraments, the Holy Eucharist *is* Jesus Christ, contained wholly and completely in the Sacrament. Jesus Christ is here on earth, in every tabernacle throughout the world. Not only is He alive, He is communicating His graces to all who receive Him in the Sacrament of the Holy Eucharist.

Jesus lived quietly for thirty years in Nazareth. Then for three years, He publicly went about the area on the east coast of the Mediterranean Sea, teaching, preaching, and preparing for the greatest event in human history. Jesus Christ, the Son of God, gave mankind the greatest gift of all time: the Sacrament of the Holy Eucharist.

Jesus had been preparing His Apostles for three years during His visible stay on earth to open the eyes of their faith, their hearts, and their minds to receive Him. When Jesus healed the blind, He also was opening the eyes of their faith. When Jesus healed the deaf, He also was healing the ears of their hearts. When Jesus performed the miracle of the loaves and fishes, He was not only feeding the hungry people; Jesus was also preparing the Apostles to better understand what He was about to do at the Last Supper on Holy Thursday night, the night before He died.

Jesus Christ instituted the Sacrament of the Holy Eucharist at the Last Supper the night before He died. Anyone who knows he is dying will have very important things to say to those he is leaving behind. That is just what happened the night before Jesus died on the Cross. He wanted to be with His special friends, His Apostles. They surely did not fully understand what He was about to do, but they certainly would miss Him very much. Imagine losing a friend, or a loved-one. That would be very difficult, but consider how hard it was for the Apostles to lose their Master: the Son of God Himself. What a miraculous gift they received when Jesus gave them the power to change ordinary bread and ordinary wine into His own Body and Blood, making it possible for Him to always be with them!

You might be thinking how blessed the Apostles were to have seen and spoken with and even touched Jesus. But think for a moment about how blessed we are to receive our Lord and Savior in the Sacrament of the Holy Eucharist every day!

We know that Jesus Christ is truly present in the Holy Eucharist because of the following words which Jesus Christ said.

"At that time, Jesus said to the crowds of the Jews: My Flesh is real Food and My Blood real Drink. The man who feeds on My Flesh and drinks My Blood abides in Me and I in him. Just as the Father Who has life sent Me and I have life because of the Father, so the man who feeds on Me will have life because of Me. This is the Bread which came down from Heaven. Unlike your ancestors who ate and yet died, the man who feeds on this Bread will live forever" (John 6:55-59).

Living Bread That came down from Heaven, have mercy on us.
Sacred Host, have mercy on us.

True (T) or false (F)

__T__ 1. The Holy Eucharist is Jesus Christ.

__T__ 2. At our Baptism, we became supernaturally alive.

__F__ 3. Jesus Christ is partially contained in the Holy Eucharist.

__F__ 4. Jesus Christ lived on earth for twenty-five years before teaching and preaching.

__F__ 5. Jesus restored sight to the blind just so they would be able to see.

__F__ 6. Jesus restored hearing to the deaf only so they could hear again.

__T__ 7. The Last Supper was on the night before Jesus died.

__T__ 8. Jesus Christ instituted the Holy Eucharist on Holy Thursday night.

__F__ 9. The Apostles were more privileged than we are because they saw and s poke with Jesus.

__F__ 10. Jesus performed the miracle of the loaves and fishes only to feed the hungry people.

The Holy Eucharist is a Sacrament and a sacrifice. In the Holy Eucharist, under the appearances of bread and wine, the Lord Jesus Christ is contained, offered, and received. Jesus Christ instituted the Sacrament of the Holy Eucharist at the Last Supper on Thursday night, the night before He died on the Cross. The Apostles were present at the Last Supper when Jesus instituted the Sacrament of the Holy Eucharist.

Jesus instituted the Sacrament of the Holy Eucharist when He took ordinary bread, blessed it, broke it, and said to His Apostles: "Take and eat; this is My Body." Then Jesus took a cup of wine, blessed it, and giving it to His Apostles, He said: "All of you drink of this, for this is My blood of the new covenant which is being shed for many unto the forgiveness of sins."

At the Last Supper with the Apostles, Our Lord Jesus Christ changed ordinary bread and ordinary wine into His own Body and Blood. He then provided a means for all Catholics to receive the Holy Eucharist for all time. He ordained the Apostles as the first bishops by commanding them: "Do this in remembrance of Me."

The Apostles who were present were: Peter, Andrew, James son of Zebedee, John, Philip, Bartholomew, Thomas, Matthew, James son of Alphaeus, Jude Thaddeus, and Simon. They were the Apostles who were to pass on the Sacramental priesthood to millions of priests and bishops into the future and even to the end of time. Ten of the original Apostles died martyrs. John, the youngest Apostle, lived to a very old age, writing his Gospel, letters, and the Book of Revelation, or the Apocalypse.

St. Paul wrote in his first letter to the Corinthians: "Brethren: I received from the Lord what I also handed on to you, that the Lord Jesus, on the night in which He was betrayed, took bread and having given thanks, broke it and said: 'This is My Body which is for you. Do this in remembrance of Me.' In the same way, after the supper, He took the cup saying, 'This cup is the New Covenant in My Blood. Do this whenever you drink it, as a remembrance of Me.'

"Every time, then, that you eat this Bread and drink this cup, you proclaim the death of Jesus until He comes. So, whoever eats the Bread or drinks the cup of the Lord unworthily will have to answer for the Body and Blood of the Lord. A man should first examine himself. Only then should he eat of the Bread and drink of the cup. For he who eats and drinks without recognizing the Body, eats and drinks a judgment against himself." [I Cor. 11: 23-29]

We must use very careful language when we speak about the Holy Eucharist. When the priest pronounces the words of consecration, "This is My Body" and "This is My Blood" or "This is the cup of My Blood," over ordinary bread and wine, what was the *substance* of bread and of wine no longer exists. Only the appearances of bread and wine remain. What are we saying? When we receive the Holy Eucharist, what tastes and looks and smells like bread and wine is not bread and wine. After the words of consecration, the bread and wine have changed in substance to become the whole Body and Blood of Jesus Christ.

There is a big word, *transubstantiation,* that perfectly describes what happens at the consecration. The prefix "trans" means over, across, from one state to another. When we talk about transportation, we mean carrying something across or over, from one place to another.

When we speak of making the substance change over, from one substance to another, we call it *transubstantiation*. This means that at the consecration, when the priest pronounces the words, "This is My Body," the entire *substance* of the bread is changed over into the substance of the Body and Blood of Jesus Christ. What had been bread no longer is bread. In the same way, when the priest pronounces the words, "This is My Blood" or "This is the cup of My Blood," the entire *substance* of the wine is changed over into the substance of the Body and Blood of Jesus Christ.

Pope Paul VI, in his *Credo of the People of God*, explained: "Christ cannot be (thus) present in this Sacrament except by the change into His Body of the reality itself of the bread, and the change into His Blood of the reality itself of the wine, leaving unchanged only the properties of the bread and wine which our senses perceive. This mysterious change is very appropriately called by the Church *transubstantiation*."

Why did the Pope explain in such detail what happens at Mass? The Pope wanted to explain again the teaching of the Bible and the Church since Jesus first said the words at the Last Supper. The consecration at Mass is the greatest miracle on earth. Jesus Christ, Body and Blood, Soul and Divinity, comes to us at every Mass. How can we not be there to receive Him?

Holy Eucharist, Mystery of Faith, have mercy on us.
Holy Eucharist, Most high and adorable Sacrament, have mercy on us.
Holy Eucharist, Most holy of all sacrifices, have mercy on us.

Matching

___5___ 1. Institution of the Holy Eucharist

_____ 2. Substance

_____ 3. Appearances

___2___ 4. *Credo of the People of God*

_____ 5. "This is My Body"

___4___ 6. Jesus Christ

_____ 7. Transubstantiation

_____ 8. Last Supper

_____ 9. Only Priest or Bishop

_____ 10. Ordinary bread

1. What something seems to be

2. Pope Paul VI

3. Complete change of substance

4. The One Whom we receive in Holy Communion

5. When Jesus instituted Holy Eucharist

6. May Consecrate

7. Before Consecration

8. At the Last Supper

9. Words of consecration spoken by priest

10. What something is

The Holy Eucharist is a sacrament and a sacrifice. In the Holy Eucharist, under the appearances of bread and wine, the Lord Jesus Christ is contained, offered, and received.

Jesus instituted the Holy Eucharist at the Last Supper with His Apostles by taking bread, blessing it and saying, "Take and eat; This is My Body." Then He took wine, blessed it, and said, "All of you drink of this; This is My Blood." Then He commanded the Apostles: "Do this in remembrance of Me." Thus He ordained the Apostles as the first bishops of the Catholic Church.

When Jesus said "This is My Body," the entire substance of bread was changed into His Body and Blood. When Jesus said, "This is My Blood," the entire substance of wine was changed into His Body and Blood. There remained only the appearances of bread and of wine. The change of the entire substance of bread and of the entire substance of wine into the Body and Blood of Jesus Christ is called Transubstantiation.

Jesus Christ is contained whole and entire, Body, Blood, Soul, and Divinity, under the appearance of bread, as well as under the appearance of wine. In other words, after the consecration, each contains Jesus Christ whole and entire, the Body and Blood, Soul and Divinity. That is why we receive only the Host at Holy Communion. It is not necessary to drink the Precious Blood also.

Even when the consecrated Host is divided into the tiniest particles, Jesus Christ is contained, whole and entire, in every single speck of the Sacred Host, no matter how tiny. Jesus Christ is contained whole and entire in each drop of His Precious Blood. That is why the priest takes such great care when he purifies the sacred vessels after Holy Communion has been distributed. The priest makes sure that each speck which may have fallen from a Sacred Host is put into the chalice. The priest pours water into the chalice, moves it around, and then drinks the water in case there might be a single drop of Blood left in the chalice. The priest then cleans the chalice very carefully with the special white linen cloth. He is taking great care to make sure that not a single particle of the Sacred Host or a single drop of Precious Blood is left.

By His almighty power, Jesus becomes our Divine Food to help us attain eternal life. What kind of love gives itself away so completely? Only the love of Jesus Christ, Who gave Himself to the world, gives Itself away completely by becoming our Food so that we may enter eternal life.

The Holy Eucharist is central to our Catholic Faith. It is set apart from all the other Sacraments. While *all* the Sacraments give the Sanctifying Grace of Jesus Christ, the Holy Eucharist *is* Jesus Christ Himself. So powerful is His presence in the sacred Host that even non-Catholics speak of a mysterious Presence in Catholic churches.

We have seen that the appearances of bread and wine remain after the consecration. Remember that nothing remains of the bread and the wine except their appearances. Appearances refer to the taste, the color, the weight, the shape, and anything else that we notice with our senses.

The most unique change in the entire universe takes place during the Consecration of the Mass. It is the only example of a complete change of substance. Nothing else in the world compares to the change that takes place when the substance of ordinary bread and ordinary wine, after the words of consecration given by Jesus, become the Body and Blood of Jesus Christ Himself.

Transubstantiation is the complete change of substance from ordinary bread and wine to the Body and Blood of Jesus Christ. The Holy Eucharist, in other words, is the whole Christ, Body and Blood, Soul and Divinity. It is a real miracle! God gives us the gift of Himself in the form of bread and wine!

We remember that a miracle is a mystery. A mystery is something we could not even imagine until God reveals it, and after He reveals it, we can never fully understand it. That is the miracle and the wonder of the Holy Eucharist!

Holy Eucharist, Medicine of Immortality, have mercy on us.
Holy Eucharist, Sacrament of Piety, have mercy on us.

Fill in the Blanks

1. The Holy Eucharist is __Jesus____Christ__ Himself.

2. We should try to __honor_____ what we believe.

3. The __appearance____ of the bread and wine remain after the consecration.

4. Appearances are the __taste__ , __color__ , __shape__ and size of what we notice with our senses.

5. Jesus is contained whole and entire in every single __speck__ of the consecrated host.

6. Jesus is contained whole and entire in each __drop____ of His Precious Blood.

7. The most unique change in the entire universe takes place in the __consecration__ of the Mass.

8. __transubstantiation__ is a complete change of substance.

9. A __Holy____eucharist__ is something we cannot fully understand.

10. The only example of a complete change of substance is __transubstantiation__.

When God became man, He came to earth not only to save us from our sins by dying on the Cross but also to dwell on earth and be available to us in the Sacrament of the Holy Eucharist and indeed in every tabernacle in every Catholic Church throughout the world. Jesus Christ is just as present on earth in the Holy Eucharist as He is in Heaven.

A remarkable and miraculous event occurs at each and every Sacrifice of the Mass: a priest pronounces words over ordinary bread and ordinary wine and they become the Body and Blood of Jesus Christ! We should never become indifferent about such an amazing event. Our senses fail to grasp what is happening. The most miraculous event in all of human experience is the Holy Eucharist.

From the very beginning of our Church, from the time of St. Peter, priests and bishops have pronounced those same words of Consecration in one continuing, unbroken line of succession. Only the one true Church founded by Jesus Christ, the Catholic Church, has the Sacrament of the Holy Eucharist. Jesus Christ Himself, on the night before He died, spoke the words, "Do this in remembrance of Me" for the first time. From that time forward, to the present day, priests, bishops, cardinals, and popes have spoken those breathtaking words. They remind us of the sacrifice of Jesus Christ. Our Lord Jesus Christ is physically feeding us with His own Body and Blood so that we may attain eternal life in Heaven.

Why does God choose to give Himself to us in the Holy Eucharist?

Jesus Christ gives us His own Body and Blood in the Holy Eucharist for several reasons:

> first, to be offered as a *sacrifice* commemorating and renewing for all time the sacrifice of the Cross;

> second, to be received by the faithful people in *Holy Communion*;

> third, to remain *present on our altars* as the proof of His love for us, and to be worshiped by us.

To answer that question more fully, we turn to the *Catechism of the Catholic Church*. The section on the Holy Eucharist is divided into three main categories: The Holy Eucharist as *Sacrifice*-Sacrament, *Communion*-Sacrament and *Presence*-Sacrament.

First, the Holy Eucharist is a *sacrifice*. As sacrifice, Jesus Christ gave His Body and Blood on Calvary; He continues to give His own Body and Blood on the altar at every Mass. "As sacrifice, the Eucharist is offered in reparation for the sins of the living and the dead, and to obtain spiritual or temporal benefits from God" (*Catechism of the Catholic Church*, n. 1414).

When Jesus Christ died on the Cross, He offered Himself to His Heavenly Father for all mankind that we might be saved from our sins. Jesus commanded that the same sacrifice occur

at Mass when the priest, who is acting as another Christ, offers the sacrifice of the Body and Blood of Jesus Christ to our Heavenly Father.

Second, the Holy Eucharist is *communion* of souls with God. "Communion with the Body and Blood of Christ increases the communicant's union with the Lord, forgives his venial sins, and preserves him from grave sins." (*Catechism of the Catholic Church*, n. 1416).

How blessed we are to receive the true Body and Blood of our Lord Jesus Christ when we receive Holy Communion at Mass!

Finally, the Holy Eucharist is God's continuing *presence* with us in the tabernacle as proof of His love, and as an opportunity for us to worship and adore Him. "Because Christ Himself is present in the Sacrament of the altar, He is to be honored with the worship of adoration." (*Catechism of the Catholic Church*, n. 1418).

We may not often think about what the *presence* of Jesus really means. We may have become so used to seeing the tabernacle in Church that we scarcely realize *Who* is present behind that little tabernacle door. We should always acknowledge the Presence of Jesus Christ by genuflecting before we enter the pew. We should visit Jesus in the tabernacle whenever we pass by a Catholic Church, or bow our heads and make the Sign of the Cross.

Pope John Paul II established perpetual Eucharistic adoration in St. Peter's Basilica in Rome. He wanted our Lord to be adored day and night in Rome, the seat of the Catholic Church. Not only in Rome, but also in Catholic churches all over the world, adoration of the Blessed Sacrament takes place often, sometimes 24 hours a day, and seven days a week.

How we need our Lord! We need to adore Him, to praise Him, and to love Him. We need to thank Him for all of the blessings and graces He has given to us. We ask Him for what we need in the prayer of petition. We pray especially for the grace to live out our lives doing His holy will. Finally, we need to make reparation. What is reparation? It means repairing the damage and injury done by sin. Spend a few minutes with our Lord in prayer and adoration. This is an indispensable means to bring grace to us and to a spiritually starving world.

Holy Eucharist, most wonderful of all miracles,
have mercy on us.

Holy Eucharist, sweetest Banquet at which angels minister,
have mercy on us.

Holy Eucharist, Priest and Victim,
have mercy on us.

Matching

6	1. Sacrifice-Sacrament
8	2. Perpetual adoration
2	3. Holy Communion
1	4. Sacrifice of the Mass
7	5. Communion-Sacrament
3	6. Pope John Paul II
9	7. Reparation
4	8. We thank our Lord
10	9. Presence-Sacrament
5	10. Petition

1. Holy Communion

2. Same as Christ's sacrifice on Calvary

3. Established perpetual adoration in Rome

4. For all blessings and graces received

5. Prayer of asking God for what we need

6. The Mass

7. Forgives venial sins

8. Adoring our Lord all day and all night

9. Repairing damage resulting from sin

10. Tabernacle

The Holy Sacrifice of the Mass

The Mass is primarily a sacrifice. It is a sacrifice of the New Law in which Jesus Christ, through the ministry of the priest, offers Himself to God in an unbloody manner under the appearances of bread and wine.

What is the New Law? The New Law is the Law of Jesus Christ rather than the previous Law of Moses. There is a stress in the New Law on the love of God and neighbor and the following of Christ. The Old Law, also known as the Old Testament or the Old Covenant, was God's covenant or promise with His chosen people. The Old Law was the customs and laws that the Jewish people practiced before the coming of Jesus Christ.

What is the difference between the Old Law and the New Law? The New Law is the fulfillment of the Old Law for Christians and makes it possible for us to receive divine grace. Jesus said, "I come not to abolish the Law but to fulfill it." We could not obtain Heaven, nor could we live our supernatural life without divine grace. The sacrifice of Jesus Christ on the Cross makes all that possible.

Jesus continues to offer Himself to God the Father in the Holy Sacrifice of the Mass. He commanded that this be done when, first, He told His Apostles that the bread and wine were to be changed to His own Body and Blood. Second, He told His Apostles to eat His Body and Drink His Blood. Third, He commanded them to continue offering this Sacrifice of His Body and Blood when He said, "Do this in remembrance of Me."

The Second Vatican Council of the Church teaches, "At the Last Supper, on the night when He was betrayed, our Savior instituted the Eucharistic Sacrifice of His Body and Blood.

"He did this in order to perpetuate [continue] the sacrifice of the Cross throughout the centuries until He should come again.

"[And he did this in order] to entrust to His beloved Spouse, the Church, a memorial of His death and resurrection: a Sacrament of love, a sign of unity, a bond of charity, a paschal banquet in which Christ is consumed, the mind is filled with grace, and a pledge of future glory is given to us" (*Constitution on the Sacred Liturgy*, n. 47).

The same sacrifice of Jesus Christ on the Cross about two thousand years ago, is continued in time, throughout the centuries, and repeated every time the Holy Sacrifice of the Mass is offered.

When we attend Mass, do we think about what is actually happening on the altar? We may not realize that the Consecration is the same thing that happened on Calvary when Jesus Christ died on the Cross for our sins. On Calvary, Jesus Christ offered Himself, Body, Blood, Soul, and Divinity, to His Heavenly Father out of love for us. When we go to Mass, we are witnessing once again the sacrifice of Calvary, an act of love by Jesus Christ for the entire human race. The Mass is the Sacrifice of Love for all people of all times.

The word "Mass" is from the Latin word *missio*, a Latin word which means, "sending." The faithful are *sent* to put their Faith into practice and to *send* to others what they learned from the Mass.

The faithful people are to use the graces they have received in the Holy Sacrifice of the Mass, the Holy Eucharist, *to become holy for others*. We are to *send* or to give to others what we have received from the Mass.

From the first century, new Christians gathered together to participate in the most Holy Sacrifice of the Mass. As we shall see, there is only one difference between the Sacrifice of Jesus Christ on Calvary and the Sacrifice of the Mass: on Calvary, Jesus Christ shed His blood; at the Mass, there is no shedding of blood. Nevertheless, the same sacrifice takes place each and every time a Mass is offered.

Heart of Jesus, in Whom the Father was well pleased, have mercy on us.
Heart of Jesus, in Whom dwells all the fullness of Divinity, have mercy on us.

Fill in the Blanks

1. The Mass is primarily a ___Sacrifice___.

2. Jesus wants to continue the Sacrifice of Calvary through the ___Mass___.

3. The Old Law is also known as the Law of ___God___.

4. The New Law is the Law of ___Jesus___ ___Christ___.

5. Jesus Christ offered Himself, Body, Blood, Soul, and ___divinity___ to God the Father out of love for us.

6. The sacrifice of the Mass is the same as the sacrifice of Jesus Christ on the ___Cross___.

7. The word "Mass" means ___sending___.

8. Jesus entrusted the Sacrifice of the Mass to His beloved spouse, the _____.

9. The ___New___ Law is the fulfillment of the ___Old___ Law.

10. We should pay close attention when we attend ___mass___.

The Mass is the sacrifice of the New Law in which Jesus Christ, through the ministry of the priest, offers Himself to God in an unbloody manner under the appearances of bread and wine.

What is a sacrifice? A sacrifice is the offering of a victim, by a priest, to God alone. The victim must be destroyed in some way to acknowledge that God is the Creator of all things.

In order to study the meaning of sacrifice to God, we return to the story of Adam and Eve, our First Parents. We remember that before they sinned, they lived in God's presence, frequently communicating with Him. They were perfectly happy. Then, when they sinned, Adam and Eve not only lost God's friendship, but also cast a dark shadow over the entire human race. Everyone inherited their Original Sin.

However, God did not abandon Adam and Eve and the rest of mankind. God made a promise to send a Redeemer to save them from their sins. In the first book of the Bible are the words of that promise. Addressing the serpent devil who had tempted Adam and Eve to sin, God said, "I will put enmities (make enemies) between you and the woman, and between your seed and her seed; she shall crush your head, and you shall lie in wait for her heel" (Genesis 3:15). The woman and her seed are Mary and her Divine Son. What was God telling Adam and Eve? He was promising a Redeemer who would someday bring grace and peace to all mankind.

Right from the beginning of mankind, God commanded that sacrifices be offered to Him. This was the Old Law. The Chosen People, the Hebrew people, were to worship God properly. In return, God would bless them in many ways. The Hebrew people offered things that were most valuable, such as their best animals and best grains. Offering sacrifice was to demonstrate to God their realization of God's power over creation, and man's dependence on God for everything. Sacrifice also was to show sorrow for sin and to express love for God. Sacrifice was a way to beg God for His mercy, and to express "fear" of His just punishments.

Cain and Abel, the two sons of Adam and Eve, offered sacrifices to God as God commanded. However, Cain's sacrifice was less pleasing to God because Cain did not choose to give his best to God. God knew Cain's heart was not filled with love for Him. On the other hand, Abel had offered to God his "first things," his best animals. God was pleased with Abel's sacrifice. Later, Cain killed his brother Abel out of envy.

Throughout the Old Testament history, the Hebrew people offered animal and food sacrifices to God. Finally, the exact right moment in time arrived. Jesus Christ, the Son of God, became Man, and offered to God the greatest sacrifice of all time. He offered Himself, by suffering and dying on the Cross, thus becoming the Perfect Sacrifice. Jesus Christ, the Son of God, gave Himself unto death on the Cross for the sins of all mankind, once and for all.

The sacrifices of the Old Law or Old Testament times before Jesus came, were imperfect sacrifices. The animals and grains could only be a symbol, could not truly make up for the sins of mankind against the Creator.

In the Bible, the entire Letter to the Hebrews is about the Priesthood of Jesus Christ, Who "offered one single sacrifice for sins, has taken His place forever at the right hand of God" (Hebrews 10:12). Jesus Christ has taken His place as the eternal High Priest Who even to the present day intercedes with His Heavenly Father for our sins through the Holy Sacrifice of the Mass.

God had made a promise or covenant with the Hebrew people through Abraham. If they obeyed His law, He would bless them; if they disobeyed His Law, they would suffer the effects of their sins. After many centuries of disobedience, it was clear that most of the people could not obey the law on their own. After allowing the people to see that they could not obey the Law on their own, God established the New Law with the death and resurrection of His Son. The Perfect Sacrifice is the sacrifice of Jesus Christ, the Son of God, which for all time makes satisfaction for the sins of the world.

Heart of Jesus, Delight of all the saints, have mercy on us.
Jesus, Meek and Humble of Heart, make our hearts like unto Thine.

True (T) or false (F)

___T___   1. The Mass is the sacrifice of the New Law.

___F___   2. Adam and Eve never lost God's friendship.

___F___   3. Jesus offers Himself to God in an unbloody manner in the sacrifice in the Mass.

___T___   4. God made a promise to send a Redeemer.

___T___   5. "I will put enmities between you and the woman."

_____   6. The book of Romans in the Bible tells us about the Priesthood of Jesus Christ.

_____   7. The Hebrew people were commanded to make sacrifices.

_____   8. Sacrifices in the Old Testament expressed man's dependence on God.

___T___   9. At the perfect moment in time, the Son of God died for our sins.

_____   10. The Sacrifice of Jesus Christ in the Mass is the Perfect Sacrifice.

The Mass is the sacrifice of the New Law, in which Jesus Christ, through the ministry of the priest, offers Himself to God in an unbloody manner, under the appearances of bread and wine.

The principal priest in every Mass is Jesus Christ. Jesus Christ offers to His Heavenly Father, through the ministry of His ordained priest, His Body and Blood, which were sacrificed on the Cross.

A priest is the minister of Divine Worship in the Mass, the highest act of sacrifice to God. A priest is a man authorized and anointed to act as an intermediary between God and man. Only a priest can offer a true sacrifice to God.

In the Holy Sacrifice of the Mass, Jesus Christ offers Himself to His Heavenly Father *through the person of the priest*. On Calvary, when Jesus died on the Cross, we can easily see that He was the Victim sacrificed for our sins. However, Jesus was also the *priest* of the Sacrifice of the Cross.

Jesus, as the Priest at Mass, offers His Body and Blood, which were sacrificed for us on the Cross. Jesus is the principal Priest Whose action takes place through His ordained priest. The priest is called by the Church "another Christ." The priest is acting in the Person, or in the place, of Jesus Christ. At each Mass, it is truly Jesus Christ Who extends His hands over the bread and wine along with the priest we see on the altar.

We have seen that in the Old Testament times, before the Son of God came into the world, sacrifices were offered to God to show recognition of God's power and authority over man, and also to make up for man's sins. In the Old Testament times, sacrifices were to include the shedding of blood and the destruction of the animal. Why? Because without the shedding of blood, the animal sacrifice was not complete and the animal—considered valuable—could be retained and used either as food or as a beast of burden. So the animal sacrifice was the complete surrender to God of something that was precious to the people.

The basic purpose of the sacrifice of Jesus Christ on the Cross is the same under the New Law. The Son of God gave His life by the shedding of His Precious Blood and His death. Meaning what? Without the shedding of Christ's Blood to redeem us and open the gates of Heaven, we could not obtain eternal life in Heaven. The sacrifice of Jesus Christ was perfect. Man no longer had to offer an imperfect animal as a sacrifice in order to make reparation to God and obtain His mercy.

To whom was the sacrifice of the Cross offered? It was offered to God the Heavenly Father. In every Sacrifice of the Mass, the same (not a new) sacrifice is offered to God the Heavenly Father. How is this so? The sacrifice is renewed again and again each time the priest speaks the words of consecration.

The only difference between the Sacrifice of the Mass and the Sacrifice of the Cross on Calvary is that the Mass is unbloody because Jesus Christ is now in Heavenly glory. He can no longer suffer in His own Body. He therefore does not die again and again at every Mass. He cannot die again because His glorified Body can never again feel pain, suffering, or death.

The Mass repeats and renews the sacrifice with the same outcome: the offering to our Heavenly Father of the Victim, Jesus Christ, in the Sacrament of the Holy Eucharist. The priest is standing in the place of Jesus Christ as offering the Perfect Sacrifice. God the Father is accepting that perfect sacrifice in every Mass throughout the world.

The Mass is the same sacrifice as the sacrifice of the Cross, because in the Mass the Victim is the same, Jesus Christ; and the principal priest is the same, Jesus Christ.

When we attend the Holy Sacrifice of the Mass, in a mystical way, we are truly at the foot of the Cross at Calvary. Jesus Christ died only once, yet His Sacrifice is for all times until the end of time.

Heart of Jesus, bruised for our offenses, have mercy on us.
Heart of Jesus, pierced with a lance, have mercy on us.
Heart of Jesus, Victim for our sins, have mercy on us.

191

Multiple Choice

_a_   1. A priest is _____ who offers sacrifice.
  - a) an ordained man
  - b) any man who chooses
  - c) a woman

_c_   2. A priest offers sacrifice to
  - a) acknowledge God's power.
  - b) make up for sin.
  - c) a and b.

_b_   3. There is/are _____ offering Mass.
  - a) a deacon and a priest
  - b) one priest
  - c) both Jesus Christ and a priest

_b_   4. The priest at Mass is
  - a) another Christ.
  - b) acting in the place of Jesus Christ.
  - c) a and b.

_c_   5. The main sacrifices in the Old Testament were
  - a) minerals.   b) people.   c) animals.

_a_   6. The sacrifice of Jesus Christ _____ the sacrifices of the Old Testament.
  - a) replaced
  - b) was the same as
  - c) was equal to

_a_   7. The sacrifice of the Mass is offered to
  - a) Jesus Christ, the Son of God.
  - b) the people.
  - c) God our Heavenly Father.

_b_   8. The sacrifice of the Mass is _____ the sacrifice of Jesus Christ on Calvary.
  - a) the same as
  - b) something like
  - c) different from

_a_   9. The only difference between the Sacrifice of the Mass and the Sacrifice of the Cross on Calvary is that
  - a) the Mass is unbloody.
  - b) the Mass is a symbol.
  - c) the Mass is in a building.

_c_   10. When we attend the Holy Sacrifice of the Mass, we are truly present at
  - a) the Ascension.   b) the Transfiguration.   c) the foot of the Cross.

193

We have learned that the sacrifice of the Mass is the sacrifice of the New Law in which Jesus Christ, through the ministry of the priest, offers Himself to God, in a unbloody manner, under the appearances of bread and wine.

We have learned that Jesus is the principal Priest as well as the Victim in the Sacrifice of the Mass. We have learned that the Mass is the same sacrifice as the sacrifice of Jesus on the Cross of Calvary. In the Mass, the Victim is the same, Jesus Christ; and the principal Priest is the same, Jesus Christ.

We have learned that the sacrifice of the Mass is different in some way from the sacrifice on the Cross. On the Cross, Jesus was physically slain and physically shed His blood, while at Mass there is no physical shedding of blood. On the Cross, Jesus *gained merit* and satisfied for the sins of mankind. In the Mass, He *applies the merits* to us of His death on the Cross.

There are four purposes for the Sacrifice of the Mass. We will explore each one. First, the Sacrifice of the Mass is offered *to adore God* as our Creator and Lord. The Mass is the perfect prayer. No matter how well we say our prayers, and how much our hearts are turned to God when we say them, our prayers are not perfect. Only the Mass can accomplish the perfect adoration, honor, and praise that God deserves. Why? While our prayers are precious to God, we are mere human creatures. The Mass, however, is the offering of Jesus Christ, the Son of God, to His Heavenly Father.

Second, the Mass is a perfect way *to thank God* for the many graces and favors He has given us. We may not often think about how blessed we are. We have only to look at our life to know how much God loves us and takes care of us. We have a family who loves us, a nice home to live in, clothes to wear, and food to eat. The greatest gift that God gives us, however, is the gift of Divine Grace. Provided we live out our baptismal promises, pray, and receive the Sacraments often, we have the assurance that we will be happy with Him in Heaven forever.

Third, we go to Mass *to ask God* for His blessings on all men. When we ask for anything, we should pray that it would be according to His will. Jesus told His disciples: "Ask, and you will receive. Seek, and you will find. Knock and it will be opened to you. For everyone who asks, receives. He who seeks, finds. The one who knocks, it shall be opened [for him]" (Matthew 7:7-8). Jesus is telling us that we should trust Him.

Finally, we go to Mass *to satisfy for sin*, for our own sins and the sins of others. The Mass has been commanded by God for the purpose of repairing the damage done by sin. The Sacrifice of the Cross, re-enacted in the Mass, is God's plan to satisfy for the many sins committed the world over, every day, every moment. Reparation means making up with greater love for the failure to love and the failure to obey God's Laws.

How should we assist at Mass? We should assist at the Holy Sacrifice of the Mass with reverence, attention, and devotion. We should unite ourselves with the priest in offering the Holy Sacrifice of the Mass, and we should receive Jesus Christ in the Holy Eucharist, or Holy Communion, with great love.

We best unite ourselves with the priest in offering the Holy Sacrifice by joining our minds and hearts to Jesus, by following the Mass prayers with the missal, and by reciting or chanting the Mass responses.

As we have seen, the Holy Sacrifice of the Mass and the Sacrifice of Jesus Christ on the Cross are the same sacrifice. Jesus Christ offers Himself to His Heavenly Father in the Mass just as He did on Calvary. Jesus Christ is atoning for sin in the Mass just as He did on Calvary. There is, of course, one important difference.

On Calvary, Jesus Christ physically shed His Precious Blood. Jesus, the Son of God, as God, could not die. That is impossible. God always was and He always will be. As a Man, however, the Son of God could die. In fact, that is why the Son of God became Man, so He could die for us to save us from our sins and open the gates of Heaven. We have seen that, unlike Calvary, the Mass is an *unbloody* sacrifice. The Mass *continues* the Sacrifice of Calvary down through the ages.

While the sacrifice of Jesus Christ on Calvary atoned for our sins once and for all, the Mass *continues in time* the Sacrifice of Jesus Christ on Calvary. In the Mass, Jesus Christ *applies* the infinite merits and satisfaction for our sins that He won on Calvary.

Heart of Jesus, of infinite majesty, have mercy on us.
Heart of Jesus, Holy Temple of God, have mercy on us.

Fill in the Blanks

1. The Sacrifice of the Mass and the Sacrifice of Jesus Christ on the Cross are the ___Same___.

2. On Calvary, Jesus Christ shed His ___blood___.

3. The Mass is a ___holy___ sacrifice.

4. The Sacrifice of the Mass ___happind___ in time the Sacrifice of Jesus Christ on Calvary.

5. Jesus Christ applies for us the ___infinite___ merits and satisfaction He won on Calvary for our sins.

6. At Mass, we should unite ourselves with the ___Priest___ who is offering the Holy Sacrifice.

7. We should ___lisin___ attentively to what the priest is saying.

8. The Sacrifice of the Mass is offered to _____ God as our Creator.

9. The Mass is a perfect way to ___thak___ God for His many favors.

10. We attend Mass to _____ for our sins.

Holy Communion is the receiving of Jesus Christ in the Sacrament of the Holy Eucharist.

To receive Holy Communion worthily, we must be without mortal sin. We also need to have the right intention, and we need to obey the Church's laws on fasting before receiving Holy Communion.

To receive Sanctifying Grace more abundantly, we should receive Jesus with great love and devotion. We should have the intention of freeing ourselves from any habitual venial sins. Also, we should also say a fervent Act of Contrition before receiving Jesus in Holy Communion. This tells Jesus that we are sorry for our sins and have the intention of not wanting to sin again.

Let us reflect for a moment on the fact that God made us from nothing. God uses nothing when He creates a human soul. He also keeps us in existence every second. If God were to abandon us for even one second, we would sink back into nothingness. We need the continual intervention of God to keep us in existence.

How does God keep us in existence? Just as our parents feed us so that we can stay alive physically, so God feeds us with His very Self to keep us alive spiritually.

Holy Communion is Food for our souls. Our Lord Jesus Christ nourishes us at Mass as members of His Church, the Mystical Body of Christ. It is no accident that when we receive Holy Communion at Mass, we are with other members of the Church. We are brothers and sisters in Christ. Just as Jesus Christ fed the multitudes during His visible stay on earth, so He feeds us with His own Body and Blood as we are gathered together in a family of believers, His Church.

To receive Our Lord worthily in Holy Communion, *we must be free from mortal sin.* We are so blessed to be able to receive our Lord Himself in Holy Communion. How terrible it would be to invite Him into a soul stained with mortal sin! Such an act would be a grave sin in itself, the sin of *sacrilege.* Moreover, as we have learned, the soul in mortal sin is dead without God's grace; it is impossible for something dead to benefit from something that is alive.

When we receive Holy Communion, we also should have an *intention of not committing any more sins.* Of course, venial sins should not keep us from receiving Holy Communion. The Mass begins with a penitential prayer in which we express sorrow for our sins; the Confiteor is the prayer we say to tell God that we are sorry for offending Him.

The Church also requires that we intend to receive the Body and Blood of Jesus Christ with love and devotion. When we attend Mass and Holy Communion, our *intention should be to increase our love of God,* and to ask Him to help us to love others because of our love for Him. We should have devotion and reflection as we prepare to receive the most precious Body and Blood of Our Lord Jesus Christ.

Fasting is important when we receive Our Lord in Holy Communion. We fast to properly prepare ourselves spiritually. For a period of time, we do without physical food for our bodies as we concentrate on receiving our spiritual Food, Jesus Christ, Who gives us the supernatural graces we need for our souls.

In the past, the Church required that people fast from all food and drink from midnight before receiving Holy Communion. This rule was relaxed to three hours, and then to one hour. Why? The Church shortened the fast in order to allow many people to be able to receive Holy Communion. At the present time, we are required to fast from all food and drink—except water—for one hour before we receive Holy Communion. Taking medicine does not break the fast.

Say an Act of Contrition before receiving Holy Communion. Memorize one of the Prayers Before Holy Communion, found in a missal, which are usually written by one of the saints. A popular one is the Prayer Before a Crucifix.

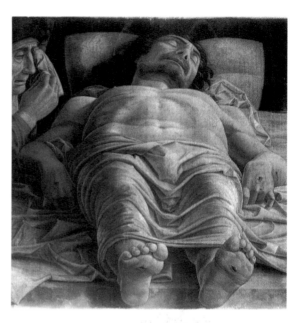

"Look down upon me, Good and Gentle Jesus, while before Thy face I humbly kneel. With a burning soul, I pray and beseech Thee, to fix deep in my heart lively sentiments of Faith, Hope, and Charity, True Contrition for my sins, and a Firm Purpose of Amendment. While I contemplate with great love and tender pity, Your five most precious wounds, pondering over them within me and calling to mind the precious words which David Thy prophet said to You, my Jesus: They have pierced My hands and My feet. They have numbered all My bones. Amen."

True (T) or False (F)

_____ T 1. God used nothing to create.

_____ T 2. If God left us to ourselves, we would cease to exist.

_____ T 3. The Church is our guide in properly receiving the Sacraments.

_____ T 4. We go to Mass and Holy Communion as a family of believers.

_____ F 5. The rules of the Church on receiving Holy Communion are optional.

_____ F 6. We must fast from all food 12 hours before we receive Holy Communion.

_____ T 7. We must be free from mortal sin to receive Holy Communion.

_____ T 8. We may take water anytime before receiving Holy Communion.

_____ T 9. A sick person may take medicine anytime before Holy Communion.

_____ T 10. Holy Communion properly received increases our love for God and others.

Holy Communion is the receiving of Jesus Christ in the Sacrament of the Holy Eucharist. To receive Holy Communion worthily, one must be free from mortal sin, have the right intention, and obey the Church's rules on fasting before Holy Communion. To receive the graces from Holy Communion, one should receive with devotion, and intend to free himself of venial sins.

We should prepare ourselves to receive Holy Communion by thinking about Our Lord Jesus Christ and the sacrifice He made for us by suffering and dying on the Cross. We should make a fervent Act of Contrition. Other prayers the Church encourages us to say are the Acts of Faith, Hope, and Charity. The Prayer Before a Crucifix is a popular prayer to say before Holy Communion.

The Church has set down regulations we must follow regarding the proper reception of Holy Communion. Why? When we walk down the aisle to receive Holy Communion, we are approaching God Himself, the Creator of Heaven and earth.

In the not-too-distant past, the Church required fasting from all food and drink from midnight before receiving Holy Communion. At the present time, we must fast from food and drink (except water) for only one hour before we receive our dear Lord in Holy Communion. This means we must neither eat anything nor drink anything but water during that time.

There are three exceptions to this rule. First, when someone is in danger of death, he may receive Holy Communion whether he has fasted or not. Secondly, if there is danger to the Blessed Sacrament, such as in time of war or attack by criminals, a person is allowed to consume the Blessed Sacrament to protect Our Lord. Finally, a sick person who takes medicine within an hour of receiving Holy Communion is not breaking the fast.

The rule used to be that Holy Communion could be received only once a day. However, the Church wants to encourage reception of Holy Communion when a person attends a second Mass, especially for an Ordination Mass or a Nuptial Mass. At the present time, anyone may receive Holy Communion a second time the same day, *but only if the person has attended the Mass*. Someone who has received earlier in the day may not simply walk into the middle of a second Mass and receive Holy Communion. A person must have actually *attended the second Mass* to receive Holy Communion again at the second Mass.

It is important to properly prepare for such a wonderful event as receiving the Son of God, Our Lord Jesus Christ, in Holy Communion. We should never receive Holy Communion carelessly or thoughtlessly. We should pray acts of Faith, Hope, and Charity and especially an Act of Contrition, for God Himself is coming to us.

When it is not possible to receive Holy Communion, the Church encourages frequent spiritual Communion. We may say the following prayer or one like it:

> *"O Jesus, I turn toward the holy tabernacle where You live hidden for love of me. I love You, my God. I cannot now receive You in Holy Communion. Come nevertheless, to visit me with Your grace. Come spiritually into my heart. Purify it, sanctify it, render it like unto Your own. Amen."*

Multiple Choice

_b_ 1. When we receive Holy Communion, we are truly
  a) receiving a host.
  b) receiving the Son of God Himself.
  c) receiving the priest's blessing.

_c_ 2. In the not-too-distant past, the Church required _____ before receiving Holy Communion.
  a) fasting for one hour
  b) fasting for one half-hour
  c) fasting from midnight

_b_ 3. In our day, we must fast _____ from all food and drink.
  a) for thirty minutes
  b) for one hour
  c) for three hours

_a_ 4. We _____ drink water any time before receiving Holy Communion.
  a) may   b) may not   c) should not

_b_ 5. It is now permitted to receive Holy Communion twice a day
  a) when someone attends only part of the second Mass.
  b) when someone attends a second Mass.
  c) when some misses part of the first Mass.

_a_ 6. A sick person may take medicine _____ before Holy Communion.
  a) anytime
  b) up to an hour
  c) up to two hours

_a_ 7. To receive Holy Communion worthily, one must be free from
  a) mortal sin.   b) venial sins.   c) all sins.

_a_ 8. We should prepare ourselves to receive Our Lord in Holy Communion by
  a) saying an Act of Contrition.
  b) by speaking to the person next to us.
  c) by wearing our best clothes.

_a_ 9. The Church encourages receiving Holy Communion
  a) whenever we attend Mass.
  b) at least once a month.
  c) especially at Christmas time.

_c_ 10. Before receiving Holy Communion, we should
  a) focus on what we are about to do.
  b) give our full attention to receiving our Lord worthily.
  c) a and b.

Holy Communion is the receiving of Jesus Christ in the Sacrament of the Holy Eucharist.

To receive Our Lord worthily, we must be free of mortal sin. We also should have the right intention, that is, to receive Jesus with great love and devotion. In addition, we need to obey the rules of the Church concerning fasting before receiving Holy Communion.

In order to obtain the most abundant graces, we need to make a commitment to try to not commit any more sins. We should prepare ourselves by saying Acts of Faith, Hope, and Charity, but especially an Act of Contrition. The Act of Contrition is very important because we are telling Jesus not only that we are sorry for our sins, but we want to amend our lives. We say "But most of all because they offend Thee, my God, Who are all good and deserving of all my love. I firmly resolve with the help of Thy grace to sin no more and to avoid the near occasions of sin."

After receiving Our Lord Jesus Christ in Holy Communion, we should spend time in prayer, adoring Him, thanking Him, promising to continue to love and obey Him, and asking for blessings for ourselves, our family, and others.

For about fifteen minutes after Holy Communion, we are the closest to Our Lord that we will ever be in this life. His Body and Blood remain about fifteen minutes, and therefore we should give Him the honor of our fullest devotion to His holy Presence. Nothing else you will do during the day can compare in importance with these precious moments you spend with Jesus.

One of the most popular prayers for reflection after Holy Communion is the *Anima Christi*: "Soul of Christ, sanctify me; Body of Christ, save me; Blood of Christ, inebriate me; Water from the side of Christ, wash me; Passion of Christ, strengthen me. Oh good Jesus, hear me; within Thy wounds, hide me. Let me not be separated from Thee. From the evil enemy, defend me. At the hour of my death, call me and bid me come to Thee, that with Thy saints, I will praise Thee forever and ever. Amen."

What are the effects of receiving Holy Communion worthily? The Sacramental graces we receive are different from the graces we receive from the other Sacraments because we are receiving the Son of God, Jesus Christ Himself. We, therefore, receive the special grace to love God with the greatest intensity possible. Our hearts and minds become resting places of His Holy Presence. We receive the grace of loving our neighbor with greater intensity. We are able to perform greater acts of charity toward others.

We receive an increase in Sanctifying Grace every time we receive Holy Communion. We recall that

Sanctifying Grace is infused for the first time into our souls at Baptism. Holy Communion is the Food that keeps our souls alive in that grace. Just as we must eat to live, so we must receive Holy Communion to nourish our souls, and keep them alive in sanctifying grace.

There are a number of effects of receiving Holy Communion. Did you know that *all our venial sins are removed* when we receive Holy Communion worthily? How powerful is the Sacrament of Holy Eucharist! God's Presence in our souls is so strong, venial sins are driven away!

Holy Communion also strengthens us to avoid mortal sins in the future. Holy Communion keeps us in God's holy friendship and keeps our wills strong to fight temptation. We are less likely to commit even the smallest sin when we receive Holy Communion. In addition, we are able to be more generous with others.

Holy Mother Church is very wise. Holy Mother Church declares that we must—if we are to remain in good standing with the Church— receive Holy Communion at least during Easter time each year. However, the Church encourages us to receive Holy Communion every time we attend Mass. Furthermore, we are encouraged to attend Mass daily if at all possible.

Jesus, Living Bread Which came down from Heaven, have mercy on us.
Jesus, Who has loved us with an everlasting love, have mercy on us.
Jesus, Who has given Thy Flesh for the life of the world, have mercy on us.

Matching

___5___ 1. *Anima Christi*

_____ 2. After Holy Communion

___7___ 3. Holy Communion

___10___ 4. Love of God and neighbor

___2___ 5. Act of Contrition

___3___ 6. Venial sins removed

___4___ 7. Tendency to commit sin

___6___ 8. At Easter time

___1___ 9. To receive worthily

___8___ 10. Fasting

1. Spend time in prayer

2. Tells God we are sorry and will amend our lives

3. When we receive Holy Communion

4. When we are obliged to receive Communion

5. *Soul of Christ*; prayer after Communion

6. Must be free from mortal sin

7. Receiving Jesus Christ

8. No food up to one hour before receiving

9. Decreased after Holy Communion

10. Increased with Holy Communion

Holy Communion is the receiving of Jesus Christ in the Sacrament of the Holy Eucharist.

To receive Jesus worthily, we must be free of mortal sin, we must receive Him with love and devotion, and we must follow the Church rules on fasting.

To receive the most graces from receiving Jesus in Communion, we should be fervent and devoted to Jesus. We should say our prayers with love. We should make fervent Acts of Love and pray the Act of Contrition before receiving Holy Communion. A popular prayer to say after we have received Our Lord is the Prayer Before a Crucifix.

After Holy Communion, we should keep in mind that Jesus is still fully present inside us for about 15 minutes. We should spend this time in prayer and devotion. This is the time to thank God for all His gifts to us.

The Church encourages us to receive Holy Communion at each Mass we attend. The Church encourages us to attend Mass more than once a week, even daily if we can. Daily Communion is highly recommended by the Church.

Many families try to go to Mass on Saturdays when Dad is home and can go too. In addition, some families try to attend Mass on Fridays, since that is the day on which Jesus died on the Cross. Some families pick a special feastday during the week and attend on that day. Going to Mass these days gives children the opportunity to see the sacred events at the altar, as sometimes on Sunday young children cannot see the priest because he is hidden by the crowd.

The Baltimore Catechism tells us that "It is well to receive Holy Communion often, even daily, because this intimate union with Jesus Christ, the Source of all holiness and the Giver of all graces, is the greatest aid to a holy life."

When families cannot attend Mass during the week, Mother Angelica's television station, EWTN, presents the Mass each day, four times a day. One of the sisters reads the Spiritual Communion prayer for those who cannot attend Mass. EWTN is offered on cable and on satellite, as well as on short-wave radio. EWTN offers a great deal of information, prayers, and meditations on its web site.

Memorize the Act of Spiritual Communion: My Jesus, I believe that You are present in the Most Holy Sacrament. I love You above all things, and I desire to receive You into my soul. Since I cannot at this moment receive You sacramentally, come at least spiritually into my heart. I embrace You as if You were already here, and unite myself wholly to You. Never permit me to be separated from You. Amen.

Father John Hardon, one of the greatest modern theologians, encouraged home schooling families to attend daily Mass. He even encouraged families to attend twice a day whenever possible because of the constant pagan influences of our society. Father Hardon taught that Jesus in Holy Communion will help our intellect to know what God wants us to do, and will help strengthen our will to do what God wants us to do.

We should show our gratitude to Our Lord for remaining always on our altars in the Holy Eucharist. We can do this by visiting Him at church, by showing reverence when we are in church or when we are passing by a Catholic church. We can show our gratitude by attending parish devotions, such as Benediction of the Blessed Sacrament.

Many parishes have perpetual adoration, or sometimes adoration on weekends, or on the first weekend of the month. We should attend these devotions as often as possible.

When Jesus was in the Garden of Gethsemane, He asked Peter, James, and John to pray one hour with Him. This has been the motivation for so many to feel called to spend one hour a week in church visiting with Jesus and meditating in gratitude. We benefit greatly by spending time away from the world in His holy Presence, to adore and praise Him; to pray to Him for others who need our prayers so desperately; to thank Him for all He has done for us and our family; to repair for our sins and the sins of the whole world.

These special visits and times of meditation, reflection, and adoration help us to see everything from the viewpoint of eternity, where Jesus Christ awaits us in the blessed Heavenly paradise for which we were made.

From a little pamphlet written by Father Lukas Etlin, who is being considered for canonization, comes the following meditation:

"Jesus is ever with us in the holy Tabernacle. He is with us in the fullness of His Godhead, and in the splendor of His glorified Humanity. He has erected His dwelling upon the altar, and He finds His delight among the children of men. Full of infinite love for us and full of most touching compassion for our weakness and poverty, He offers us the immeasurable riches of His Divine treasures of grace.

"O wonderful Mystery of Divine Love! Thou containest Jesus, the Source of all grace, the most precious Treasure! All the mysteries of His life, Passion, and death are united in one. All the merits He has acquired are gathered here, gathered for you, happy soul, for each one of us. Here is contained the Incarnation, the Redemption, all the graces of sanctification and blessedness, yes, all that Jesus gave, could give, and wished to give, all that He is and has. The Father has given us everything.

"Streams of graces and blessings flow from the living and personal Presence of our Divine Savior in the holy Tabernacle into the hearts of those who approach Him with humility and confidence. As a flood of rays emanates from the sun and diffuses over the whole earth, so do the rays of grace flow from the Sacred Host and sink into every faithful contrite heart" (*The Holy Eucharist, Our All,* by Father Lukas Etlin, TAN Books, pp. 12-13).

Jesus, Who has loved us with an everlasting love, have mercy on us.

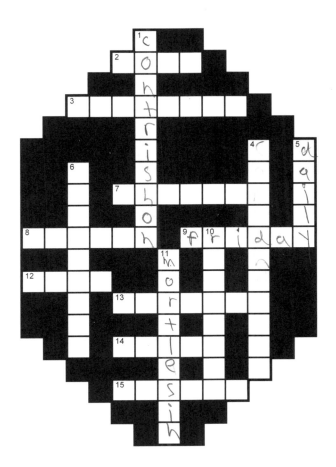

Across

2 Jesus asks us to pray one __ with Him. (4)

3 Our hearts must be faithful and __. (8)

7 Jesus is present inside us for __ minutes after receiving Him. (7)

8 one of the greatest modern theologians: Fr. John __ (6)

9 the day on which Jesus died (6)

12 Mother Angelica's tv station (4)

13 To receive the most graces, we should be __ and devoted to Jesus. (7)

14 Jesus is the source of all __. (5)

15 We should make frequent __ to Our Lord in the Blessed Sacrament (6)

Down

1 The most important prayer to say before Holy Communion is the Act of __. (10)

4 We show our gratitude by attending __ of the Blessed Sacrament. (11)

5 We should attend Mass __ if we can. (5)

6 If we cannot receive Jesus, we should make an Act of __ Communion. (9)

10 We should be __ in church. (8)

11 To receive Jesus worthily, we must be free of __ __. (6,3)

Penance is the Sacrament by which sins committed after Baptism are forgiven through the absolution of the priest.

As we have seen, the Sacraments do the same things for our souls as the necessities in our lives do for our bodies. Just as Holy Communion is food for the soul, so the Sacrament of Penance is medicine for the soul. Why do we need medicine for our souls? Because God knows how weak we are and how much we need the healing power of the Sacrament of Penance.

On Easter Sunday night, after Jesus rose from the dead, He appeared to His Apostles. They were badly shaken over the events of the past few days, during which they had seen their Master beaten, scourged, and crucified. They were already priests because Jesus had ordained them just three nights before on Holy Thursday. When their Master walked into the room in His splendid glorified Body, they were at once astonished and overjoyed.

Jesus said to them, "'Peace be to you. As the Father has sent me, I also send you.' Then Jesus breathed on them, and He said to them, 'Receive the Holy Spirit. Whose sins you shall forgive, they are forgiven them; and whose sins you shall retain, they are retained'" (John 20:21-23). Thus Jesus instituted the Sacrament of Penance. He gave the Apostles, and every priest and bishop who would follow throughout the centuries until the end of time, the power to forgive sins in His name.

God forgives sins in the Sacrament of Penance through His priests. This is the way God wants sins forgiven. To neglect to receive the Sacrament of Penance on a frequent basis can not only cause emotional distress when one is in sin, but deprives one of the opportunity to have counseling from a priest. When one does not receive this Sacrament, it is likely that a person will fall into carelessness and a habit of committing sins.

The priest forgives sins with the words, "I absolve you from your sins in the name of the Father, and of the Son, and of the Holy Spirit. Amen." These are the most consoling words in the English language. These extraordinary words, said by the priest representing Jesus Christ, so filled with meaning and power, give us the assurance that we have indeed been forgiven. Whatever the sin, the sinner is assured of God's infinite mercy and forgiveness.

You know that whenever you have done something wrong toward someone, you don't feel well until you have said you are sorry to the person you offended. With the Sacrament of Penance, you are able to tell God you are sorry, and with the consoling words of God through the priest, you know you are forgiven of your offense.

When Jesus established the Sacrament of Penance on Easter Sunday night, He was showing the way He wanted people forgiven of their sins. Jesus knew we needed the consolation of hearing the words of forgiveness. Some people like to say that they can confess their sins private to God. However, Jesus knew that confessing our sins aloud to a priest gives us consolation and makes us humble. We would not learn humility if we confessed our sins quietly in prayer.

Jesus established the Sacrament of Penance because He wants us to use it! When we hear the consoling words of forgiveness, we are assured that we receive the Sacramental graces of the Sacrament of Penance just like any other Sacrament. A priest can give us the assurance that we have been forgiven. He can also give us spiritual advice. He can tell us how we can avoid sin in the future and give us helpful instructions and counsel. We thank God for the mercy He has shown in giving us the Sacrament of Penance!

St. John Vianney, the Cure of Ars, spent hours in the confessional hearing confessions from people who came from great distances to receive his helpful counsel. He is a patron of confessors. Let us ask him to pray for us when we go to Confession.

St. John Vianney, wise director of souls, pray for us.
St. John Vianney, favored with the gift of miracles, pray for us.

Fill in the Blanks

1. Penance is the Sacrament by which sins committed after Baptism are forgiven through the _absolution_ of the priest.

2. Jesus Christ instituted the Sacrament of Penance on _Easter sunday_ night.

3. Jesus gave His Apostles the _sacriminte_ to forgive sins in His Name.

4. Confession of our sins to a priest makes us _forgiven_.

5. The Sacrament of Penance gives us Sacramental _grase_.

6. The priest in confession gives us _realeaf_ that our sins have been forgiven.

7. As the Holy Eucharist is Food for the soul, the Sacrament of Penance is _____ for the soul.

8. Jesus knows we are in need of the _grate_ power of the Sacrament of Penance.

9. "Whose sins you shall forgive, they are _forgiven_ them; and whose sins you shall retain, they are _relatned_."

10. A famous saint and patron of confessors is _St. John_.

Penance is the Sacrament by which sins committed after Baptism are forgiven through the absolution of the priest.

The priest has the power to forgive sins from Jesus Christ. On the evening of His Resurrection, Jesus appeared to His Apostles in the Upper Room. He said to His Apostles and to their successors in the priesthood: "Receive the Holy Spirit; whose sins you shall forgive, they are forgiven them; and whose sins you shall retain, they are retained."

The priest has the power to forgive sins through Jesus Christ. He forgives sins with the words: "I absolve you from your sins in the name of the Father, and of the Son, and of the Holy Spirit. Amen."

One time Jesus was preaching and healing people inside a home. It was very crowded and no one else could enter the house. A paralyzed man had been brought to the house by his friends. They were carrying him on a cot. They were anxious to have him cured by Jesus. They decided to climb on the roof and lower him down through a hole in the roof. It must have taken a great deal of effort to raise the man on a cot onto the roof. They carefully lowered him down through the hole.

When Jesus saw the poor paralyzed man being lowered down, He could read the mind of the man. He knew what the man really wanted. Jesus said, "Be of good heart, Son, thy sins are forgiven thee." This was the real cure, the spiritual cure, for which the man had come! His friends were very surprised! They thought Jesus would cure the poor man! Some of the enemies of Jesus were sitting in the house, and they said, "How can He forgive sins? Only God can forgive sins!"

Jesus immediately said, "Which is easier to say? Thy sins are forgiven, or arise and walk?" Then Jesus said, "So that you may know that the Son of Man [Himself] has power on earth to forgive sins," He turned to the sick man and said, "Arise, take up thy bed, and go back to thy house!"

Jesus forgave the man his sins. It is terrible to be sick in the body, but it worse to be sick in the soul. A person suffers much more from being in sin and not being forgiven, than suffering from a bodily illness. This is why Jesus instituted the Sacrament of Penance, so that we can be forgiven and not suffer from a lifetime of feeling guilty and not knowing if we have been forgiven.

There are several effects or fruits of the Sacrament of Penance, worthily received. As with all the Sacraments, the Sacrament of Penance gives Sanctifying Grace. Once we have received the Sacrament of Penance, our soul is restored to the state it was in before we committed sin. Sanctifying Grace *increases* the life of God in us if we were in venial sin. If we were in mortal sin, Sanctifying Grace *restores* the life of God in our souls.

Once we have received absolution in the Sacrament of Penance, our sins are forgiven. No matter how serious the sin or how long we have been falling into sin, we are forgiven. If we have committed mortal sin, the eternal punishment is removed and at least part of the temporal punishment is also removed. By the Sacrament of Penance, we are strengthened in grace to avoid sin in the future.

Finally, through the Sacrament of Penance, whatever merits have been lost by sin are restored. In other words, our souls are refreshed, strengthened, restored, and renewed.

In 1943, Pope Pius XII wrote, "We will that the pious practice of frequent confession, which was introduced into the Church by the inspiration of the Holy Spirit, should be earnestly advocated. By it, genuine self-knowledge is increased, Christian humility grows, bad habits are corrected, spiritual neglect and tepidity are resisted, the conscience is purified, the will strengthened, a salutary self-control is attained, and grace is increased in virtue of the Sacrament itself" (*Mystici Corporis*, 88).

What wonderful promises! We do not realize how important is the Sacrament of Penance! The Pope was telling us the Sacrament of Penance is not only for the removal of sins, but also for gaining so many more blessings from the wonderful and consoling Sacrament of Penance.

St. John Vianney, who did preach in words of fire, have mercy on us.
St. John Vianney, inflamed with zeal, have mercy on us.

True (T) or False (F)

__T__ 1. The Sacrament of Penance gives us Sanctifying Grace.

__F__ 2. If our sins are very serious, they may not be forgiven.

__T__ 3. Pope Pius XII wrote in his encyclical that he wanted frequent confession.

_____ 4. The Pope said that we will know ourselves better.

__T__ 5. The Sacrament of Penance makes us grow in humility.

__T__ 6. The Sacrament of Penance helps us to have more self-control.

__T__ 7. "The Son of Man has power on earth to forgive sins."

__T__ 8. We should be truly sorry for our sins.

__T__ 9. Jesus said to the paralyzed man, "Thy sins are forgiven thee."

__T__ 10. The story of the paralyzed man illustrates how much God wants to forgive us our sins.

Penance is the Sacrament by which sins committed after Baptism are forgiven through the absolution of the priest. The priest has the power to forgive sins from Jesus Christ Himself. He said to His Apostles and to their successors: "Receive the Holy Spirit; whose sins you shall forgive, they are forgiven them; and whose sins you shall retain, they are retained."

The consoling words of the priest are given to the penitent in the confessional after he confesses his sins. The priest, as the instrument of Jesus Christ, forgives sins with the words: "I absolve you from your sins in the name of the Father, and of the Son, and of the Holy Spirit. Amen."

There are five main effects from the reception of the Sacrament of Penance worthily. First, the penitent receives Sanctifying Grace. If the penitent has been in mortal sin, Sanctifying Grace is restored. If the penitent has been in venial sin, Sanctifying Grace is increased.

The second major effect of the Sacrament of Penance is the forgiveness of sins.

In the Bible, the Parable of the Prodigal Son illustrates God's desire to forgive us, based on His love and mercy for each one of us. In the story, a father has two sons. The younger son went off to spend his inheritance money, but he wasted it all. Soon he had nothing left. He also committed many sins. In the end, he was so hungry he had to eat what the pigs were eating.

One day, the younger son decided he had enough of living in sin. He said to himself, "I will arise and will go to my father and say to him, "Father, I have sinned against Heaven and before you." The son started walking on the road to his home. His father had been looking out the window for months,

waiting for his son to return home. As soon as the father caught sight of his son coming down the road, he was so overjoyed, he ran out to his son in the road, and threw his arms around him. The boy asked forgiveness and his father forgave him immediately and completely (cf. Luke 15:11-32).

Jesus told this story to illustrate how much God our Heavenly Father wants to forgive us when we commit sin. Along with the mercy of God is deep love for us, so deep we will never really understand it. How much God loves us! How much we should love Him in return!

In addition to receiving Sanctifying Grace, and having our sins forgiven, there are additional effects or fruits from receiving the Sacrament of Penance worthily. If the penitent has confessed a mortal sin, all the eternal punishment due is remitted or taken away. If the penitent has confessed venial sins, all or part of the temporal punishment due is taken away.

An additional effect of the Sacrament of Penance is the grace to help us to avoid sin in the future. This is a very important reason to go to Confession on a regular basis, to obtain the graces needed, the Sacramental Graces, to help us to avoid sin.

Another effect of the Sacrament of Penance is to restore the merits from good works if they have been lost by mortal sin. The Church teaches that if a person is in mortal sin, his soul is "dead." If a soul is dead, like a dead body, even if the person does something good like an act of charity, no graces or merits can be earned from that act.

What is our part? What is our duty and responsibility so that we may receive the effects of the Sacrament of Penance? We have the duty to prepare ourselves to receive the Sacrament of Penance *worthily*. First, to receive the Sacrament of Penance worthily, we should carefully examine our conscience. How? We need to review the Ten Commandments and the Laws of the Church. This review will help us recall all the sins we have committed since our last Confession.

The most important part of a good confession is sorrow for our sins. Unless we are sincerely sorry for having offended God, we cannot be forgiven of our sins. Moreover, we must be firmly resolved to not sin again. That does not mean that we will not sin again. No. God knows how weak we are. All He wants us to do is our best. We are all called to be saints. What is a saint? A saint is a sinner who keeps on trying.

Then we must confess our sins to the priest in the Sacrament of Penance. We must tell our sins honestly, frankly, and simply. We must not accuse anyone but ourselves in our confession even if someone else helped us to commit a sin.

Finally, we must perform the penance the priest assigns as soon as possible after leaving the confessional. Most people, when they leave the confessional, walk up to a pew near the altar and kneel down and say their Penance right away. Jesus is happy to see that we are willing to do the penance the priest gives us, and we are willing to do it right away. This shows Jesus that we are truly sorry for our sins, and are willing to do penance to make up for our sins.

There is a beautiful prayer that priests used to say, and perhaps many still do, after giving absolution to the penitent. The priest says: "May the Passion of Our Lord Jesus Christ, the merits of the Blessed Virgin Mary and of all the saints, whatever good you may perform, and whatever you may suffer, count toward the remission of sin, the increase of grace, and the reward of life eternal. Amen."

St. John Vianney, enlightened by the light from Heaven, pray for us.
St. John Vianney, fortified by divine visions, pray for us.

Fill in the Blanks

1. Penance is the Sacrament by which sins committed after __baptisum__ are forgiven through the absolution of the priest.

2. The priest has the power to forgive sins from __people__

3. "Receive the _____. Whose sins you shall forgiven they are forgiven them; whose sins you shall retain, they are retained."

4. "I __absolv__ you from your sins in the name of the Father, and of the Son, and of the Holy Spirit. Amen."

5. A main effect from the Sacrament of Penance is the restoration or increase of __Sanctifying__ Grace.

6. The main goal of the reception of the Sacrament of Penance is the __forgivnes__ of sins.

7. If the penitent has committed mortal sin, the Sacrament will remit all the _____ punishment due to sin.

8. If the penitent has committed venial sin, all or part of the temporal _____ will be remitted by the reception of the Sacrament of Penance.

9. The Sacrament of Penance helps us to _____ sin in the future.

10. The Sacrament of Penance restores the merits of our _____ _____ if they have been lost by mortal sin.

Penance is the Sacrament by which sins committed after Baptism are forgiven through the absolution of the priest.

We have learned about the effects of receiving the Sacrament of Penance worthily. The main effect, of course, is the forgiveness of sin.

We know that the first step to receive the Sacrament of Penance worthily is to *examine our conscience*. What is an examination of conscience and why is it so important? First, let us think about the meaning of conscience. Our conscience is that little voice that God puts in each one of us to keep us alert to the Laws of God. Our conscience helps us to understand what is right and wrong according to the Laws of God. The examination of conscience is a review of our past actions so that we might realize if we have committed any sins against God's Laws. With a good examination of conscience, we make a sincere effort to recall all the sins we have committed since our last worthy confession.

How often should we examine our consciences? We should examine our consciences every evening, preferably just before we go to sleep. Each evening, we should reflect on our actions, words, and thoughts of the day to remember our sins. We will not make much progress in the spiritual life without a daily examination of conscience.

Before we examine our conscience, we should say a brief prayer, or simply ask God to help us to know our sins, to be sorry for our sins, and to confess them to Him in Confession, with sincere sorrow.

What should we do when we discover that we have sinned? We should immediately ask God's forgiveness by saying an Act of Contrition. Then we should thank God for the grace He has given us to be able to know our sins. We should be neither too easy nor too demanding on ourselves, but simply and honestly go over our behavior in the light of the Commandments of God, and of the Commandments of the Church.

We should particularly think about our sins in relation to our state in life. For instance, as a student, we have certain duties related to our studies. As a member of a family, we have certain duties regarding helping with younger children, or helping with chores around the house.

How do we perform the examination of conscience? First, we consciously place ourselves in God's holy presence. Did you know you can be in someone's company and not be aware of their presence because our thoughts are miles away? That is why we should turn our thoughts deliberately toward God when we say any prayer.

Next, we begin an honest evaluation of our actions. "Did I fail in my duty to love my parents, my brother or sister, my friends?" "Did I deliberately eat or drink too much?" "Did I take something that did not belong to me?" Reflecting on the Commandments of God and the Church is our best guide.

Finally, we say an Act of Contrition, telling God how sorry we are that we have failed to be obedient to Him. We must remember particular sins to tell the priest in our next confession. Finally, we must thank God for the grace He has given us to know how we have offended Him.

St. John Vianney, tender friend of the young,
pray for us.
St. John Vianney, wise director of souls,
pray for us.

Fill in the Blanks

1. The examination of conscience is _____ of our past sins.

2. _____ is the Sacrament by which sins committed after Baptism are forgiven.

3. Our _____ helps us to know what is right and wrong.

4. We should examine our consciences at least _____.

5. When we realize we have sinned, we should immediately ask for God's _____.

6. We should be _____ in reviewing our behavior.

7. We should review the _____ of God to examine our consciences.

8. We should place ourselves in God's holy _____.

9. The main effect of the Sacrament of Penance is the _____ of sin.

10. At the beginning and end of our examination of conscience, say an Act of _____.

To receive the Sacrament of Penance worthily, we must have contrition for our sins. Contrition is sincere sorrow for having offended God. Contrition also means that we hate the sins we have committed, and we have a firm purpose to sin no more.

We cannot expect God to forgive us unless we have true contrition for our sins. We must be truly sorry for our venial sins as well as our mortal sins for God to forgive us those sins.

One day Bill entered a store in order to steal a video game. The manager saw him take the video and slip it under his coat. The store owner immediately went to Bill and asked him to give it back. We can imagine three possible behaviors by Bill.

Bill is angry that he was caught stealing.

Bill is sorry because he does not want to be punished.

Bill is deeply sorry because he realizes it is wrong to steal, and he has offended God and the storeowner.

Which of Bill's three behaviors would the storeowner most like to see? Wouldn't we all agree that the third behavior is the only one of the three that shows perfect contrition? If we would like to see that kind of contrition from those who offend us, all the more should we have that kind of contrition for having offended God. Yet God is so merciful that in Confession he only requires the minimum of imperfect contrition for the forgiveness of sin.

The *Catechism of the Catholic Church* tells us "among the penitent's acts, contrition occupies first place. Contrition is 'sorrow of the soul and detestation [intense hatred] for the sin committed, together with the resolution not to sin again [firm purpose of amendment]" (n. 1451). In other words, before God, we must have true sorrow for our sins. In our example above, only the third attitude, while not erasing the crime or the punishment due the crime, gave complete satisfaction to the storeowner for what Bill had done.

There are several qualities which are required for contrition or sorrow to be true. The first requirement is that contrition needs to be *interior*. This means we must have true sorrow in our heart, not merely on our lips. It means that at least we *want* to be sorry even if we don't always *feel* sorry. How many times have we heard people *say* they are sorry, but their actions do not match their words. Have you heard the phrase, "Actions speak louder than words!"? God knows if our contrition is true and honest sorrow.

A second quality which is required for our contrition to be true is that our sorrow is supernatural. If the only reason we are sorry for our sin is because we were caught in the sin, then our sorrow is merely natural sorrow. Our sorrow is supernatural when, with the help of God's grace, our sorrow arises from motives which spring from faith and not merely from natural motives. When we tell the priest and Our Lord in Confession we are sorry for our sins, we should try to be sorry based on what God has told us, either about the danger of eternal loss of our soul or about how much sin displeases and offends Him.

When we read about the saints who went before us, we are inspired to be like them. One of the best ways we can imitate the saints is to do what they did: to be sorry for our sins, not merely because we are afraid of being punished by our parents, but because of what God has told us, either about the danger of eternal loss of our soul or about how much sin displeases and offends Him. This is an important part of true contrition.

You may have heard of the great Saint Augustine, who lived from 354 to 430. Augustine was the son of a pagan father and a Christian mother, Monica. He was born in Africa and attended schools both in Carthage and in Rome. Monica had taught him his catechism at home, and he was a Christian until he was sixteen. At that age, the pagan influences of the bad schools turned him away from God, and for the next fourteen years, he lived an evil life.

However, Augustine finally met St. Ambrose, the Archbishop of Milan, who began to gently instruct Augustine in the Catholic Faith. Augustine, then a teacher at the university, soon became convinced of the existence of God, and the need of an absolute authority, an infallible teaching Church to interpret Scripture. Augustine was truly sorry for his evil life, and became deeply remorseful for his sins. He realized his sin of pride because of his great intellect. He turned to a life of prayer and service to the poor. After a time, he was ordained a priest. In spite of his becoming world famous for being a scholar, and in spite of his writing the book *City of God,* the story of his conversion, he remained humble and contrite for his sins for the rest of his life.

Augustine's true contrition was evident when he turned from his sinful practices and lived a life of prayer and service to the poor. His actions showed both interior and supernatural sorrow.

St. Augustine, pray for us to have true interior and supernatural contrition.

Matching

_1_	1. Contrition		Necessary in Sacrament of Penance
_8_	2. *Catechism*		Sincere sorrow for offending God
_4_	3. Sorrow for sin		Had true contrition; wrote *City of God*
_9_	4. Confession of our sins		Not supernatural contrition
_3_	5. St. Augustine		Unless we are truly sorry for them
_6_	6. All the saints		Says that contrition is of first importance
_10_	7. Regret of being caught		May be forgiven without confession
_2_	8. Sorrow arising from faith		Supernatural contrition
_5_	9. No forgiveness of sins		Only good if we are truly sorry
_7_	10. Venial sins		Had supernatural sorrow

According to the *Catechism of the Catholic Church,* contrition is the most important part of the Sacrament of Penance. Contrition is sincere sorrow for having offended God, hatred for the sins we have committed, and a firm purpose of sinning no more. God will not forgive any sin unless we have true contrition for it.

True contrition has four qualities. The first quality is that it should be *interior*. There is a difference between merely saying we are sorry with our lips, which is exterior, and being truly sorry in our hearts for something we have done wrong. We do not necessarily have to *feel* sorrow, but we should at least will or desire to be sorry for what we have done to offend God. We should ask God for more grace to have true sorrow for our sins.

True contrition is *supernatural*. True contrition does not come from merely natural sorrow. Natural sorrow means we fear the human consequences of our sins, such as being punished by our parents. Supernatural sorrow is sorrow based on motives that spring from faith and not merely natural motives. We are sorry *because we believe what God has told us* about the dangers of Hell or *because we believe what He has told us* about how sin offends Him.

True contrition is *supreme*. What is *supreme* sorrow? To answer that question, consider for a moment what is the most terrible thing that can happen? Some people might think that a natural disaster, such as an earthquake in which many people die, is the worst thing that can happen. Others might think that a war which destroys people, their homes, and families is the most terrible thing that can happen. Still others might think that a disease such as cancer is the worst thing that can happen to

anyone. Yet, nothing is as horrible as mortal sin. Earthquakes, wars, fatal diseases can certainly bring *physical* harm to people but they cannot kill the *immortal* soul. We should hate sin above every other evil in the world because it can bring about the loss of eternal happiness with God in Heaven.

Our sorrow is supreme when we hate sin above every other evil. Our sorrow is supreme when we are willing to endure any suffering rather than offend God in the future by sin. Many people have been put in jail for many years because they would not lie or be bribed to commit a sin. Many martyrs have died because they refused to commit a sin, such as worship a false god. These saints truly hated sin above every other evil.

Finally, true contrition should be *universal*. This means we are sorry for *every mortal sin* we have committed, if we have any. When we go to confession, we should end the pronouncement of our sins by saying "and for all the sins of my past life, I am very sorry." What are we saying? We are telling God and the priest that we are very sorry for *all* of our past sins and intend to never commit *any* sin ever again. We should prefer to please God more than we love our sins.

It may sound strange to imagine that we love our sins. That is what we are doing, however, when we continue to commit the same sins over and over again. We prefer our love of anger, envy, pride, gluttony, laziness, disobedience, or other sins to our love for God. Even if we fall again and again into the same sins, but we are sorry for our sins and keep trying to do His will, God will always forgive us. He loves us and He is rich in mercy. How blessed we are to have the Sacrament of Penance which allows us to look into our hearts to see where and how we have strayed from God's love!

We might make the mistake of thinking that venial sins, though regrettable, are not that important. However, every sin offends God. Every sin we commit also offends the Mystical Body of Christ, the Church. The worst thing that can happen is sin. The best thing we can do to

remedy our sins is to be as deeply sorry for them as we can be. We should try to have sorrow for *all* our sins (both mortal and venial) when receiving the Sacrament of Penance.

We might ask why should we confess venial sins when they are forgiven by receiving Holy Communion worthily? Pope Pius XII gave us many reasons to go to confession frequently. He reminded us that venial sins can lead to more serious sins. Venial sins weaken our resolve to love God and others. Venial sins also merit temporal punishment, in this world or in the next, in Purgatory.

If we have the misfortune to fall into mortal sin, we must have true contrition for that sin. When we go to confession, we must be determined to never commit that sin again. Without contrition, there is no forgiveness of sin.

How we need the Sacrament of Penance! The more we turn to God in the Sacrament, the more at peace we will be in His love. One of the ways we can thank God for the gift of the Sacrament of Penance is by going to confession at least once a month, and even twice a month or weekly, if we want to follow the saints.

Pope John Paul II explained contrition in one of his teachings. He said, "[Contrition is] a clear and decisive rejection of the sin committed, together with a resolution not to commit it again, out of the love which one has for God and which is reborn with repentance. Understood this way, contrition is therefore the beginning and the heart of conversion" (*Reconciliation and Penance*, n. 31).

The Holy Father is telling us that our sorrow for sin is part of our conversion. What is conversion? Conversion is a turning or changing from the state of sin to the state of being sorry for sin. Conversion is moving from a careless faith to an eager faith. When we are very sorry for sin, we are experiencing a kind of conversion or a closer union with God.

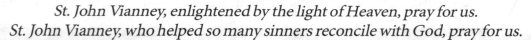

St. John Vianney, enlightened by the light of Heaven, pray for us.
St. John Vianney, who helped so many sinners reconcile with God, pray for us.

Fill in the Blanks

1. __Contrition__ is the most important part of Confession.

2. Our contrition for sin is __forgiven__ when it comes from the heart.

3. Our contrition for sin is __supernatural__ when our motives are from faith.

4. Our contrition for sin is __supreme__ when we hate sin above all else.

5. Our contrition for sin is __universel__ when we are sorry for every mortal sin we may have committed.

6. Every sin, even venial sin, __offends__ God.

7. Pope __Pius XII__ gave us reasons for receiving Penance frequently.

8. Venial sins can __lead__ to more serious sins.

9. Venial sins merit __temporal__ punishment.

10. Pope __John Paul II__ said that contrition is the beginning and heart of conversion.

Contrition is sincere sorrow for having offended God. Contrition also means we hate the sins we have committed, and we have a firm purpose of sinning no more. God will not forgive us our sins if we do not have true contrition. We must be sorry for all our venial sins as well as our mortal sins.

For our contrition to be true sorrow, it must be interior, from our hearts, and not just our lips. Our sorrow for sin must be supernatural; it arises from motives of faith. Our contrition must be supreme; we hate our sins because sin is the worst evil in the world. Our contrition must be universal; we are sorry for *all* our mortal sins (assuming we've committed some).

Real sorrow for sin is evidenced by our avoidance of sin in the future. When we are truly sorry for our sins, we are determined never to commit them ever again. We must decide in our wills to avoid sin in the future. Each time we are tempted, we must pray and ask God for the grace to resist sin. If we fail in our resolve to avoid sin, we must turn to the ever-willing love and mercy of God Who knows us better than anyone else. He is always ready to forgive us our sins if we are truly sorry and will truly try not to sin again.

Today we will consider perfect and imperfect contrition. Our contrition is imperfect when we are sorry for our sins because the sins are hateful or because we fear God's punishment. An example of imperfect contrition follows: It is a Saturday afternoon. I am watching a movie about the apparitions of Our Lady at Fatima. When I come to the part where Our Lady shows Hell to Jacinta, Lucia, and Francisco, I gasp in horror, get out of my chair, and — forgetting to turn the VCR off — run straight to the church and into the confessional. I then proceed to confess my mortal sin. I tell the priest that I am very sorry for this sin "because I don't want to go to Hell when I die. That would be terrible!" I am sorry for my sins only because I fear God's punishment; therefore, my contrition is imperfect. Nonetheless, my sin is forgiven since imperfect contrition is sufficient for the forgiveness of sins in the Sacrament of Reconciliation or Confession.

What is perfect contrition? In our example above, suppose that, after finishing the movie on Fatima, I watch a movie about the Passion of Our Lord. After the movie, I am sorry for my sins because I now realize how much they hurt Jesus, the Incarnate God, and for this reason I am sorry for my mortal sin. God then immediately forgives me of my mortal sin, but I cannot receive

Holy Communion worthily until I go to confession and obtain absolution for this mortal sin. I still have a healthy fear of Hell, but the main reason I am sorry is because I have offended God. This is perfect contrition.

We immediately see that perfect contrition is far better than imperfect contrition. Why? Because God is the Supreme Being Who is above all creatures, He created us and He loves us. We owe Him perfect contrition. God is good and He gave us all that we are and all that we have. However, He knows that we are weak and far from perfect. That is why He went to the Cross and suffered a horrible death: to save us from our sins. Our primary reason for being sorry always should be that we have offended God.

Here is another example of perfect and imperfect contrition. John leaves the house with his friends, telling his mother that he will be home for dinner at 6 o'clock. John decides he and his friends are having so much fun, they will go to the ballpark. Time goes by and before he realizes it, it is 7 o'clock; however, instead of going home, John decides to go to his friend's house to watch a movie.

John gets home at 9:30. His mother is very upset and tells him he will not be allowed to go out for a week. John is sorry, but not because he has worried his mother. He is sorry only because he will be punished. This is imperfect contrition. Later on, however, as John reflects on what he has done, he begins to be sorry that he has hurt his mother.

John's mother was very worried that something might have happened to him. Now his sorrow is motivated by love for his mother, his contrition is now perfect. He tearfully apologizes to her for what he has done and tells her he won't ever do it again. His mother's heart melts at his sorrow and her love for him deepens. She accepts his apology. When we are able to see clearly enough past our own selfish motives, we are then better able to see the pain we have caused to someone we love.

The *Catechism of the Catholic Church* tells us, "When it [contrition] arises from a love by which God is loved above all else, contrition is called 'perfect' (contrition of charity). Such contrition remits venial sins; it also obtains forgiveness of mortal sins if it includes the firm resolution to have recourse to Sacramental Confession as soon as possible" (n. 1452).

The *Catechism* also notes the following: "The contrition called 'imperfect' is also a gift of God, a prompting of the Holy Spirit. It is born of the consideration of sin's ugliness or the fear of eternal damnation and the other penalties threatening the sinner (contrition of fear)…By itself, however, imperfect contrition cannot obtain the forgiveness of grave sins; but it disposes one to obtain forgiveness in the Sacrament of Penance" (n. 1453). God loves us so much, that even imperfect contrition will suffice for the forgiveness of our sins in the Sacrament of Penance. Nevertheless, we should try to have perfect contrition whenever we go to Confession because perfect contrition is more pleasing to God.

Multiple Choice

_____a_____ 1. Contrition means
- a) sorrow for sin.
- b) ignorance of sin.
- c) sadness over sin.

_____c_____ 2. Imperfect contrition is
- a) fear of punishment.
- b) sorrow for offending God.
- c) fear of being caught.

_____b_____ 3. Perfect contrition arises out of
- a) fear of punishment.
- b) our love for God.
- c) fear of being caught.

_____b_____ 4. If I confess my mortal sin(s) only because I am afraid of going to Hell, then my contrition is
- a) perfect.   b) imperfect.   c) a & b.

_____c_____ 5. Contrition means
- a) we hate the sin.
- b) we resolve not to commit the sin again.
- c) a & b

_____a_____ 6. When we offend our parents, we
- a) should be perfectly sorrowful.
- b) should be somewhat sorrowful.
- c) need not be sorry at all.

_____a_____ 7. Perfect contrition _____ mortal sin.
- a) takes away
- b) covers over
- c) partially removes

_____b_____ 8. It is sufficient in Confession to have
- a) imperfect contrition.
- b) perfect contrition.
- c) firm purpose of amendment.

_____c_____ 9. When we have committed a mortal sin, we should
- a) be immediately sorry for having offended God.
- b) go to confession as soon as possible.
- c) a and b.

_____b_____ 10. Imperfect contrition without Confession _____ obtain forgiveness of mortal sins.
- a) can   b) cannot

We have learned that contrition is sincere sorrow for having offended God. True contrition includes a hatred for our sins, and a firm purpose of sinning no more. God will not forgive us our sins unless we have true contrition.

We have learned that our sorrow must be from our hearts, and we should be sorry primarily because we have offended God. Our contrition is supreme when we hate sin above every other evil. Our contrition is universal when we are sorry for every mortal sin we have ever committed.

In our last lesson, we learned about perfect contrition, which means we are sorry for our sins because we have offended God, Whom we should love above all things for His own sake. Our contrition is imperfect when we are sorry for other reasons. Although we should try to have perfect contrition, imperfect contrition is sufficient for a worthy confession.

Children usually do not commit mortal sins. Parents help children to be good. However, a child could commit a mortal sin if he purposefully hurt a younger child or hit his mother. A child could commit a mortal sin by telling a terrible lie about someone or by stealing a large amount of money from someone who needed it. A child could commit a mortal sin by purposefully refusing to go to Mass on Sunday.

If one has the misfortune to fall into mortal sin, hopefully, he will immediately pray for the grace of true contrition, or someone else has prayed and obtained this grace for him. Once a person is sorry for having committed a mortal sin, he should immediately say an Act of Contrition. After all, if a person dies with a mortal sin on his soul, he will go to Hell forever. For all eternity, he will be in Hell.

When the person says his Act of Contrition, he should say it this way so it is a Perfect Contrition. "O my God, I am heartily sorry for having offended You because I love you above all things, and above all things, I want to live and die in Your holy love." The person can have a mortal sin removed immediately only if he has perfect contrition, that is, he is sorry because he offended God. However, there is one more condition. The person MUST have a sincere purpose of going to confession as soon as possible, which means within a week's time.

We should point out that if the mortal sin was committed with another person, it would be a good deed to save the other person from Hell by telling him or her to say an Act of Contrition and to go to Confession. A person should continue to pray for anyone with whom he has committed a mortal sin.

Anyone in mortal sin, even after an Act of Perfect Contrition, may NOT go to Holy Communion. A person who has committed a mortal sin may go to Holy Communion only after going to Confession.

Remember that in the definition of contrition, we learned that we must have a firm purpose of sinning no more. If a person does not have a purpose of not committing that sin again, obviously

he is not truly sorry for committing the sin. Someone who steals money from people at work, confesses it on Saturday, and then does it again the following week, is not truly sorry!

Sometimes children confess getting angry at their brothers and sisters, but commit the sin again the following week. The question is, "Did the boy or girl *try* not to commit the sin?" God is willing to forgive people their sins over and over again, but He expects people to *try* not to commit sin again. That is why the Church says people should avoid persons, places, or things which tempt people to sin again! There are places where children gather who use terrible language, or who talk proudly about committing sins, or who plan on committing sins such as lying, stealing, taking drugs, going to bad movies, looking at bad pictures, and so on. Good people stay away from persons, places, and things which can lead one into sin.

Parents often say to their children: "I am sorry but you cannot go to that movie." They might say, "I am sorry but you cannot go to that mall without me." They might say, "I am sorry, but you cannot go anywhere with that boy again." Parents are protecting their children by keeping them away from occasions of sin. It would be a sin for a parent *not* to keep their children away from occasions of sin.

The Church declares that the Sacrament of Penance must include *sorrow* for our sins with a *firm purpose of amendment,* otherwise there will be no forgiveness for sin. A firm purpose of sinning no more is a sincere desire, a sincere resolve not only to avoid sin, but to avoid the near occasions of sin. Just as our interior attitude when receiving Holy Communion is important because the place where Our Lord will visit must be as pure as possible, so the better our interior attitude in the Sacrament of Penance, the more graces will be obtained from the Sacrament.

Most of the saints experienced perfect contrition in their lives for the sins they had committed. Contrition is a sign of humility. St. Paul's conversion is an example of perfect contrition for sin. We recall that St. Paul was formerly known as Saul. He was responsible for the deaths of many Christians. Then one day, he received an explosion of grace. It was so powerful that he was thrown from his horse. For three days, Saul was blind. When the scales were removed from his eyes, he realized what he had done. He was deeply sorry for having offended God and spent the remainder of his life loving and serving Our Lord Jesus Christ. God rewarded him with the gift of martyrdom. As we know, St. Paul wrote most of the epistles, or letters, in the New Testament.

St. John Vianney, faithful adorer of the Blessed Sacrament, pray for us.
St. John Vianney, who gives joy to those who ask you, pray for us.

Fill in the Blanks

1. True contrition includes a _forgivnes_ for our sins.

2. True contrition means we have a firm purpose to _Sin_ no more.

3. Our sorrow must be from our _hearts_ – not just from our lips.

4. We must be sorry primarily because we have offended _GOD_.

5. Parents help _Kid's_ to be good.

6. When a person is sorry for committing a mortal sin, he should immediately say an _our father_.

7. If a person has a mortal sin, he must go to _Confetion_ before going to Holy Communion.

8. God is willing to forgive people their sins over again, but people must _Promise_ not to commit the sin again.

9. We must _avoid_ persons, places, and things which tempt us to sin.

10. We must avoid the near _that_ of sin.

Take this week to review the lessons from this quarter.

Day 1

Review lessons for weeks 19 and 20.

Day 2

Review lessons for weeks 21 and 22.

Day 3

Review lessons for weeks 23 and 24.

Day 4

Review lessons for weeks 25 and 26.

Day 5

Take the Third Quarter Test.

Confession is the telling of our sins to an authorized priest in order to obtain forgiveness of sins.

The *Catechism of the Catholic Church* tells us, "Confession to a priest is an essential part of the Sacrament of Penance" (n. 1456).

We have seen that on Easter Sunday night, Jesus Christ immediately upon His appearance before His startled Apostles, said to them, "Peace! Whose sins you shall forgive, they are forgiven them; and whose sins you shall retain, they are retained" (John 20:23). Why did Jesus say those words before He said anything else to his disciples? Notice that His very first word was "peace." Those of us who have been to Confession know the special kind of peace that comes from confessing our sins and being forgiven by God.

The words of Jesus Christ to His Apostles oblige us to confess our sins to a priest. He cannot forgive us our sins if we do not confess them. God can and does forgive us our venial sins when we tell Him we are sorry. We are *required* to confess our mortal sins to a priest even if previously we asked God for forgiveness, so that we can have the assurance that our sins are forgiven. The Sacrament of Penance was instituted by Jesus Christ, so it is obvious that that is the method He has chosen for us to be forgiven.

When we go to Confession, we should think about Jesus as the Good Shepherd. The Good Shepherd cares about each one of his sheep, and does let one go astray. Jesus wants us to think of Him this way. One day, some of His enemies were complaining that he associated with sinners, even eating with them. That was when Jesus told us the parable of the Lost Sheep which we can read in the Gospel of Luke, chapter 15.

"What man of you that has a hundred sheep, and if he loses one of them, does not leave the ninety-nine in the desert, and go after the one that was lost until he finds it? And when he has found it, he lays it upon his shoulders, rejoicing. Coming home, he calls his friends and says to them, 'Rejoice with me, because I have found my sheep that was lost!' (Luke 15: 4-6).

"I say to you that even so [likewise], there will be joy in Heaven upon one sinner that does penance, more than upon ninety-nine just who need not penance" (Luke 15:7). And after a second parable, Jesus said, "…there shall be joy before the angels of God for one sinner doing penance" (Luke 15:10).

God gave each one of us a conscience. This is a little voice inside us that tells us or reminds us that something is wrong, that is, against the Commandments of God. When our conscience bothers us, we should think about Jesus, the Good Shepherd, warning us not to go astray and get lost. He loves us so! But if we do go astray, like a Good Shepherd, He will come after us, calling us back again and again. He will not rest, and we will not rest, until we are happy again in His loving arms. If we are in sin, we cannot be happy, we cannot be at peace, until we go to Confession.

Because of Original Sin, our minds are not as smart as Adam's before his sin, our wills are not as strong but are inclined to commit sin. So Jesus gave us His Catholic Church, with all the Sacraments to help us. Jesus established the Sacrament of Penance or Reconciliation by giving His priests the power to forgive sins in His Holy Name. Obviously, the priests must judge if a person is truly sorry and should have his sins forgiven. The priest cannot know our sins unless we confess them to him.

We must have mortal sins forgiven in Confession. While venial sins may be forgiven in other ways, we are encouraged to confess them. However, mortal sins must be confessed in Confession to be forgiven. Do you remember the ten lepers who asked Jesus to be cured? He said to them, "Go show yourselves to the priests!" So many times, when it appears that people are asking for a physical cure, they really need a spiritual cure. Often, disease and illness cause people to reject God or to despair or to lose their Faith. That is why Jesus often told people to have their souls cleansed first!

The Church encourages going to Confession at least once a month. However, the Church also teaches that twice a month, or once each week is even better. Being in the habit of going to Confession every week brings an abundance of graces and rapid growth in the spiritual life. No one can explain this, but those who go to weekly Confession know inside them the wonderful peace that comes from such regular and close time with Jesus.

Remember the story of the Prodigal Son? When he was living in sin and eating with the pigs, he suddenly came to his senses and ran down the road back to his father's home, asking for forgiveness. Never let yourself live in the dirt and mud of the pigs! Go to Confession quickly if you are dirty in sin! Your Father in Heaven loves you more than you can ever understand! He welcomes you with open and loving arms! There in His arms you can find eternal peace!

St. John Vianney, confessor of confessors, pray for us.
St. John Vianney, ardent lover of the sinner, pray for us.

Fill in the Blank

1. We must confess our sins to an authorized _Priest_.

2. Confession to a _Priest_ is an essential part of the Sacrament of Penance.

3. Jesus Christ instituted the Sacrament of Penance on _Easter night_

4. The first word Jesus said to His Apostles was _Peace_.

5. We are required to confess our _mortal_ sins in Confession.

6. When we go to Confession, we should think about Jesus as our Good _Shepherd_.

7. God gave each one of us a _soul_.

8. "Whose sins you shall forgive, they are _forgiven_ them."

9. We need not confess _our_ sins, but we are encouraged to confess them.

10. The Church encourages us to go to Confession at least once a _month_.

Confession is the telling of our sins to an authorized priest for the purpose of obtaining forgiveness.

We must confess our sins because Jesus Christ obliged us to do so when He said to the Apostles and their successors: "Whose sins you shall forgive, they are forgiven them; whose sins you shall retain, they are retained." It is necessary to confess every mortal sin. Though it is not necessary to confess venial sins, it is better to do so because a habit of venial sins can lead to mortal sins.

Today we will learn about what makes a good confession. A good confession must be *humble, sincere* and *entire*. What do we mean by a *humble* confession? We make a humble confession when we have carefully looked into our hearts and we realize we are guilty of offending God. Because of our fallen human nature, it is very difficult to see ourselves truthfully and humbly. We tend to make excuses for our own behavior. If we pray and ask for the grace to see ourselves as God sees us, we should be humble because of our guilt against God Who loves us. Being humble means we are ashamed and sorry for having offended our all-loving, all-good, and all-merciful God. St. Augustine was humble when he realized his sins, and went to live in a monastery and spent his time helping the poor even though he had been a famous and well-known university professor.

A good confession is *sincere*. A sincere confession means that we tell the truth without excuses. We must be honest, frank, and direct. We must not be tempted to excuse our behavior. We should never make excuses to the priest for what we have done. We must be sincere in confessing our sins honestly. St. Paul could have said, "Well, I persecuted the Christians because that is what I was told to do by my Roman military superiors! So it was not really all my own fault!" If we do not realize and recognize our own guilt, we are not sincere in expressing our sorrow and contrition in Confession!

A good confession is *entire*. We must confess *all mortal sins*. We must tell their kind, and the number of times we have committed the sin. It is a further mortal sin to omit a mortal sin in Confession. When we kneel before the priest and honestly and sincerely bare our souls to God, He is very merciful and loving. God does not cease loving us no matter what we do. Withholding sins and making excuses for our behavior is an expression of pride. God wants to give us His mercy and grace.

Our confession is entire when we confess all our mortal sins, telling their kind and the number of times we have committed each sin. We may tell venial sins as well; in fact, the Church encourages us to confess venial sins. However, our confession is entire only if we confess all mortal sins. We are required to confess mortal sins. We are not allowed to receive Holy Communion until all mortal sins are confessed.

Usually when a child has a mortal sin to tell, it involves missing Mass on purpose, hitting a parent, abusing a brother or sister, or a grandparent. Sometimes children tell serious lies about someone, or sometimes children steal money from their parents or someone in the family. For a sin to be mortal, it must be a serious sin, the person must know it is a serious sin, and the person must intend to commit the sin.

We must not deliberately conceal a mortal sin in Confession. Not only is that sin not forgiven, of course, but the penitent has committed a second mortal sin, the sin of sacrilege. The next time the person goes to Confession, he must confess: first, the sin he did not confess; second, the sin of sacrilege; and third, any other mortal sins confessed or not confessed since the last good Confession!

If you are going to Confession, you must confess all the mortal sins you have committed. You are not the first person to commit that kind of sin. Keep in mind that God and the priest have heard these sins before. Remember only God knows who you are, the priest does not.

What if we sincerely forget a mortal sin? Sometimes a person is so concerned about one mortal sin, that he can sincerely forget to confess another mortal sin. Perhaps a person confesses that he committed a mortal sin twice, and then after the Confession, remembered a third time. These would certainly not be sins of sacrilege, but we must tell that sin in Confession if it again comes to mind.

Keep in mind that it is *supposed to be difficult* to tell the priest the wrong we have done, said, and thought. This shows that we have shame, and shame is a good thing to have. Why? Because we are supposed to be ashamed of the sins we commit against our all-loving God!

Father John Vianney, the Curé of Ars, was so good at counseling people in Confession, that people traveled from miles around to go to him for confession. The small town of Ars was filled to overflowing because of the numbers who came to see him. In the book *The Curé of Ars*, by Mary Fabyan Windeatt, published by TAN Publishers, Father Vianney says these words:

"I was besieged with crowds of men and women who wanted to go to Confession. Some of these were deep in mortal sin…. 'Actually each of these pilgrims wants just one thing,' I thought, gazing out at the vast throngs in the church, in the grounds, in the public square. "Peace of mind and heart! Oh, dear Lord! Won't You please let them find it here in Ars?"

"In just a short time, this little prayer was answered… Ars actually became the sanctuary of peace. And why? Because God renewed my startling powers to read men's hearts, and no troubled soul ever came to me for help without being comforted and strengthened.

"Thus, within or without the confessional, I could sense the dreadful stain of sin upon certain people's souls, even when these same people pretended to be leading good lives. To prove my knowledge, it was permitted that the past and the future should open up before me, and I would utter such amazing words of advice, of warning, of encouragement, that the sinners would no longer dare to conceal anything from me. Then, through the mercy of God, I would show them in what a detestable condition their souls were, and with just a few words, excite in them a deep love for the Heavenly Father, a sorrow for having offended Him, and a desire to lead a thoroughly Christian life. …

"It isn't enough to pray for one's penitents," I declared. "We must also be willing to suffer for them, to fast, to go without sleep, to practice difficult mortifications. Ah, the pastor who does not pray and suffer to make saints among his people is in great danger of being a complete failure" (pp. 163-164).

St. John Vianney, pastor of pastors and confessor of confessors, pray for us.

Confession is the telling of our sins to an authorized priest for the purpose of obtaining forgiveness. We must confess our sins because Jesus Christ obliges us to do so in the words spoken to His Apostles: "Whose sins you shall forgive, they are forgiven them; and whose sins you shall retain, they are retained." The priest cannot forgive sins unless we tell them to him.

It is required that we confess every mortal sin. Venial sins need not be confessed, but the Church encourages us to do so because if venial sins become a habit, they can lead to mortal sin.

A good confession must be humble and sincere. A good confession also must be entire. This means that all mortal sins must be confessed, telling their kind and the number of times we have committed each sin. We must be careful not to conceal any mortal sin. Not only would this sin not be forgiven, but it is an additional sin of sacrilege to conceal a mortal sin. A person who knowlingly conceals a mortal sin must go back to confession, confess the concealed sin, confess the sin of sacrilege, and confess any other mortal sins committed since the last good Confession.

When we sin, we should have a recognition of our own guilt. What do we mean by guilt? Guilt is what we incur before God when we have sinned. For example, I can *feel* guilty when I have lied to someone, but I truly *have* the guilt of the sin I have committed. Two things happen whenever we sin: we take on guilt and punishment due for our sin. When we go to Confession, the guilt and eternal punishment is removed for confessing a mortal sin. Some of the temporal punishment is removed also. When we confess venial sins, some of the temporal punishment is removed.

If someone drives through a red light on purpose, he is guilty of breaking the law. At the same time, punishment is due. The usual punishment is paying a fine. The judge may decide the guilty person must pay $100 for going through a red light. In a similar way, punishment is due for our sins against the Ten Commandments of God.

We must never worry that the priest will ever reveal our sins. In the first place, the priest does not know who it is in the confessional. Secondly, the priest listens to confessions for a couple of hours at a time; he would never remember all the sins he hears in an afternoon! Thirdly, the priest is bound by the *seal of the Sacrament of Penance* not to reveal anyone's sins.

Priests never reveal what they have heard in Confession. It is called the seal of Confession or the seal of the Sacrament of Penance. No human being has a greater responsibility to keep a secret. Priests, such as St. John Nepomucene, have gone to their deaths rather than reveal the sins they have heard in confession.

After we have confessed our sins to the priest in the Sacrament of Penance, the priest gives us a penance that we may make atonement to God for our sins. The penance also helps us to avoid sin in the future, and the penance makes some satisfaction for the temporal punishment due to our sin. As one priest told the children, the penance should be said immediately after we leave the confessional. It should be said slowly and devoutly because it is the means of taking away part of the punishment we deserve, and which God, in His justice, must demand.

There are two kinds of punishment due to sin: the eternal punishment of hell due to unforgiven mortal sin, and temporal punishment, lasting for only a time, due to venial sins and due to forgiven mortal sins. Temporal punishment must be given either on earth or in Purgatory. The Sacrament of Penance takes away eternal punishment for forgiven mortal sins, but does not take away all temporal punishment.

God requires temporal punishment for sin to satisfy His justice, to teach us the great evil of sin, and to warn us not to sin again. We must pay the debt of temporal punishment either in this life or in Purgatory. We can satisfy the debt of our temporal punishment to some extent by doing the penance the priest gives us.

As we have seen, two things happen every time we sin: we acquire guilt, and we deserve punishment. We have seen that guilt is the condition of a person who has sinned. He is, therefore, more or less separated from God and liable for punishment. When the priest says the words of absolution, one's sins are forgiven. However, one still must make reparation for what one has done.

Suppose I break an expensive dish because I became angry and threw it on the floor. My mother is upset; I tell her I am very sorry. She accepts my apology, but says that I must earn the money to replace the dish. That is how I must make reparation for what I have done. It is the same in Confession. I have been forgiven, but I must still atone for my sin by accepting the penance the priest assigns to me.

St. John Vianney, priest, pray for us to make a good confession.

Fill in the Blank

1. Confession is the telling of our sins to an authorized priest for the purpose of obtaining _forgiveness_.

2. It is required that we confess every _mortle_ sin.

3. A good confession must be entire, meaning we must confess _every_ mortal sins.

4. To conceal a mortal sin knowingly is the sin of _Sacrilege_

5. When we confess our sins, the guilt and only _part_ of the punishment is removed.

6. The priest is bound by the _Seal_ of the Confessional not to reveal anyone's sins.

7. After we have confessed our sins, the priest gives us a _Penance_ to atone for our sins.

8. The penance helps us to _avoid_ sin in the future.

9. The penance should be said immediately after leaving the _Confessionle_

10. One kind of punishment due to sin is the eternal punishment of _hell_ due to unforgiven mortal sin.

Confession is the telling of our sins to an authorized priest for the purpose of obtaining forgiveness.

We know that we must confess our sins in a formal manner to a priest in the Sacrament of Penance because of the words which Jesus Christ spoke to His Apostles: "Whose sins you shall forgive, they are forgiven them; whose sins you shall retain, they are retained." These words oblige us to confess our sins to a priest.

The Church has declared that every mortal sin must be confessed because it would be like lying to God if we said we were sorry, yet omitted confessing a mortal sin. Venial sins should be confessed also, though it is not necessary to confess any venial sin.

We know that our confession should be humble, sincere, and entire. We know that it is good to have a sense of shame and guilt, but this should never lead us to omit telling a mortal sin in Confession. This would be a grave sacrilege.

Even though we do our penance after Confession, we know that there is still punishment due to sin. Eternal punishment due to mortal sin is entirely wiped away when we receive absolution or forgiveness from God in the Sacrament of Penance. However, some temporal punishment, either in this world or in Purgatory, is still due for both mortal and venial sins.

Why does God still require temporal punishment? Because offending God is a very serious matter. Our sins have offended our Creator, Who loves us so much He suffered and died on the Cross for us. God requires temporal punishment to satisfy His justice, to teach us the great evil of sin, and to warn us not to sin again. We must pay the debt of temporal punishment either in this life or in Purgatory.

All of us suffer in this life in some way, which is one way to pay back our debt for our sins. We can offer up our sicknesses and pains, our being too cold or too hot, our discomfort during the day, our difficulties, our chores, our school work. The Morning Offering, which the Church encourages to say at the beginning of each day, declares: "O God, I offer Thee all my prayers, works, joys, and sufferings for this day." The Offering goes on to give several reasons, one of which is: "in reparation for my offenses."

Temporal punishment is the penalty that God, in His justice, imposes on us for our sins. We must undergo temporal punishment either here on earth or, if satisfaction is still incomplete when we die, our punishment will be in Purgatory. When the priest gives us a penance to perform, it remits only part of the temporal punishment due to our sins. What can we do to remit more of the temporal punishment due to our sins? Besides the penance imposed after confession, there are several other means of satisfying the debt of our temporal punishment.

Voluntary penance is not only very good for the soul; it can remit all of the temporal punishment still due to our sins.

What is voluntary penance? Voluntary penance is what we can do on our own to discipline our bodies and our souls. It also heals the effects of sin. Jesus told us that, "If any man would come after Me, let him deny himself and take up his cross and follow Me" (Matthew 16:24). By accepting and not complaining about the daily trials and difficulties, we are accepting the daily crosses which are the steps which lead us to Heaven.

What exactly can we do to satisfy the debt we have incurred for the sins we have committed? St. Thérèse of Lisieux did what she called her "Little Way." Every single action she performed, no matter how small, she elevated it by offering it to God. Washing dishes became a prayer because she offered it to God. Mother Teresa of Calcutta called this doing "something beautiful for God." We can all offer everything we do as a prayer to God. We need not perform heroic deeds in order to expiate the temporal punishment due to our sins. The simplest deeds performed with love for God and others become penitential acts directed toward God.

Many of the saints have taught that it is better to do our penance in this world rather than suffer the pains of Purgatory in the next world. The Church encourages us to attend Mass, even daily if possible. We should be saying plenty of prayers every day, such as the Rosary. We should abstain, especially on Fridays, by giving up meat, candy, desserts, or whatever our parents say. We should give to the poor whenever possible, or help the poor by helping to take care of their children.

The Church recommends specific things we can do to satisfy the debt of our temporal punishment: prayer, attending Mass, fasting, almsgiving [giving to the poor], the works of mercy, the patient endurance of sufferings, and indulgences.

St. John Vianney, inflamed with zeal, pray for us.
St. John Vianney, tireless teacher of catechism, pray for us.

Fill in the Blank

1. Even though we do our penance after Confession, we know there is still ___Punishment___ due to sin.

2. ___there's___ punishment, either in this world or in Purgatory, is still due for sin.

3. Punishment is still due to satisfy God's ___justice___.

4. Punishment is still due to teach us the great ___lesson___ of sin.

5. Punishment is still due to ___teach___ us not to sin again.

6. We can offer up our daily ___aches___ and pains.

7. The Church encourages us to say the ___rosary___ at the beginning of each day.

8. Voluntary penance can remit ___all___ the temporal punishment due to sin.

9. "If any man would come after Me, let him deny himself and take up his ___cross___ and follow Me."

10. To satisfy our debt, the Church recommends attending ___Mass___, doing the works of ___mercy___, and patiently enduring our daily ___life___.

Today we will learn about how to prepare ourselves to make a good confession, and how to begin our confession.

The Sacrament of Penance is not to be taken lightly. It is not to be quickly squeezed in between your Saturday afternoon soccer game and your visit to the store. The Sacrament of Penance is truly a wonderful meeting event between you and God. It is a Sacrament, and we should receive it with a good and holy attitude.

Many families have a schedule for when the family goes to Confession. The Church recommends at least once a month, but many Catholic families go twice a month, and some even go every week. Some families have the Confession schedule on the family calendar so that other events can be scheduled around it.

To prepare for the Sacrament of Penance, consider spending fifteen minutes reading over the meaning of the Sacrament of Penance from a catechism. Some churches have little booklets for children to review the Ten Commandments. TAN Publishers publishes a booklet for children called *My Confession Book*, written by Sister Andrine Welters. It contains little prayers for before and after Confession, as well as a review of the Ten Commandments for children.

Parents can help children prepare before going to Confession. Parents can remember times of disobedience, laziness, impatience, or arguing with siblings which sometimes children forget. Parents can help their children reflect on their spiritual life, and even suggest specific areas needed for improvement. A regular schedule for Confession gives both parents and children a regular opportunity to have such discussions.

Before going to Confession, read a prayer specifically written to help you make a good Confession. Prayers are included in many prayer books and missals. Some are by saints. These especially help in developing a sense of sorrow for sin, and a firm purpose not to commit those sins again.

Sister Andrine suggests the following prayer: *Come Holy Spirit, enlighten my mind that I may clearly know my sins; touch my heart that I may be sorry for them, and better my life. Amen.*

Sister Andrine suggested a few questions which children might ask themselves about the Ten Commandments: For the First Commandment: Did I willfully allow myself to be distracted during prayers? Did I bother others during prayers? For the Second Commandment: Did I use God's Holy Name in anger? Did I make fun of holy things? For the Third Commandment: On Sundays or holy days, did I come late to Mass or miss Mass through my own fault? Did I talk to others during Mass?

For the Fourth Commandment: Did I disobey my parents? Was I mean to my parents? For the Fifth Commandment: Did I fight or quarrel with others? Was I mean to other boys and girls? Was I angry with others? Did I try to get even with others?

For the Sixth and Ninth Commandments: Did I tell bad stories or listen to bad talk? Did I look at bad pictures or bad books? For the Seventh and Tenth Commandments: Did I steal anything? Did I help someone else steal something? Did I damage someone's property? Did I cheat on a test? For the Eighth Commandment: Did I tell a lie? Did I talk about the sins of others?

Once you have done a review, look at Jesus on the Cross, and tell Him how sorry you are for offending Him. Practice making a good Act of Contrition before you go into the Confessional.

We should begin our confession by kneeling down and making the sign of the Cross. We should then say to the priest: "Bless me, Father, for I have sinned. It has been [whatever number] weeks since my last Confession."

St. John Vianney, tender friend of children, pray for us.

Fill in the Blank

1. The Church recommends going to Confession at least once a __month__.

2. Many families have a __schedule__ for when the family goes to Confession.

3. Some time should be spent reflecting about the __sins__ committed since the last Confession.

4. Children should talk to their __parents__ before going to Confession.

5. Parents can suggest specific areas needed for __confession (reflection)__

6. Confession should be on a __weekly__ schedule.

7. It is a good idea to read a __prayer__ to help make a good confession.

8. We must try to develop a sense of __sorrow__ for sin.

9. We must have a firm purpose not to __comit__ that sin again.

10. We should begin our confession by saying, "Bless me, Father, for I have __sined__."

Before we enter the confessional, we should prepare for our confession by taking the time to examine our conscience. We do this by reviewing the Ten Commandments. We should ask the Holy Spirit to help us. Looking at Jesus on the Cross, we should be sorry for our sins. Then we should practice our Act of Contrition.

We begin our confession by saying: "Bless me, Father, for I have sinned." Then we say how long it has been since our last confession.

Then we must tell any mortal sins, and the number of times each mortal sin was committed. While we are encouraged to confess venial sins as well, the Church *requires* that we confess all mortal sins.

It is very important that we confess all mortal sins. If we go to Confession and deliberately not confess a mortal sin, we commit a second mortal sin of sacrilege. The next time we go to Confession, we must confess our sin of sacrilege PLUS all the mortal sins we have committed since our last good confession.

We are forbidden to receive Holy Communion if we have committed a sacrilege, or any other mortal sin. We must go to Confession first.

We might ask, "How do we know a sin is mortal?" Usually a person knows by his conscience that he has committed a mortal sin. A mortal sin is a serious matter, such as stealing a large amount of money or deliberately missing Mass on Sunday.

If we cannot remember the exact number of times the mortal sin was committed, we must give the number as nearly as possible, or say how many times a week or a month we committed the sin.

If we have committed no mortal sins since our last Confession, we should confess our venial sins. The Church encourages us to confess venial sins because venial sins offend God also. Confessing venial sins will help us avoid committing these sins again. This is important because venial sins can lead to mortal sins. Also, if we love God, we want to tell him we are sorry we offended Him by committing venial sins.

For those of us who love God, we try hard not to commit a mortal sin. Most of us, from week to week, will be confessing venial sins.

St. John Vianney told his friends that it is important to pray for sinners. No one can do anything without the grace of God. He said that the conversion of sinners begins with prayer and ends with penance. St. John Vianney often asked the children in his parish to pray for sinners. He told another priest: "If you can get the children in your parish to join you in praying for these poor sinners, in offerings sacrifices for them, real wonders will take place. O, my friend, how many amazing stories I could tell you of what the little ones at my parish have accomplished through their prayers and sufferings."

St. John Vianney said he could not impress enough on people the importance of these things. God is so good and so merciful to those He has made. When people, especially children, beg Him in prayer for a certain grace, then add suffering or sacrifice to the prayer, what can He do but grant what is asked of Him?

Every time we go to Confession, let us remember in our prayers to pray for sinners who need to go to Confession. St. Augustine's mother prayed for him for many years, but he finally returned to the Catholic Church and became a great saint.

The Sacrament of Penance, the opportunity to be forgiven by God of our sins, is so great that priests will hear confessions from anyone at almost any time. The Church teaches that priests must encourage the people to come to the Sacrament of Penance and must make themselves available to hear confessions each time a person reasonably asks for it.

When a priest is in the confessional box, ready to hear confessions, he is like the Good Shepherd looking for his sheep, as in the story Jesus told. As the priest waits for people to come to confession, the priest is like the father waiting for his son in the story Jesus told of the Prodigal Son. The priest is like the Good Samaritan in the story Jesus told. The Good Samaritan came along and found a man half dead, beaten by robbers, lying in the road. The Good Samaritan took care of him, bound up his wounds and took him to safety in an inn. In the same way, the priest is ready to help bind up the wounds of sin on our souls. He wants to heal our souls in the name of Jesus Christ, and take us back to safety in the loving arms of Holy Mother Church.

St. John Vianney, wise director of souls, pray for us.
St. John Vianney, who did help so many in the way of virtue, pray for us.

Fill in the Blank

1. Before we enter the confessional, we should ask the __Holy Spirit__ to help us.

2. We should start our confession by making the Sign of the __Cross__.

3. We should say, "Bless me, Father, for I have __sinned__.

4. We must start our confession by telling __how long__ it has been since our last confession.

5. We are required to confess all __mortal__ sins, and their __number__.

6. If we deliberately not confess a mortal sin, we commit a sin of __sacrilege__.

7. If we have deliberately not confessed a mortal sin, we may not receive Holy __Communion__

8. If we cannot remember the exact number of times we have committed a mortal sin, we must give the number as __close__ as possible.

9. The priest waits in the confessional like the __father__ waits, looking for his son to return.

10. St. John Vianney asked the __children__ in his parish to pray for poor sinners.

To make a good confession, we must confess all our mortal sins, being sure to give the number of times that we have committed the sins. The Church encourages us to confess our venial sins as well, though it is not necessary to confess any of them.

We should end our confession with the words: "For these and for all the sins of my past life, I humbly ask pardon, penance, and absolution." This is a traditional ending. Our catechism tells us to end our confession by saying: "I am sorry for these and all the sins of my past life." This is a popular shorter ending.

Once the penitent has finished confessing his sins, it is not unusual for the priest to ask a question. Sometimes when children go to confession, they do not speak clearly or loudly enough, and the priest needs to ask a question. Sometimes a priest is not clear about a sin, and may ask a question about it. It is important to be truthful and answer the questions as accurately as possible.

Sometimes a priest will give advice about how to avoid committing that sin again. We must listen to the priest very carefully.

Then the priest gives a penance. The penance is usually prayers, such as saying some Our Fathers or some Hail Marys. Sometimes the priest will tell us to say a decade of the Rosary or make a Stations of the Cross. Sometimes the priest may say to do something special for a member of our family. For example, if we have hurt a brother or a sister, the priest may tell us to do something to make up for our sin.

Be sure that you listen carefully to the penance, and that you repeat it silently so that you will not forget it. After the priest tells us our penance, we should say "Yes, Father," so that the priest knows that we heard him and we are agreeing to do the penance.

It is important to be grateful that we have received a penance. After all, the penance is usually very small in comparison to the sins we have committed.

St. John Vianney heard a number of sinners' confessions as they came to kneel in the confessional at Ars, France. Father heard confessions in nearby parishes also, and eventually those people came to see Father Vianney in Ars. The visits from those from other times meant Father was hearing confessions for hours every day. Catherine, who helped Father in the church, said one day, "You are making our little church famous, Father. There have never been so many people coming here for Confession before!"

People came and stood in lines a long time to hear advice and counseling from Father Vianney in Confession. People recognized "great" sinners who had not been to confession in many years.

Father told those in his parish that, with the exception of the Mass, "There is no prayer which touches the Heart of God more effectively than the prayers of the young and innocent. O, if boys and girls could only know what power they have to do good for souls… to win the most wonderful graces for themselves and for others."

Father Vianney told the people to have the children pray for the sinners who live in the area of the parish. The prayers of the children would help convert the sinners. "If you can get the little ones to pray and make sacrifices for the sinners in this town," Father said, "and if you can get to make sacrifices too, how much easier it will be to turn our village into a holy place." When they asked if the children should say any special prayer, he said, "Ask the children to say just one Hail Mary each day for the conversion of the people in our parish."

Father Vianney reported that several weeks after the children started their prayers and sacrifices for the conversion of sinners in the parish, certain farmers who usually missed Mass on Sundays started coming to Mass. Others who did servile work on Sunday, began to change their habits. Several of the young girls who were spending time in dancing and going to parties began to change their lives. Several of the men gave up drinking and gambling in the four taverns in the town. Some of the taverns owners actually complained!

St. John Vianney, confessor of children, pray for us.

Fill in the Blank

1. When we confess our mortal sins, we must give the _number_ of times.

2. "For these and for all the sins of my _past_ life, I humbly ask pardon, penance, and absolution."

3. Sometimes the priest asks _question_ after the person has confessed his sins.

4. Children should be sure to speak _clearly_ and loudly enough for the priest to hear.

5. Sometimes a priest will give _advice_ about how to avoid committing that sin again.

6. We must _commfes_ to the priest very carefully.

7. The penance the priest gives us is usually _prayers_.

8. After the priest gives us our penance, we should say "Yes, Father," so the priest knows that we have _heard_ to do the penance.

9. We should be _grateful_ that we have a penance to do.

10. The penance is very small in comparison to the _sins_ we have committed.

We prepare for our confession by examining our conscience, by reviewing the Ten Commandments and thinking about ours sins. We pray to the Holy Spirit to help us remember our sins. We look at Jesus on the Cross and reflect about how much we do not want to offend Him.

In the confessional, we tell the priest how long it has been since our last confession. Then we tell the priest all of our mortal sins and how many times we committed these sins. Then we may tell the priest some or all of our venial sins, and the number of times we committed them.

We should end our confession by saying, "I am sorry for these and for all the sins of my past life, and I ask penance, pardon, and absolution." We can say the short form: "I am sorry for these and all the sins of my past life." Then we listen to the priest if he asks us any questions, and we must answer him truthfully and accurately. We listen if the priest gives us any advice or counseling, like St. John Vianney did.

Then the priest will give us our penance. We must listen carefully so we can say the penance after we leave the confessional. The penance is usually several prayers, the Our Father, the Hail Mary, a decade of the Rosary, or perhaps a reading from the Bible.

Then the priest will ask us to say a good Act of Contrition. We must say the Act of Contrition quietly, but in a tone he can hear. This should be a very sincere prayer because Jesus is listening in the confessional. Jesus is listening for us to say we are sorry for our sins.

As we are saying the Act of Contrition, we should be speaking to God from our hearts. The first line of the Act of Contrition is: "O my God, I am heartily sorry for having offended Thee." This means that with all our heart, we are truly sorry we have sinned against our Loving God.

We go on to say that we "detest all our sins." This means we hate our sins, and we do not want to commit them again. Then we say that we detest our sins because we fear the just punishment of God, or because of the loss of Heaven and the pains of Hell. In other words, we know that because of our sins, especially if they are mortal, we could lose eternal life in Heaven and may even suffer eternity in Hell.

"But most of all, I detest my sins because they offend Thee, my God." This is the overwhelming reason why we are sorry for our sins. We know that we have offended God Who made us and Who loves us beyond all human understanding!

Then we tell Jesus in our Act of Contrition: "You are all good and deserving of all my love." By this statement in our Act of Contrition, we are acknowledging the Perfect Goodness of God, and that He deserves our total loving commitment. He is deserving of all our love, and not deserving of our disobedience to His Commandments!

"I firmly resolve with the help of Thy grace to confess my sins, to do penance, and to amend my life." Another form of this final line of the Act of Contrition is: "I firmly resolve with the help of Thy grace to sin no more and to avoid the near occasions of sin."

Thus we end our Act of Contrition by saying that we resolve, that we are determined, that we promise, that we will try our best that, with God's help through the Sacraments, we intend to sin no more, to avoid the near occasions of sin, and to amend our lives.

After we say the Act of Contrition, the priest will say the words of absolution, absolving us from our sins in the name of the Father, the Son, and the Holy Spirit.

When we leave the confessional, the first thing we should do is kneel down in church and say the prayers the priest gave us for our penance.

After confession, we want to truly try during the next week or two weeks before the next confession to not commit those sins again. It is not enough to say we are sorry in confession, and to say we are sorry because God is so good to us. Actions speak louder than words. Our actions must be to avoid the occasions of sin and to work very hard, with determination, not to commit these sins again.

God knows we are weak, and that it is a constant struggle, but we must persevere and keep up the struggle! St. Paul wrote in his letters to the people in the different churches that life is like a race. We need to keep running, keep jumping over the hurdles or obstacles. We need to persevere and keep at it. The prize is eternal life.

St. John Vianney, pastor of conversions, pray for us.

Matching

_7_ 1. Preparation for confession	1. How long it's been since my last confession
_10_ 2. "Bless me, Father, for I have sinned."	2. We should confess venial sins
_1_ 3. Number of weeks or months	3. We have committed mortal sin
_3_ 4. We must say how many times	4. Before the priest gives absolution
_2_ 5. If no mortal sins to confess	5. The way we should end our confession
_5_ 6. "For all the sins of my past life, I am very sorry"	6. Right after leaving confession
_9_ 7. Listen to the priest	7. Examination of conscience
_4_ 8. The Act of Contrition	8. Once a month or even more often
_6_ 9. Do penance priest gives	9. While he gives advice
_8_ 10. Frequent confession	10. How we begin our confession

Do you remember about two lessons back we learned about two kinds of punishment due to sin? We discussed eternal punishment in Hell for those who die in mortal sin. We also discussed temporal punishment, which we must work on in this world or we will need to suffer in Purgatory for a time. We can reduce the temporal punishment due in this world by taking up our cross, saying prayers, doing acts of charity, and attending Mass.

We begin this week with a remarkable and fascinating topic: indulgences. An indulgence is the remission granted by the Church of the temporal punishment due to sins already forgiven.

Many people today have forgotten about indulgences. Yet those who gain indulgences lessen the time they must spend in the fires of Purgatory for punishment still due to sins we have committed. Indulgences are based on ways the Church has decided for us to remove the temporal punishment due to sin. Because they are the result of the Church's decision, rather than our own, they merit more than our own ideas for remitting sin.

Recall that two things happen when we sin: 1) we take on guilt, and 2) we deserve to be punished. The Sacrament of Penance removes all the guilt due to sin. When we have made a good confession, all of the guilt and the eternal punishment that was due to mortal sin is removed. However, temporal punishment is still due our forgiven mortal and venial sins! Here the Church is more generous than we can imagine.

The Church has a treasure-trove of priceless gifts. It is called the Spiritual Treasury of the Church. Indulgences come from the Spiritual Treasury of infinite satisfaction merited by Jesus Christ Himself, and the superabundant satisfaction of the Blessed Mother and the saints.

Pope Paul VI wrote that indulgences are "The remission before God of the temporal punishment due to sins forgiven as far as their guilt is concerned, …[the Church] authoritatively dispenses and applies the treasury of satisfaction won by Christ and the saints" (Pope Paul VI, *Apostolic Constitution on Indulgences*).

What was Pope Paul VI saying? He was telling us the Church dispenses from her spiritual treasury what we need in order to enter more fully into God's presence. We see that the saints also are included in God's plan, but how?

The *Catechism of the Catholic Church* tells us, "In the communion of saints, 'a perennial link of charity exists between the faithful who have already reached their Heavenly home, those who are expiating their sins in purgatory, and those who are still pilgrims on earth. Between them there is, too, an abundant exchange of all good things'" (n. 1475).

We recall what we learned about the Mystical Body of Christ, which consists of all the saints in Heaven, those in Purgatory, and those on earth. Known as the Church Triumphant, the Church Suffering, and the Church Militant, all three parts of the Church are mystically joined together. While we are still on earth, we need and receive help from the souls in Heaven.

The *Catechism* continues, "In this wonderful exchange, the holiness of one profits others, well beyond the harm that the sin of one could cause others. Thus recourse to the communion of saints lets the contrite sinner be more promptly and efficaciously purified of the punishments for sin" (Ibid).

The Church is teaching here that holiness of individual members of the Church can help others who are members of the Church. We can pray for the souls in Purgatory to help them lessen their time there, and the souls in Heaven can pray for us to lessen our temporal punishment due to sin.

Many people today forget about praying for the souls in Purgatory. This is very sad because these are people who may be relatives we do not know about, people in our family who died long ago and are still suffering. St. John Chrysostom wrote: "Let us help and commemorate them [the souls in Purgatory]. If Job's sons were purified by their father's sacrifice, why would we doubt that our offerings for the dead bring them some consolation? Let us not hesitate to help those who have died and to offer our prayers for them" (Ibid. n. 1032).

St. John Vianney, enlightened by the light of Heaven,
pray for us.

St. John Vianney, devoted servant of the Immaculate Heart of Mary,
pray for us.

Fill in the Blank

1. An indulgence is the ___remission___ of the temporal punishment due to forgiven sins.

2. Indulgences are granted by the ___Church___.

3. Two things happen when we sin. We incur ___guilt___ and ___Punishment___.

4. Confession removes the ___guilt___ of our sins.

5. After Confession, ___temporal___ punishment is still due our forgiven sins.

6. The Church has a Spiritual ___treasury___.

7. Pope ___Paul___ ___VI___ wrote *Apostolic Constitution on Indulgences.*

8. The Church on Earth is known as the Church ___Militant___.

9. The Church in Purgatory is known as the Church ___Suffering___.

10. The Church in Heaven is known as the Church ___triumphant___.

An indulgence is the remission granted by the Church of the temporal punishment due to sins already forgiven.

There are two kinds of indulgences, plenary and partial. A plenary indulgence is the remission of *all* temporal punishment due to sin. What does "temporal" mean? It comes from the Latin word for "time." The opposite of time is eternity. Do not forget that if one dies in mortal sin, the punishment is *eternal* suffering and *eternal* separation from God.

Sacramental Confession removes this barrier and restores us to full communion with Our Lord. What still remains, however are the wounds left by our sins. Temporal punishment is God's remedy for healing those wounds. A plenary indulgence removes all of the temporal punishment still due to sins forgiven. With a plenary indulgence just earned, a person could go directly to Heaven without spending time in Purgatory. Of course, only God knows the human heart, and a person must have truly earned the indulgence with an honest heart.

A partial indulgence removes *some* of the punishment still due our sins after they have been forgiven in Sacramental Confession. We have the assurance that our Mother, the Holy Church, takes care of all our needs, and can be relied upon for all the help we need to obtain Heaven.

Only Catholics can gain indulgences. This is because indulgences are given by the Church usually in fulfilling the conditions of receiving the Sacrament of Penance and the Sacrament of the Holy Eucharist. Certain conditions must be fulfilled. There must be sorrow and repenting of sin, there must be confession of sin, and there must be a willingness to do penance.

The Church gives indulgences because of the words of Our Lord to St. Peter, the first Pope: "I will give to thee the keys of the kingdom of Heaven; and whatsoever thou shalt bind on earth shall be bound also in Heaven; and whatsoever thou shalt loose on earth, shall be loosed also in Heaven" (Mt. 16:19). The word "whatsoever" means that the Church, as inspired by the Holy Spirit, can retain or "loose" the punishment due to sin.

The Pope has the right to dispense the treasures of the Church. The Treasury of the Church is made up of the merits of Jesus Christ and the merits from the superabundant penances of the Blessed Virgin Mary and of the saints. The saints, by their sufferings and martyrdoms, earned a greater atonement of merits or satisfactions than they needed to expiate for their own sins. Thus the Church has a spiritual bank, a spiritual fund of merits and satisfactions which she can dispense to whom she wills.

St. John Vianney spoke about sinners who were converted because of the graces earned by others. Father Vianney earned graces for sinners due to sleepless nights because of visits from the devil! The devil would come and make constant scratching noises. He would come and shake his room! As written in *The Curé of Ars,* published by TAN Publishers, Father's bedroom "rose and fell as though it were the desk of a ship at sea. The walls creaked and groaned. Downstairs there were the thunderous blows on the front door, the rattling of the handle, the tugging at the lock."

For months, the devil tormented Father Vianney, especially at night to keep him awake. He finally realized what was happening when no one else heard the noises he heard. "It's the devil and his angels who are making this commotion. They're angry because I've been trying to convert my parish … now they want to frighten me so that I'll go away from Ars…" Father's terror faded as he realized that whenever the devil tormented him, it was a sign that a great sinner would be coming to make his Confession the next day (pp. 100 to 106).

Father Vianney's sufferings at the hands of the devil make the point that we can help each other in the Mystical Body of Christ. We can offer up our sufferings, our aches and pains, our discomforts, for the conversion of sinners. We can also do certain penances and earn indulgences for ourselves and those in Purgatory. We cannot gain indulgences for other living persons, however.

St. John Vianney, fighter of demons, pray for us.
St. John Vianney, compassionate toward sinners, pray for us.

Fill in the Blank

1. An indulgence is the remission granted by the Church of the
   temporal _Punishment_ due to sins already forgiven.

2. There are two kinds of indulgences: _Plenary_ and
   Partial.

3. If one dies in mortal sin, the punishment is _eternal_ suffering and separation from God.

4. Only _God_ knows for sure when an indulgence is actually gained because only He knows the human heart.

5. _Catholics_ alone can gain indulgences.

6. To gain indulgences, there must be _Confeson_ of sin.

7. The Church gives indulgences because of the words of Our Lord to _St. Peter_.

8. "I will give to thee the _keys_ of the kingdom of Heaven; and _whatsoever_ thou shalt bind on earth shall be bound also in Heaven."

9. The Church can retain or _loose_ the punishment due to sin.

10. The _treasury_ of the Church is made up of the infinite merits of Jesus Christ as well as superabundant satisfaction of the Blessed Mother and the saints.

The Church, by means of indulgences, remits the temporal punishment due to sins already forgiven. A plenary indulgence remits all the temporal punishment due to sin. A partial indulgence remits part of the temporal punishment due to sin.

The Church remits the temporal punishment due to sin by applying from her Spiritual Treasury part of the infinite merits and satisfaction for sin earned by Jesus Christ and His sufferings and death on the Cross. The Blessed Virgin Mary and the saints also have earned merits which are in the Spiritual Treasury. They all earned more merits than were necessary for their own salvation, which were added to the Treasury to help other members of the Church.

The superabundant satisfaction of the Blessed Mother and of the saints is that which they gained during their lifetime, and often by their martyrdoms. They gained more merits or satisfactions than they needed for themselves. The Church dispenses or applies these merits from the Spiritual Treasury to those who are members of the Church and who fulfill certain conditions.

We have seen that our sins must have a penalty either on earth or in Purgatory, even after they have been forgiven in Sacramental Confession. We also have seen that there is a Treasury of merits the Church provides as the means to obtain indulgences. That treasury is drawn from the infinite merits of Jesus Christ and the superabundant merits of the Blessed Mother and the saints. We ourselves can add to that treasury whenever we perform good works out of love for God and neighbor.

St. Thomas Aquinas, Doctor of the Church, said that the "effect of Sacramental absolution is the removal of a man's guilt… But when a person gains an indulgence, he pays the penalty he owes for his faults out of the common stock of the Church's goods."

The Church has the power to set down the rules for indulgences. From about the year 1063 under Pope Alexander II, indulgences were measured in days or years. The first plenary indulgences were granted to those fighting against the enemies of the Church in Spain, and later to the Crusaders who were fighting to keep the Holy Land from the enemies of the Church.

Following the Second Vatican Council (1962-1965), satisfaction for sin or indulgences are not measured in days or years but according to the extent of love of God and neighbor with which a work is performed.

We should think about gaining indulgences for ourselves and especially for the souls in Purgatory. Remember that the First Great Commandment is to love God, and the Second Great Commandment is to love our neighbor as ourselves. Certainly loving the suffering souls in Purgatory by earning indulgences for them is a great work of mercy.

The following commentary is based on *Read Me or Rue It*, a pamphlet on Purgatory, by Father Paul O'Sullivan, published by TAN Publishers.

When we read in the Gospel the words which we expect to hear on Judgment Day, "For I was hungry and you gave me to eat, I was thirsty, and you gave me to drink," we think about helping our neighbors in this world. However, the suffering souls in Purgatory are part of the Mystical Body of Christ, and we must not forget them in our works of mercy. We can earn indulgences only for ourselves and for the souls in Purgatory.

We have a duty to help others, especially those in most need. While we think about the poor and the sick primarily, certainly those in Purgatory are in urgent need. They are suffering the intense fires of Purgatory. God's justice demands that they suffer in Purgatory, yet He and the Church have given us on earth the possibility of lessening their time of sufferings. We can shorten their time of sufferings by our indulgenced prayers and good works.

We can be assured that the holy souls in Purgatory who are released to eternal glory will not forget us when they are in Heaven. They will have a great desire to pray for those who helped them escape the fires! We can be sure that they will be praying for us from Heaven. St. Catherine of Bologna once said, "I received many and very great favors from the Saints, but still greater favors from the Holy Souls."

St. Gertrude, on her deathbed, said that Our Lord Himself appeared to her and told her that "in exchange for all she had done for the Holy Souls, He would take her straight to Heaven, and would multiply a hundredfold all her merits" (p.21).

St. Gertrude, lover of the Holy Souls, pray for us.
St. Gertrude, strong protector of all who venerate you, pray for us.

Fill in the Blank

1. The Church, by means of _indulgences_ remits the temporal punishment due to sin.
2. The Church dispenses the merits which are in the Spiritual _treasury_ of the Church.
3. Infinite merits were earned by _Jesus Christ_
4. The Church dispenses the superabundant _merits_ earned by the Blessed Mother and the saints.
5. Our sins must have a penalty either on earth or in _Purgatory_.
6. _St. Thomas_ said that "when a person gains an indulgence, he pays the penalty he owes for his faults."
7. The _Church_ has the power to set down the rules for indulgences.
8. Pope _Alexander_ granted plenary indulgences to those fighting against the enemies of the Church.
9. The _Crusaders_ were fighting to keep the Holy Land from the enemies of the Church.
10. Following the Second Vatican Council, indulgences are not _measured_ in days or years.

Many people do not realize what a great Spiritual Treasury the Catholic Church has, a Treasury filled with indulgences to give us remission of the temporal punishment due to sin. As Father Paul O'Sullivan said, "God in His infinite mercy and compassion offers us a most wonderful and easy means for lessening or canceling our Purgatory. He offers us most abundant Indulgences in exchange of some small act of devotion" (*How to Avoid Purgatory*, p. 19).

When the Blessed Mother appeared to St. Catherine Labouré in France, she appeared with bright rays of light streaming out from her fingers. Some of her fingers did not have rays of light. The Blessed Mother said that the rays represented graces she was sending to people to help them, but that the fingers without rays represented graces to give but were not requested. Let us take advantage of the indulgences which the Church has to help us obtain eternal life in Heaven.

To gain an indulgence, we must be in the state of grace. Anyone living in mortal sin cannot obtain any graces or benefits or indulgences. Just as a dead body cannot benefit from medicine, likewise a dead soul cannot benefit from spiritual medicine.

Anyone who wants an indulgence must specifically have the intention of fulfilling the requirements and have the intention of gaining the indulgence. The person must perform the specific works or say the prayers as required by the Church to obtain the indulgence. The person also must pray for the intentions of the Pope.

We cannot gain indulgences for other living persons, but we can gain indulgences for anyone in Purgatory. The Church teaches that only we ourselves and the souls in Purgatory can benefit from indulgenced works. Recall that the souls in Purgatory know they are saved but they cannot enter God's presence until they are purified of the effects of their sins. We have seen that the poor souls have no way to pray for themselves; they must rely upon our prayers and sacrifices to help them reach Heaven. They are very grateful for our prayers and sacrifices for them.

Many Catholics do not realize the magnificent benefits in gaining indulgences. It is truly incredible that we can obtain a plenary indulgence which remits *all* of the punishment due to sin. If we should die after obtaining a plenary indulgence, we would go straight to Heaven!

When we realize the gravity of sin and its consequences, we are more apt to seek and perform indulgenced works. Imagine a large box that is closed but unlatched. Inside the box are contained the most beautiful sparkling gems and rare jewels filled all the way to the top. They are worth a priceless fortune. Now imagine that people know it is there, but they do not open the box. That is what it is like when we do not take advantage of indulgences that the Church offers. The Church holds a treasury of gifts of satisfaction for sin but few realize it.

The external conditions for gaining a plenary indulgence are that we must receive Sacramental Confession and Holy Communion within eight days of the works being performed for the indulgence. Also, we must include praying one Our Father, one Hail Mary, and one Glory Be for the intentions of the Holy Father. If any one of these conditions is not satisfied, the indulgence is only partial. One of the best reasons for going to confession often, even once a week, is because it is one of the conditions for earning indulgences.

Reading the Bible for fifteen minutes, saying the Rosary, and making the Stations of the Cross are just a few of the devotions for gaining a plenary indulgence. In the past, a specific number of days were applied to indulgenced prayers or works. While the number of days are not specific any longer, many Catholics perform the indulgenced work or say the prayers, and ask for the traditional remission of days. Just saying the ejaculation, "Sacred Heart of Jesus, I place my trust in Thee," gave 300 days indulgence. The "days" were a period of time referring to indulgenced acts of reparation during the Middle Ages.

John goes to confession on Saturday. Sunday morning before Mass, he goes to Church where he makes the Stations of the Cross around the Church. He receives Holy Communion and prays for the intentions of the Holy Father. John has fulfilled the conditions to gain a plenary indulgence. One Sacramental confession suffices for eight days before or after one wishes to accomplish an indulgence. Once we understand sin and its consequences, we should be very eager to gain indulgences.

St. Philomena, patron for St. John Vianney, pray for us.

True (T) or False (F)

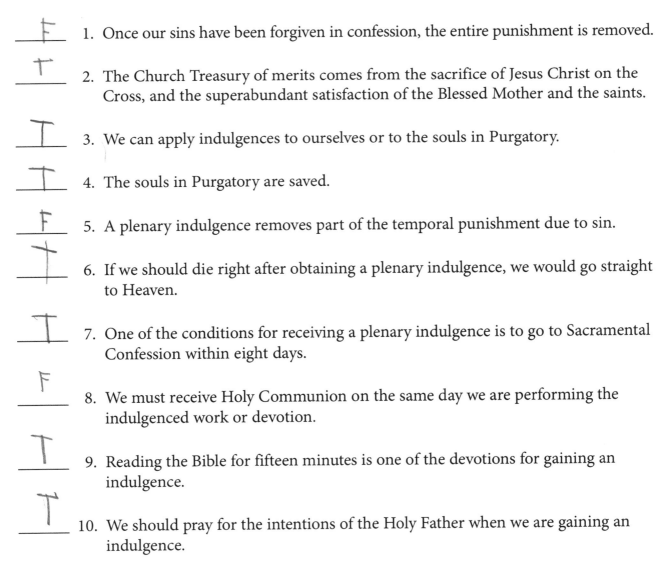

____F____ 1. Once our sins have been forgiven in confession, the entire punishment is removed.

____T____ 2. The Church Treasury of merits comes from the sacrifice of Jesus Christ on the Cross, and the superabundant satisfaction of the Blessed Mother and the saints.

____T____ 3. We can apply indulgences to ourselves or to the souls in Purgatory.

____T____ 4. The souls in Purgatory are saved.

____F____ 5. A plenary indulgence removes part of the temporal punishment due to sin.

____T____ 6. If we should die right after obtaining a plenary indulgence, we would go straight to Heaven.

____T____ 7. One of the conditions for receiving a plenary indulgence is to go to Sacramental Confession within eight days.

____F____ 8. We must receive Holy Communion on the same day we are performing the indulgenced work or devotion.

____T____ 9. Reading the Bible for fifteen minutes is one of the devotions for gaining an indulgence.

____T____ 10. We should pray for the intentions of the Holy Father when we are gaining an indulgence.

Anointing of the Sick or Extreme Unction is the Sacrament which, through the anointing with blessed oil by the priest, and through his prayer, gives health and strength to the soul, and sometimes to the body, when we are in danger of death from sickness, accident, or old age.

All Catholics who have reached the age of reason and are in danger of death from sickness, accident, or old age should receive the Sacrament of Anointing of the Sick, formerly called Extreme Unction.

There are many wonderful effects from the Sacrament of Anointing of the Sick. The first effect is an increase of Sanctifying Grace. The second effect is comfort in sickness, and strength against temptation. The third effect is preparation for entrance into Heaven because this Sacrament removes venial sins, and cleanses our souls. The fourth effect is health of body when it is good for the soul.

This Sacrament takes away even mortal sin when the sick person is unconscious. However, before lapsing into unconsciousness, the person must have made an act of contrition (perfect or imperfect) after committing the mortal sin.

This Sacrament formerly was called Extreme Unction. "Extreme" refers to those who have an extreme disability or are likely to die; "unction" means oil. The *Catechism of the Catholic Church* tells us, "Over the centuries, the Anointing of the Sick was conferred more and more exclusively on those at the point of death. Because of this, it received the name 'Extreme Unction'" (n. 1512). Now, however, although those at the point of death are certainly candidates for receiving this Sacrament, the Church regards this Sacrament in a wider sense, such as when someone is very old or seriously ill.

What is the Sacrament of the Anointing of the Sick? When people are very sick, their spirits sometimes fall under the weight of their illness and they lose hope. It is a time when all they may think about is their pain. They can become exhausted and may be more vulnerable to attacks by the devil. The purpose of the Sacrament is to revive the sick person into awareness that he is not alone, God is with him. The Sacrament gives him hope and strength to carry on. Sometimes the person is healed of his sickness and his health is restored.

Because of the sin of Adam, we all suffer and die. In God's glorious plan, however, suffering and death are to be patiently endured and even embraced. Suffering is a very important means to become holy. Nothing impure can enter Heaven (Rev. 21:27). Suffering with resignation purifies the soul and makes it holy and more pleasing to God. This Sacrament enables the sick person to accept God's healing grace and not rebel against his pain and suffering.

St. Philomena, mirror of heroic virtues, pray for us.
St. Philomena, miraculously cured in prison, pray for us.

Fill in the Blank

1. The Sacrament of Extreme Unction is now called the Sacrament of the _anointing_ of the _sick_.

2. The priest anoints the sick person with blessed _oil_.

3. Through the prayer of the priest, the person's soul receives health and _strength_.

4. This Sacrament is primarily for people in danger of _death_.

5. The first effect of this Sacrament is an increase in _sanctifying grace_.

6. The second effect of this Sacrament is comfort in sickness and strength against _temptation_.

7. This Sacrament removes _venial_ sins.

8. The fourth effect sometimes is _health_ of the body.

9. This Sacrament takes away mortal sin if the person is _unconscious_ and has made an Act of Contrition (perfect or imperfect) after sinning.

10. The purpose of the Sacrament is to help the person remember that _God_ is with him.

The Sacrament of Anointing of the Sick is the Sacrament which, through the anointing with blessed oil by the priest, and through his prayer, gives health and strength to the soul, and sometimes to the body, when we are in danger of death from sickness, accident, or old age.

The blessed oil used for the anointing is olive oil that has been blessed by the bishop on Holy Thursday. As the priest anoints the sick person with the blessed oil, he prays: "Through this holy anointing, may the Lord in His love and mercy help you with the grace of the Holy Spirit." The sick person responds, "Amen." The priest says: "May the Lord, Who frees you from sin, save you and raise you up." The sick person responds, "Amen."

If we are in the situation of being in danger of death, we should prepare to receive this Sacrament as we prepare for all the Sacraments. When the priest comes, we should make a good Confession by preparing properly for the Sacrament of Penance. We also should say the prayers of the Acts of Faith, Hope, and Charity, as well as other prayers, such as the Our Father and the Hail Mary.

In addition, we should prepare to receive Jesus in the Sacrament of the Holy Eucharist. If the person is conscious, he receives three Sacraments in this order: 1) Confession, 2) Anointing of the Sick, and 3) the Holy Eucharist.

Perhaps the hardest thing for the person who is in danger of dying is to accept the will of God. This may be especially difficult for those who suffer for a period of months with such diseases as cancer. Accepting God's will is the best way for a person to prepare to receive the Sacrament of Anointing of the Sick.

A person who is seriously ill, or family members of a person who is seriously ill, should call a priest even if there is no danger of death. One of the duties of a priest is to visit the sick. Even if the priest decides not to administer this Sacrament, he may give the sick person the Sacrament of Penance and the Sacrament of the Holy Eucharist.

The Sacrament of the Anointing of the Sick gives grace and is a great consolation to those who are suffering the extraordinary pain of illness or injury. It enables them not only to bear their cross of pain and suffering, but it also makes them stronger spiritually.

The Sacrament of Anointing of the Sick increases Sanctifying Grace, and strengthens us against the temptation to despair. If we open ourselves in complete submission to God's will, He will give us the grace we need to endure and even to embrace whatever crosses He sends us. Such submission to Our Lord will gain us happiness in this life and eternal bliss forever in Heaven.

Throughout the Gospels we read many instances of Jesus healing people. He healed the sick, the deaf, the blind, the lame, even those who were possessed by the devil. In all cases, Jesus wanted their souls to be purified. In the same way, God wants us to be pure when we are ready to enter into His presence when our lives here on earth are complete.

If a person dies suddenly, a priest should be called because the priest is allowed to give absolution and to give the Sacrament of Anointing of the Sick. This means that even though a person has died, since no one is sure when the soul leaves the body, the soul may still be present and he would receive the benefits of the Sacrament. If there is any doubt as to whether the sick person has reached the age of reason, or is dangerously ill, or is dead, the Sacrament of Anointing of the Sick is to be administered.

Priests are always ready to serve. On a very cold night in April of 1912, the ocean liner Titanic, while on her way to New York, hit an iceberg and sank in the North Atlantic Ocean, killing over one thousand people. A priest aboard had spent his last hours administering the Sacraments of Penance, the Holy Eucharist, and Anointing of the Sick. Eventually, he himself was plunged into the icy ocean. No one knows how many people he helped, but each one will be eternally grateful to him and to God. Thanks to him, everyone he helped in this way most certainly died a happy death.

St. Joseph, patron of a happy death, pray for us.
St. Joseph, loving foster-father of Jesus, pray for us.

Fill in the Blank

1. The Sacrament of Anointing of the Sick is the Sacrament which through the anointing with blessed oil by the priest, and through his __Prayers__, gives health and strength to the __Soul__, and sometimes to the body, when we are in danger of __death__ from sickness, accident or old age.

2. We should prepare for the Sacrament of Anointing of the Sick by making a good __Confession__.

3. We should prepare for this Sacrament by saying Acts of __faith__, __Hope__, and __charity__.

4. Family members should call a priest when someone is seriously __ill__, even if he is not in danger of death.

5. If a person dies suddenly, the priest is allowed to give __absolution__ and the Sacrament of Anointing of the Sick.

6. Priests are always ready to __serve__.

7. This Sacrament gives grace and is a great __consolation__ to those who are suffering the extraordinary pain of sickness or injury.

8. Throughout the Gospels, we read many instances of Jesus __healing__ people.

9. This Sacrament strengthens sick people against the temptation to __sin__.

10. God will give us the grace to endure and even to __bear__ the crosses He sends us.

Holy Orders is the Sacrament through which men receive the power and grace to perform the sacred duties of bishops, priests, and deacons.

For a man to receive the Sacrament of Holy Orders worthily, it is necessary that he be in the state of grace, and be of excellent character. Secondly, he must be of the age and have the education that the Church requires. Thirdly, the man must have the intention of devoting the rest of his life to the priesthood or diaconate. Fourthly, the bishop must call the man to the Sacrament of Holy Orders. It is the bishop who ordains a man through the Sacrament of Holy Orders.

The effects of the Sacrament of Holy Orders are first, to increase Sanctifying Grace. The second effect is to give Sacramental Grace which gives the priest or deacon God's constant help as he carries out his vocation.

The third effect of the Sacrament of Holy Orders is that it gives the soul a special mark or character which lasts forever. For priests and bishops this character is a special sharing in the priesthood of Jesus Christ. At a lower level of Holy Orders, men who become deacons receive the imposition of hands "not unto the priesthood, but unto the ministry." (CCC 1569). The Sacrament of Holy Orders also marks deacons with an indelible character, but not in the sharing of the priesthood. The deacon's permanent mark "configures" or shapes them to Jesus Christ in service to the bishop and priest. While the priest and bishop are the two degrees of participation in the priesthood of Christ, the deacon's role is to serve the bishop and priest (CCC 1570).

When the bishop lays his hands on the heads of the men who have studied and prepared to receive and now request the Sacrament of Holy Orders, they receive the grace and spiritual power to teach, to sanctify, and to rule the people of God. From the time of his Ordination, each bishop, priest, and deacon is marked with a special character, like the characters of the Sacraments of Baptism and Confirmation.

A priest receives special powers that no one else in the world has. *The priest has the power to change ordinary bread and wine into the Body and Blood of Jesus Christ.* He also has the power to absolve sins in the Sacrament of Penance, and to anoint the sick in the Sacrament of the Anointing of the Sick. Priests and deacons also witness marriages and perform baptisms.

Jesus Christ Himself ordained the very first bishops. All bishops and priests, throughout the ages of the Church, can be traced in an unbroken line all the way back to the twelve original Apostles. There are hundreds of bishops in the world today, many serving as heads of dioceses.

A man who has a vocation to the priesthood has been called by God to serve His Church in a supernatural way. Only a priest has the power to call Jesus Christ down on the altar; only a priest has the power to forgive sins. Because priests are so special, they must be carefully chosen. Each candidate to the priesthood must have been baptized, be morally upright, and in the state of grace. The candidate must be at least twenty-five years old, have the prescribed educational studies in the seminary, and be ready to give the rest of his life completely to the Church.

How does a young man know he has been called to become a priest? The first requirement is a sincere desire to become a priest. He also must be living a good and virtuous life, be in good health, and be of at least average intelligence. If a man is not sure if he is being called to the priesthood, he should pray and seek good spiritual direction. Only God knows how many young men have been called to serve Him in this very special way. As in all things, we must do God's will to be truly happy and find peace.

The stories of how men have become priests give an idea of how God works in lives of young men. Fr. Grogan, now in his middle seventies, has served the poor his entire life. Father Grogan says he knew he wanted to be a priest when he was seven years old. He always felt at home on the altar serving as an altar boy. His parents and the priests he served always knew he had a vocation. No one was surprised when he entered the seminary right out of high school. Father Grogan was ordained in his late twenties and has served God and His Church for the past fifty years. He now lives and works among the poor in New York City.

The majority of priests have been altar boys. They learn the prayers of the priest, and serve Mass more than once a week. They grow up getting up early and not sleeping late. They feel comfortable and even come to love serving Mass. On the other hand, some men enter professional lives, for instance as salesmen or lawyers, and find that success and money does not make them happy. God seems to direct them to daily Mass, and they start finding happiness there instead of in the world.

As we have seen, each of the Sacraments carries a special Sacramental grace. The Sacrament of Holy Orders gives unique graces that enable the priest to carry out the sometimes-difficult duties of the priesthood. Priests belong completely to God and the people. Just like Christ, their lives are totally sacrificial. From offering Mass for the people every day, to hearing confessions whenever they are asked, to performing marriages and baptisms, to teaching and preaching, to giving the Sacrament of the Anointing of the Sick, their time is not their own. The Sacramental graces of Holy Orders enable the priest to be always ready to serve and to be completely open to the people and their spiritual needs.

St. Augustine of Canterbury, great priest and Apostle of England, pray for us.
St. Dominic, priest and preacher of the Gospel, pray for us.

Fill in the Blank

1. For a man to receive the Sacrament of Holy Orders worthily, he must be in the state of _grace_.

2. The candidate to the priesthood must have the _education_ that the Church requires.

3. The candidate to the priesthood must have the intention of devoting the _rest of his life_ to the priesthood.

4. The _bishop_ must call the candidate to the Sacrament of Holy Orders.

5. It is the _bishop_ who ordains a man in the Sacrament of Holy Orders.

6. The first effect of the Sacrament of Holy Orders is to increase _Sanctifying_ Grace.

7. The second effect of Holy Orders is to give _Sacramental_ Grace to help the priest as he carries out his vocation.

8. The _Priesthood_ is a special mark which lasts forever, and gives the priest _special_ powers.

9. All bishops and priests can be traced in an unbroken line all the way back to the original _apostle_.

10. Holy Orders is the Sacrament through which men receive the _grace_ and _powers_ to perform the sacred duties of bishops, priests, and deacons.

Holy Orders is the Sacrament through which men receive the power and grace to perform the sacred duties of bishops, priests, and deacons of the Church. The effects of the Sacrament of Holy Orders are first, an increase in Sanctifying Grace, second, Sacramental Grace to help the man ordained perform the duties of the vocation, and third, a lasting character which is a sharing in the priesthood of Christ and gives special supernatural powers.

Priests serve God in a great variety of ways. There are missionary priests who go to the far corners of the world to serve the poor and teach the Catholic Faith. There are diocesan priests who serve the pastoral needs of the people in local churches throughout the world. Diocesan priests are the priests with whom we are most familiar. There are many religious orders of priests, each with a different ministry. Some of the largest are the Franciscans, Dominicans, and Benedictines. There are priests who spend their lives behind the walls of an abbey praying for the needs of the world. There are some new apostolates for priests, such as the Fatima Family Apostolate, Priests for Life, and the priests serving the Catholic television apostolate EWTN. Although there are many different kinds of work for priests, they all have the same gifts and graces of the Sacrament.

We should show reverence to all priests. Why? Priests are especially deserving of our highest respect. Their consecrated hands hold the sacred Host; their souls have the sacred character of the

priesthood; they will be priests forever. All priests are special, but some stand out among their brother priests more than others for their piety and selfless charity. Here is the story of one such priest.

Far out in the Pacific Ocean lies a beautiful paradise called the Hawaiian Islands. Among those islands, one stands out. Molokai is a particularly beautiful jewel-like island filled with lush tropical foliage and exquisitely lovely multi-colored flowers. In May of 1873, Fr. Damien, a young priest, went to this tropical paradise. Father went to Molokai because he had been hearing about the terrible plight of the lepers who were forced to live out their lives in the isolation of this small scenic island. Leprosy had plagued some of the Hawaiian people for many years. Molokai became their prison. No one wanted the lepers to communicate their horrible disease to others. Even the few doctors who ventured to the island feared touching them.

At first, Fr. Damien kept his distance from these poor people. Their disease was not only very contagious; it was unbearably repulsive. "Many a time," he wrote as he recalled these first days, "in fulfilling my priestly duties at the lepers' homes, I have been obliged, not only to close my nostrils, but to remain outside to breathe fresh air. To counteract the bad smell, I got myself accustomed to the use of tobacco. The smell of the pipe preserved me somewhat from carrying in my clothes the obnoxious odor of our lepers."

Fr. Damien was a very holy priest who was deeply conscious of not only the wretched agony of the Hawaiian peoples' disease, but of their isolation from the rest of humanity. Because they were so weak from their disease, they lived in unkempt, fetid grass shacks that did little to shelter them from the cold stormy nights. Many were unable to obtain food because they were either too weak or were refused help because of their disease. Their Hawaiian brethren treated them worse than animals. Fr. Damien wanted more than anything to give them back the dignity of their God-given humanity. The first thing he did was see to it that they had proper dwellings; he built many wooden houses with his own hands. He saw to it that their bodies were properly covered and fed. Soon Father made the decision to begin to treat the poor people with the dignity every human deserves. He began to treat their wounds with his own hands, to touch their tongues when he gave them Holy Communion and to minister to them. It was inevitable that he himself would contract the dreadful disease, and eventually he did. In his daily journal, he wrote, "I make myself a leper with the lepers to gain all to Jesus Christ. That is why, in preaching, I say 'we lepers'; not, 'my brethren....'"

More than anything, the lepers needed food for their souls. Father Damien built a Church, St. Philomena's, with his own hands and celebrated the Holy Sacrifice of the Mass with so many in attendance everyone could not fit inside the Church. He heard confessions and anointed their rotting bodies in order to prepare them for death. The disposition of these poor isolated lepers quickly rose from despair to hope. Now they had a priest to give them Holy Communion, hear their confessions, and give them the last Sacraments when the disease took their lives.

Some weeks before his death, leprosy had so ravaged Father Damien's body that he could no longer speak. He finally received his much deserved rest. On April 15, 1889, Father Damien died. It was Holy Week. Some weeks before, Father had mentioned that the Lord wanted him to spend Easter in Heaven. In June 1995, Pope John Paul II beatified Fr. Damien. He is now known as Blessed Fr. Damien, Servant of Humanity.

We should pray to God for all priests. Most will not be called to sacrifice their lives in quite the same way as Fr. Damien. Nonetheless, we should always regard priests as extraordinary men of dedication and service to God's holy Church.

Blessed Father Damien, pastor of the poor and suffering, pray for us.
Blessed Father Damien, dedicated priest, pray for us.

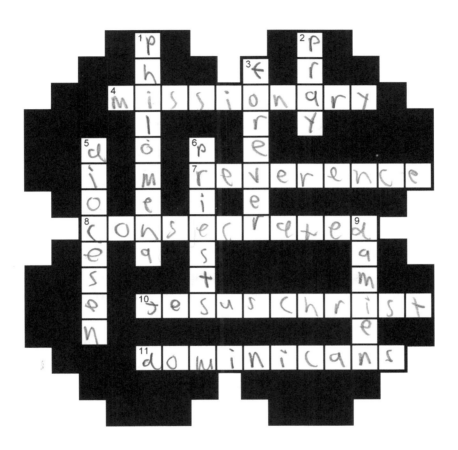

Across

4 __ priests travel the far corners of the world. (10)

7 We should show __ to all priests. (9)

8 The hands of a priest are __. (11)

10 "I make myself a leper with the lepers to gain all to __ __." (5,6)

11 Some of the largest religious orders are the Franciscans, __, and Benedictines. (10)

Down

1 Name of Molokai's leper church: St. __ (9)

2 We should __ for our priests. (4)

3 A priest is a priest __. (7)

5 __ priests serve in our parish church. (8)

6 We should thank God for our __. (7)

9 the priest who worked among the lepers: Fr. __ (6)

A wedding is a very special and holy event, for the couple being married, for their families, and for members of the Catholic community. For their wedding, the man rents a fancy tuxedo and the woman purchases a beautiful white wedding dress, often with a long train. Sometimes the dress has sequins and pearls. The bride carries flowers and wears a long veil. They invite many of their friends to attend their wedding, and have a reception after the wedding to celebrate their new life together as husband and wife. The bride and groom are totally changing their lives, and the wedding celebration makes it a religious and public event.

When two Catholic people join in the Sacrament of Matrimony, they promise each other, usually at a Nuptial Mass, before God, that they will remain faithful to each other, and they will raise their children in the Catholic Faith.

What is Matrimony? Matrimony is the Sacrament by which a baptized man and a baptized woman bind themselves for life in a lawful marriage, and receive the grace to discharge their duties.

The chief duty of the husband and wife in the married state is to be faithful to each other.

The second chief duty is to provide for the bodily and spiritual welfare of the children God may give them.

The bond of the Sacrament of Matrimony lasts until the death of husband or wife because Jesus said: "What therefore God has joined together, let no man put asunder" (Matt. 19:6).

When a couple are married in the Holy Sacrament of Marriage or Matrimony, Jesus changes their natural love into supernatural love. They are not only united to each other, they are united to each other in Christ.

The Catechism teaches: "Children are the supreme gift of marriage and contribute greatly to the good of the parents themselves... Hence, true married love and the whole structure of family life which results from it, … are directed to disposing the spouses to cooperate valiantly with the love of the Creator and Savior, Who through them will increase and enrich their family from day to day" (*Catechism of the Catholic Church*, n. 1652).

The Catholic Church is teaching us in the Catechism that the highest gift of marriage is children, and that children actually help parents to grow in the spiritual life. The whole structure of family life — mother, father, and children — actually helps mothers and fathers to be valiant, to be brave, to be courageous and unafraid in working with the loving plan of God the Father, God the Son, and God the Holy Spirit for Catholic family life. God will bless, increase, and enrich the family, each and every day for those families who "valiantly" are obedient to God's laws.

The Church reflects on marriage from the viewpoint of eternity. Marriage as taught by the Church is much more than a secular contract or legal agreement between two people. Marriage is a *sacred bond* by which God unites a man and a woman to one another for life.

It is unthinkable that the bond created by God should ever be broken. The husband and the wife are expected to remain faithful to one another not only in good times, but also in bad times.

The Sacrament of Matrimony is so holy that in the Bible we read that the union of husband and wife is like the union of Jesus Christ and His Church! In the Book of Ephesians, chapter 5, verses 25 to 33, we read: "Husbands, love your wives, *just as Christ also loves the Church, and delivered Himself up for her*... He who loves his own wife, loves himself... and let the wife respect her husband."

Love in the context of marriage means a "delivering oneself up," a giving of one person to another just as Jesus did for all of us by His sacrifice on the Cross. Jesus offered Himself to God to save us from our sins. True human love is sacrificial, too. True love is willing to do things for other people without asking for anything in return. Fathers must work to provide for the family, mothers need to care for the children. With love and prayer, and the Sacramental Graces, the couple can have a happy marriage, united with Christ, until death.

Holy angel, my guardian, pray for me.
Holy angel, my defender, pray for me.

Fill in the Blank

1. ~~Matrimony~~ is the Sacrament by which a baptized man and woman _bind_ themselves for life in a lawful marriage, and receive the _grace_ to discharge their duties.

2. The chief duty of husband and wife in the married state is to be _faithful_ to each other.

3. The second chief duty of husband and wife is to provide for the bodily _bodily_ and _spiritual_ welfare of their children.

4. The bond of the Sacrament of Matrimony lasts until the _death_ of husband or wife.

5. Jesus said: "What therefore God has _joined_ together, let no man put asunder."

6. The Catechism says that _children_ are the supreme gift of marriage.

7. Family life helps parents and children in the family to be valiant, to be _unafraid_, to be _brave_, to be _courageous_

8. Marriage is a _sacred, bond_ by which God unites a man and a woman to one another for life.

9. Husband and wife are expected to remain faithful to one another in good times and in _bad_ times.

10. True love is willing to do things for other people without _asking_ for anything in _return_.

Matrimony is the Sacrament by which a baptized man and a baptized woman bind themselves for life in a lawful marriage, and receive the grace to discharge their duties.

The chief duties of the husband and wife are to be faithful to each other, and to provide for the bodily and spiritual welfare of their children.

The bond of the Sacrament of Matrimony lasts until the death of the husband or wife because Jesus said: "What therefore God has joined together, let no man put asunder" (Matt. 19:6).

Because of the sacred bond of the Sacrament of Matrimony, the husband cannot, during the life of his wife, have another wife; nor can the wife, during the life of her husband, have another husband.

Every true marriage between a baptized man and a baptized woman is a valid Sacrament. Jesus Christ raised every marriage between baptized Christians to the level of a Sacrament. Jesus did that because He wanted to give Christian spouses and parents Sanctifying Grace, and the Sacramental Graces which can be obtained only through this Sacrament.

When did our Lord first institute marriage? At the very beginning of the human race when God made Adam and Eve, He made them "husband and wife."

When Jesus Christ came into the world, He raised marriage to the level of a Sacrament. Why? Because Jesus wanted to provide Sanctifying Grace for people to reach Heaven by the special graces found in the Sacrament of Matrimony.

Human society exists because of the Sacrament of Matrimony. Marriage is the very foundation of the family. The Catholic Church alone, the one true Church established by Jesus Christ, has authority to make regulations about and to administer the Sacrament of Marriage.

Because Baptism is required to be a member of Christ's Church, those who want to become married in the Church must first be baptized. Baptism is the very first requirement for two people when they seek the Sacrament of Matrimony. Why? Baptism is the entryway into the Church. Through Baptism, people become members of the Church and are therefore permitted to receive the other Sacraments.

The Church teaches that every true marriage must have two properties: *unity* and *indissolubility*. Unity means that a man is married to only one woman as long as she is alive; a woman is married to only one man as long as he is alive.

Indissolubility means that the marriage cannot be ended by any human authority. In other words, if the marriage between a baptized man and a baptized woman is valid, that marriage can never be dissolved by any human or Church authority.

Just as the Sacrament of Holy Orders is to help men to become holy, so the Sacrament of Marriage is to help families become holy. Our dear Lord did not create the Sacrament of Matrimony and then leave people to fend for themselves in a sinful world. He gave them special gifts to help them throughout their lives.

"By reason of their state in life and of their order, [Christian spouses] have their own *special gifts* in the People of God. This grace proper to the Sacrament of Matrimony is intended to perfect the couple's love and to strengthen their indissoluble unity. By this grace, they "help one another to attain holiness in their married life and in welcoming and educating their children. Christ is the source of this grace" (*Catechism of the Catholic Church*, 1641, 1642).

The late Bishop Fulton Sheen never tired of saying, "It takes <u>three</u> to get married: a man, a woman, and Jesus Christ." When a man and a woman stand before God and the priest at the altar, they are making magnificent promises to one another. They promise to love, honor, and obey one another during good times and bad times, in sickness and in health. They promise to love and to cherish each other and the children God will give them. They will be faithful to one another as long as they both shall live. Real love grows when it gives itself away to help others. Just as Jesus Christ gave Himself to His Church, so do married spouses give themselves to one another.

St. Anne, filled with grace, pray for us.
St. Anne, mother of the Mother of God, pray for us.

Fill in the Blank

1. Matrimony is the Sacrament by which a __baptized__ man and a __baptized__ woman bind themselves for life in a lawful marriage, and receive the grace to discharge their duties.

2. The bond of the Sacrament of Matrimony lasts until the __death__ of the husband or wife.

3. What therefore God has __joined__ together, let no man put asunder.

4. Jesus raised every marriage between baptized Christians to the level of a __sacrament__.

5. At the very beginning of the human race, God made Adam and Eve __Husband__ and __wife__.

6. Only the Catholic Church has the authority to make __regulations__ about the Sacrament of Matrimony.

7. Marriage is the foundation of the __family__.

8. Unity means that a man is married to only __one__ woman as along as she is alive.

9. Indissolubility means that the marriage cannot be ended by any __human__ authority.

10. The Sacrament of Marriage is to help families become __holy__.

Matrimony is the Sacrament by which a baptized man and a baptized woman bind themselves for life in a lawful marriage, and receive the grace to discharge their duties. The chief duties of husband and wife are to be faithful to each other, and to provide for the welfare of their children.

The bond of the Sacrament of Matrimony lasts until the death of husband or wife. Jesus Christ said, "What therefore God has joined together, let no man put asunder" (Matt. 19:6).

Every true marriage between a baptized man and a baptized woman is a Sacrament because Jesus Christ raised every marriage of this kind to the dignity of a Sacrament.

The laws of the Church require a Catholic to be married in the presence of a bishop, priest, or deacon and before two witnesses. The Church recommends that couples be married at a Nuptial Mass.

In order to receive the Sacrament of Matrimony worthily, the couple must:

· <u>Be in the state of grace</u>. As we have seen, Matrimony is a Sacrament of the living. This means the graces of the Sacrament are available only to couples who are in the state of grace.

· <u>Know the duties of married life</u>. That means they must enter into the Sacrament of Matrimony knowing they must remain faithful to one another, and they must be prepared to provide for the bodily and spiritual welfare of any children God may send them.

· <u>Obey the marriage laws of the Church</u>. The commandments of the Church say that a Catholic must be married in the presence of an authorized priest and two witnesses.

The Church requires that Catholic couples get married before a priest or deacon and two witnesses. The Church encourages couples to be married at a Wedding Mass in order to obtain all the Sacramental Graces possible.

The Church shares in and celebrates with joy the union of the newly married couple whom God has joined together. The new husband and wife are like a king and queen of a new kingdom. From their union will come children, who will increase the Kingdom of God on earth and in Heaven.

St. Anne, grandmother of Our Savior, pray for us.
St. Anne, joy of angels, pray for us.
St. Anne, refuge of sinners, pray for us.
St. Anne, mother of the sick, pray for us.

Fill in the Blank

1. Matrimony is the Sacrament by which a baptized man and a baptized woman bind themselves for _____life_____ in a lawful marriage, and receive the grace to discharge their duties.

2. The laws of the Church require a Catholic to be married in the presence of a _____priest_____ or a _____bishop_____, and two witnesses.

3. In order to receive the Sacrament of Matrimony worthily, the couple must be in the state of _____grace_____.

4. To receive the Sacrament worthily, the couple must know the _____duties_____ of the married state.

5. A chief duty of the married state is to remain _____faithful_____ to each other.

6. Another chief duty of the married state is to _____provide_____ for the bodily and _____spiritual_____ welfare of the children.

7. To receive the Sacrament worthily, the couple must obey the _____marriage_____ laws of the Church.

8. The Church encourages couple to be married at a _____church_____ in order to obtain all the Sacramental Graces possible.

9. The Church celebrates with _____joy_____ the union of the newly married couple.

10. The new husband and wife are like a _____king_____ and _____queen_____ of a new kingdom for Christ.

Matrimony is a Sacrament by which a baptized man and a baptized woman bind themselves for life in a lawful marriage, and receive the grace to discharge their duties.

God blesses homes and families who live according to the Ten Commandments and the Commandments of the Church. When couples marry in a Catholic Church at a Nuptial Mass, they are asking for the graces which will help them through the difficult times which ordinarily come in a family. The Sacrament of Matrimony helps mothers and fathers to be good practicing Catholics and to be good teachers of the Catholic Faith for their children. When God created Adam and Eve, he created them as husband and wife.

The Doctors of the Church believe that it was at the Wedding Feast of Cana when Jesus Christ raised marriage to the dignity of being a Sacrament. At the Wedding Feast of Cana, He certainly blessed and honored marriage by His very presence. It was planned by Jesus that He work His first public miracle at the Wedding Feast of Cana. This miracle was of special significance because He changed water into wine, a prefiguring of the miracle at the Last Supper, the institution of the Sacrament of the Holy Eucharist. What greater honor and blessing could He have given the new bride and groom at Cana than a gift of miraculous and most excellent, in fact, perfect wine with which to celebrate their marriage?

The chief effects of the Sacrament of Matrimony are first, an increase in Sanctifying Grace. Secondly, the couple receive Sacramental Grace. Remember that Sacramental Grace gives the supernatural help necessary to fulfill the duties of the particular Sacrament. Sacramental Grace for this Sacrament helps the couple to remain faithful to each other, to love each other, to bear with each other's faults.

The Sacramental Grace of the Sacrament of Matrimony gives parents the graces necessary to provide for the bodily and spiritual welfare of their children. It is the Sacramental Grace of the Sacrament of Matrimony which gives parents the graces necessary to educate their children in the Catholic Faith, as the primary educators of their children.

Sometimes when a young couple are planning to get married, they spend too much time thinking about the wedding ceremony and not enough time preparing spiritually for the obligations of raising a family. To prepare to receive the Sacrament of Matrimony, Catholics should pray that God has directed them to a good Catholic spouse. Secondly, Catholics should seek the advice of their parents and of their confessor. Thirdly, Catholics should practice the virtues, especially the virtue of chastity.

Catholics who are looking for other good practicing Catholics should participate in the parish activities celebrating the events of the liturgical year. Parish organizations which are dedicated to prayer and serving the needs of the community have members who should make good Catholic spouses.

To prepare for the Sacrament of Matrimony, Catholic couples should attend Mass frequently, even daily. They should receive the Holy Eucharist frequently, even daily, and should go to Confession, at least once a month. Receiving the Sacraments frequently helps young people to discern and make good judgments in selecting a spouse.

Catholics can best obtain God's blessing for their marriage by being married at a Wedding Mass or Nuptial Mass, and by receiving Holy Communion devoutly.

God personally calls each of us to a life of holiness. How best can I respond to *God's calling to live a holy life?* The best answer to this is found in the Catechism: "All Christians in any state or walk of life are called to the fullness of Christian life and to the perfection of charity.' All are called to holiness: 'Be perfect, as your Heavenly Father is perfect'.

"In order to reach this perfection, the faithful should use the strength dealt out to them by Christ's gift, so that...doing the will of the Father in everything, they may wholeheartedly devote themselves to the glory of God and to the service of their neighbor" (*Catechism of the Catholic Church*, n. 2013).

Everyone, without exception, is personally invited by our perfectly loving Creator to live a life of charity and holiness. So we can see that the vocation one chooses, in order to fulfill God's will, should be one that helps us to grow in holiness.

What is holiness? Holiness means being in the state of grace and doing God's will. Whatever vocation I choose, it should be decided upon with the foremost intent to save my soul. "Life in the Holy Spirit fulfills the vocation of man...This life is made up of divine charity and human solidarity...It is graciously offered as salvation"(*Catechism of the Catholic Church*, 1699).

St. Anne, mirror of obedience, pray for us.
St. Anne, mirror of patience, pray for us.

Fill in the Blank

1. God blesses families who live according to the ___Commandments___.
2. The Sacrament of Matrimony helps parents to be good ___teachers___ of the Catholic Faith.
3. It was at the Wedding Feast at ___Cana___ that Jesus raised marriage to the dignity of a Sacrament.
4. Jesus worked his first ___public___ miracle at the Wedding Feast.
5. The first chief effect of the Sacrament of Matrimony is an increase in ___grace___.
6. The second chief effect is the reception of ___Sacramental Grace___.
7. Young adult Catholics should ___pray___ that God directs them to a good Catholic spouse.
8. Catholics should seek the advice of their ___parents___ and their ___confessor___ when choosing a spouse.
9. Catholics can best obtain God's blessing for their marriage by being married at a ___Nuptial___ Mass.
10. "Be perfect, as your Heavenly Father is ___perfect___ ."

We have just finished studying the seven Sacraments. The Sacraments were instituted by Jesus Christ when He was on earth. The Sacraments are God's plan to give us a sharing in His Divine Life through the gift of Sanctifying Grace. All of us in the Catholic Church have the benefit of the Sacraments, and we have all received Baptism. Most of us regularly receive the Sacrament of Penance and the Sacrament of the Holy Eucharist. You may not yet have received your Confirmation.

Two of the other Sacraments are for special vocations. Young men who choose to live a special life of holiness and service to the Church may be chosen by their bishop to receive the Sacrament of Holy Orders. Many people choose to marry and receive the Sacrament of Matrimony. The last of the seven Sacraments prepares us to meet God. When people are seriously ill or near death, they should receive the Sacrament of the Anointing of the Sick.

Sacramentals, unlike Sacraments, have been instituted by the Catholic Church. The Catholic Church has this authority from Jesus Christ, Who said, "Whatever you bind on earth shall be bound in Heaven; whatever you loose on earth shall be loosed in Heaven."

Sacramentals are holy things or actions of which the Church makes use to obtain for us from God, through her intercession, spiritual and temporal favors.

For many Catholics, the Sacraments are not easy to obtain. Though Sacramentals do not give Sanctifying Grace like the Sacraments, they do give Actual Graces. In many places of the world, it is not possible for people to travel to a Catholic church to attend Mass or to receive the Sacraments. In some places, people can make the trip to church only on Sundays.

In some places and in some periods of history, Catholics have been in fear of their lives, and could not publicly attend Mass or receive the Sacraments. At the present time, Catholics in China are in danger of being imprisoned if they try to attend a Catholic Church. The saintly Cardinal Kung spent more than 30 years in prison in China. The Cardinal Kung Foundation works constantly, through prayer and exposing the truth, to help Catholics who are imprisoned in China.

Sacramentals help those suffering from persecution to receive graces and spiritual help when Sacraments are difficult or impossible to obtain. Sacramentals provide the rest of us with additional spiritual help, in addition to the Sacraments.

While Sacraments give us Sanctifying Grace, Sacramentals give us Actual Graces, which are temporary spiritual and temporal helps. Actual Grace is a supernatural help of God which enlightens our mind and strengthens our will to do good and to avoid evil. While Sanctifying Grace is permanent, and can be removed only by mortal sin, Actual Grace is

temporary. God gives us Actual Graces each day to help us, but they last only long enough to help us as long as we need them.

What are Sacramentals? Sacramentals are a variety of things and actions which have been approved by the Church. Sacramentals include blessings by priests and bishops. Sacramentals also include certain objects, such as medals, and certain actions, such as making the Stations of the Cross. Sacramentals are used to beg God's help by reason of the Church's intercession and our expressions of devotion.

Sacramentals unite us with the powerful prayers of the entire Church, the Mystical Body of Christ. Sacramentals, like the Indulgences, remind us again about the Spiritual Treasury of the Church, spiritual graces and merits available through the Church due to the merits of the sufferings and death of Jesus Christ on the Cross.

Once again we see that we are not alone in our struggle to respond to God. We have the prayers and support of the most Holy Catholic Church. It is the Church herself which has given us the Sacramentals.

The *Catechism of the Catholic Church* tells us, "Holy Mother Church has instituted Sacramentals. These are sacred signs, which bear a resemblance to the Sacraments. They signify effects, particularly of a spiritual nature, which are obtained through the intercession of the Church. By them, men are disposed to receive the chief effect of the Sacraments, and various occasions in life are rendered holy" (n. 1667).

We can see that Sacramentals should "dispose" us to receive the Sacraments. In other words, Sacramentals help us to prepare spiritually to receive the Sacraments. Our hearts and our souls are more open to the graces and the meaning of the Sacraments if we are constantly making use of the Sacramentals in our daily lives.

In the Sacraments, Jesus Christ works directly in our souls to give us grace. In the Sacramentals, we receive grace because of our own personal devotion and the intercession of the Church. Because Jesus Christ Himself instituted the seven Sacraments, no authority on earth can change them. Sacramentals, however, can be added to or changed because the Church instituted them and can change them.

St. Francis Xavier, patron of the souls of the East,
pray for the Catholic Chinese.
St. Francis Xavier, pray for the suffering Catholics in China.

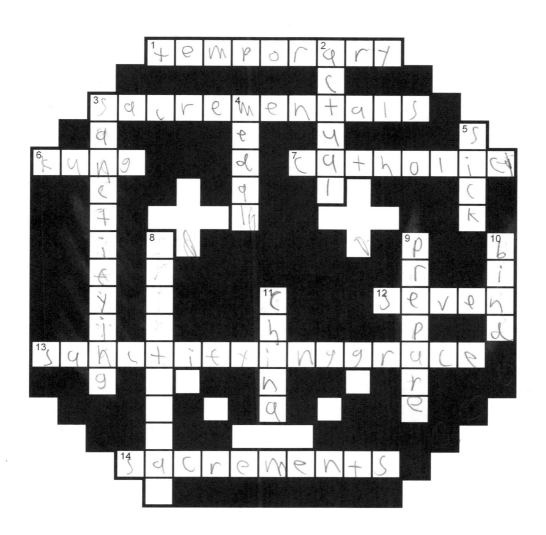

Across

1 Actual grace is a ___ spiritual help. (9)

3 instituted by the Catholic Church (12)

6 saintly Cardinal who suffered in China (4)

7 The ___ Church is the Mystical Body of Christ. (8)

12 There are ___ Sacraments. (5)

13 ___ ___ can only be removed by mortal sin. (11,5)

14 instituted by Jesus Christ (10)

Down

2 Sacramentals give us ___ grace. (6)

3 Sacraments give us ___ grace. (11)

4 a type of sacramental (5)

5 Anointing of the ___ (4)

8 Sacramentals provide ___ spiritual help. (10)

9 Sacramentals help us to ___ spiritually to receive the Sacraments. (7)

10 "Whatsoever you shall ___ on earth, shall be bound also in Heaven." (4)

11 Catholics is this country are in danger if they try to go to church. (5)

Sacramentals are holy things or actions of which the Church makes use to obtain for us from God, through her intercession, spiritual and temporal favors. The Sacramentals obtain favors from God through the prayers of the Church, offered for those who make use of them, and through the devotion they inspire.

The Sacramentals obtain favors from God through the Spiritual Treasury of the Church, the *prayers* of the Church because *prayer* is always involved in the use of Sacramentals. For example, if someone is wearing the Miraculous Medal, the medal is a very powerful Sacramental but the Blessed Mother expects us to say certain *prayers* along with wearing the medal. We are to say: "O Mary, conceived without sin, pray for us who have recourse to thee."

The Sacramentals obtain favors from God because of the *devotion* they inspire in us. For instance, as we make the Stations of the Cross, we become more *devoted* to Our Lord and His sufferings on the Cross. Our disposition becomes more loving and united with our Sweet Jesus Who suffered so for us! As we reflect on Veronica and see her wiping the face of Jesus as He lay fallen under the weight of the Cross, our *devotion* increases.

St. Francis of Assisi helps us to increase our *devotion* to Jesus by the following meditative *prayer* on one of the Stations of the Cross: "Consider how Jesus, as He passes along the way, meets the holy woman Veronica, who is in anguish at His sufferings, and wipes the sweat and blood from His Holy Face with her veil. Consider how Jesus receives her offering and miraculously leaves the impression of His Face upon it. O my Sweet Jesus, I have nothing to offer Thee but my heart. Take it and leave Your Holy Face upon it, that I may carry it through life, until death. Following in Thy footsteps, I carry my cross for Thee and with Thee."

The chief benefit obtained by the use of Sacramentals is Actual Grace. Other benefits are the forgiveness of venial sins, the remission of temporal punishment due to sin, health of body, material blessings, and protection from evil spirits.

The benefits of Sacramentals are truly amazing. The main benefit, or favor from God, of Sacramentals is Actual Grace. We recall that Actual Graces are temporary supernatural interventions by God to enlighten the mind and strengthen the will to perform supernatural actions that lead to holiness. Whenever we make use of a Sacramental, we are giving light to our minds to *discover* God's will, and strength to our wills to *do* God's will.

Think about the other benefits. Think about the forgiveness of venial sins! By receiving blessings from priests, by wearing Church-approved holy medals, by making the Stations of the Cross, for example, we can have our venial sins forgiven! The Church is very generous in giving us many different Sacramentals by which we can obtain forgiveness for our venial sins. Mortal sins can be forgiven only in Confession, but venial sins can be forgiven both through the Sacraments and through the Sacramentals.

By using the Sacramentals, we can have the temporal punishment due to sin removed! Temporal punishment is the penalty that God in His justice imposes on us. We have many opportunities to shorten the punishment due our sins through the generosity of the Church. Sacramentals take time away from what we are due to suffer as punishment for our sins, either in this world or in Purgatory. It is very important that we do all we can and take advantage of the Church's generosity because after we die, it is too late.

God often gives bodily health as a result of the use of Sacramentals. Often when we visit a shrine in honor of the Blessed Mother, such as at Lourdes, we see crutches hanging around the altar. These are evidence of the results of the bodily health that God gives those who use Sacramentals with devotion. Miracles happen frequently as a result of the devotion and prayers and use of the water of Lourdes, a wonderful and powerful Sacramental.

Other material blessings come from the use of Sacramentals. So many blessings have come from the Immaculate Conception medal given to the world by the Blessed Mother through St. Catherine Labouré that it is commonly known as The Miraculous Medal!

Sacramentals offer protection against evil spirits. Making the sign of the cross with holy water can drive away evil spirits. Saying the Holy Name, "Jesus!" is a Sacramental from which all evil spirits flee with haste! Whenever you are in trouble or in danger of sin, quickly say "Jesus! Jesus! Jesus!"

St. Francis Xavier, pray for us.

Fill in the Blank

1. __Sacramentals__ are holy things or actions, of which the Church makes use to obtain for us from God, through her intercession, __Spiritual__ and __temporal__ favors.

2. The Sacramentals obtain favors from God through the __treasury__ of the Church, offered for those who make use of them, and through the __devotion__ they inspire.

3. The chief benefit obtained by the use of Sacramentals is __actual__ Grace.

4. Sacramentals also obtain forgiveness of __venial__ sins.

5. Sacramentals also obtain the __removal__ of temporal punishment.

6. Sacramentals may obtain __health__ of body and __material__ blessings.

7. Sacramentals are a protection from __evil__ spirits.

8. __Veronica__ wiped the Holy Face of Jesus.

9. The Sacramental water of __Lourdes__ has given bodily health to many.

10. We have received the __miraculous__ from Our Blessed Mother through St. Catherine Labouré.

Sacramentals are holy things or actions of which the Church makes use to obtain for us from God, through her intercession, spiritual and temporal favors.

The Sacramentals obtain favors from God through our prayers and devotion.

The Sacramentals benefit us by giving us Actual Graces, the forgiveness of venial sins, the remission of temporal punishment due to sin, health of body, material blessings, and protection from evil spirits.

The chief Sacramentals are *blessings* from priests and bishops. Blessings by priests and bishops are very special. They call down God's favor on a person or object. Blessings sanctify, or help to make holy, people or things. We should always ask a priest or bishop for his blessing.

An important Sacramental which we don't hear about very often is *exorcisms* against evil spirits. Each diocese is supposed to have an exorcist to say special powerful prayers to remove evil spirits. Exorcisms destroy the power of evil spirits in homes or places of business, as well as around geographical areas.

"When the Church asks publicly and authoritatively in the name of Jesus Christ that a person or object be protected against the power of the Evil One and withdrawn from his dominion, it is called *exorcism*" (*Catechism of the Catholic Church*, n. 1673). Exorcisms destroy the power of the devil to control the possessed person.

The most commonly used Sacramentals are *blessed objects of devotion*. There are thousands of different blessed objects of devotion. There are millions of Miraculous Medals available for people. It has been traditional for every Catholic to own and wear at least one Miraculous Medal.

Sacramental objects are such things as holy water, crucifixes, candles, rosaries, scapulars, medals, palms (on Palm Sunday), ashes (given on Ash Wednesday), and pictures and statues of Our Lord, the Blessed Mother and the saints.

What is holy water and why is it a Sacramental? Water, blessed by a priest, calls down God's blessing on all who use it. It is a symbol of spiritual cleansing and causes us to recall the commitments we made at our Baptism. We should bless ourselves with Holy Water when we enter Church before Mass and as we leave after Mass. We ought to have holy water on hand in our homes for use during moments of physical danger and against temptations from spiritual enemies. It is a good practice to keep a holy water font by the front door of the home. Whenever we leave home, it is a good habit to dip our fingers into the font and bless ourselves.

It is important that crucifixes are kept in the home. In fact, there should be a crucifix in every room. We venerate crucifixes. They are crosses bearing the image of our crucified Savior

Jesus Christ. Some religious men and women wear a crucifix as part of their religious habit. It is good for lay people to wear them as well because they are reminders of our redemption and the infinite love Our Blessed Lord has for us.

A rosary is a Sacramental and devotional prayer that honors the Blessed Mother of God. Prayers are recited on a string of beads made up of five sets each of one large and ten smaller beads. Each set of ten beads is called a decade. We meditate on the joyous, sorrowful, and glorious events in the lives of Our Lord and His Blessed Mother while praying the Our Father, Hail Mary and Glory Be to the Father. Many popes have recommended praying the Rosary, and it is the most popular of all Catholic Sacramental devotions.

Remaining constantly mindful of the presence of Our Lord, the Blessed Mother, and the saints through pictures and statues is a good way to keep our minds and hearts properly focused. When we look at a statue or picture or icon of Our Blessed Mother, we are reminded that she is *Mother of God*. When we look at a picture of the Sacred Heart of Jesus, with the flaming Heart so filled with love for us, *we are moved to return the love God has for us.*

We should make good use of Sacramentals as a means to prepare and dispose our souls for the worthy reception of the Sacraments and to keep our minds and hearts turned always toward God.

St. Francis Xavier, model of apostolic men,
pray for persecuted Catholics around the world.
St. Francis Xavier, destroyer of idols and false gods, pray for unbelievers.

True (T) or false (F)

_F_____ 1. There are only two kinds of Sacramentals: blessings and holy water.

_T_____ 2. We should always ask a priest or bishop for his blessing.

_T_____ 3. We should keep holy water in our homes.

_F_____ 4. A crucifix is a plain cross.

_T_____ 5. A rosary is a set of beads on which we say prayers.

_T_____ 6. We meditate on the lives of Our Lord and Our Lady when we pray the Rosary.

_F_____ 7. An exorcism is when the Church publicly asks, in the Name of Jesus, that the power evil spirits be removed.

_T_____ 8. Blessed candles, ashes, palms, and medals are Sacramentals.

_F_____ 9. Sacramentals are really Sacraments.

_F_____ 10. Anyone can bless holy water.

Sacramentals are holy things or actions of which the Church makes use to obtain spiritual and temporal favors from God. The Sacramentals obtain favors from God through prayers and through the devotion they inspire.

The chief benefits obtained by the use of Sacramentals are Actual Graces, the forgiveness of venial sins, and the remission of temporal punishment due to sin.

The chief kinds of Sacramentals are blessings by priests and bishops, exorcisms, and blessed objects of devotion. The most common blessed objects of devotion used by Catholics are holy water, candles, ashes, palms, crucifixes, medals, rosaries, scapulars, and images of Our Lord, the Blessed Virgin, and the saints.

We should make use of the Sacramentals with faith and devotion. We should believe in what they represent, and treat them as signs of spiritual things.

Most of the Sacramentals have been given to us by the Church. They are often based on biblical events, such as the blessings of Jacob to his sons. Novenas, a common and popular Sacramental used both in homes and in parish churches, are based on the nine days the Apostles waited in the Upper Room for the Holy Spirit.

Some Sacramentals have a heavenly origin. The Blessed Mother appeared to St. Dominic and gave us the Rosary. The Brown Scapular was given by the Blessed Mother to St. Simon Stock. The Bible, the inspired Word of God, is a Sacramental. The Holy Face and the Shroud of Turin are Sacramentals. The miraculous image of Holy Mary of Guadalupe on the tilma of

Juan Diego is a miraculous Sacramental responsible for the conversion of eight million Aztec Indians, and millions of others since then.

When we think of Sacramentals in relation to health of body, we must remember the blessing of throats on the feast of St. Blaise. Besides novenas, we also have powerful litanies to Our Lord, the Blessed Mother, and the saints, which bring health and blessings, such as employment. Certainly novenas to St. Joseph are the most common and popular prayers for employment for fathers.

For protection against evil spirits, holding up the crucifix against the enemy is based on how St. Clare protected her convent against attacking enemies. Commonly-used Sacramentals against evil spirits are making the Sign of the Cross, saying the Holy Name of Jesus, and sprinkling holy water.

Powerful protection against evil spirits has been obtained through the St. Benedict Medal. St. Benedict performed many miracles and exercised great power over the spirits of darkness, the devils, basically by holding up the crucifix. One side of the St. Benedict Medal shows the image of the crucifix. Latin words around the crucifix are translated: "Begone, Satan! Do not suggest to me your vain things. The cup you offer me is evil. Drink your own poison!"

The power of the St. Benedict Medal is due to the merits of Jesus Christ, to the prayers of St. Benedict, to the blessing of the Church, and to the faith and disposition of the person using the St. Benedict Medal. The Medal has proved beneficial in warding off dangers from the devil, and obtaining the grace of conversion. It has obtained protection for people tormented by the devil, especially in temptations against purity. The Medal has given consolation at the hour of death. It has been a remedy against bodily sufferings, especially in regards to contagious diseases. Expectant mothers have found the St. Benedict Medal helpful for safe deliveries. The Medal has afforded protection against storms on land and sea. Domestic animals have been cured of diseases.

St. Benedict, leader of holy warfare, pray for persecuted Catholics.
St. Benedict, wonderful worker of miracles, pray for suffering Catholics.

Fill in the Blanks

1. The chief benefit obtained by the use of Sacramentals is __actual__ Grace.

2. Other benefits from Sacramentals are the __forgiveness__ of venial sins and the __remission__ of part of the temporal punishment due to sin.

3. One of the chief kinds of Sacramentals are blessings by __priests__ and bishops.

4. List six Sacramentals commonly used by Catholics __candles__, __ashes__, __palms__, __medals__, __rosaries__, __scaplars__.

5. We should make use of the Sacramentals with __respect__ and devotion.

6. Most of the Sacramentals have been given us by the __God__.

7. Some Sacramentals have a __holy__ origin.

8. The Blessed Mother gave the Rosary to __St. Dominic__.

9. The Blessed Mother gave the Brown Scapular to __St. Simon Stock__.

10. We have our throats blessed on the feast of __Blaise__.

Prayer is necessary if we love God. Prayer is a necessary way to communicate with God. We want to communicate with those we love, like our parents and grandparents. We certainly want to communicate with love with God Who made us. So if we love God, we want to communicate with Him frequently. Prayer is an act of love, lifting up our minds and hearts to God, telling Him not only that we love Him, but also our needs and concerns.

We may not yet realize the great importance of prayer. We lift up our *minds* by giving God our attention; we lift up our *hearts* by giving Him our love. Prayer is our response to all the wonderful things God has done for us, and continues to do for us. The *Catechism* states that prayer is one of the four pillars of the foundation of the Catholic Faith.

The Church says that prayer originates deep inside of us, in our hearts and souls. In the *Catechism,* we read: "…it is the *heart* that prays" (*Catechism of the Catholic Church*, n. 2562). The Catechism says that there are over 1000 references in Scripture that tell us the heart is the source of prayer. In fact, the Catechism says that if our hearts are far from God our "words of prayer are in vain" (*Catechism of the Catholic Church*, n. 2562).

The source from which our love of God issues forth is actually the Holy Spirit. "No one can say 'Jesus is Lord' except by the Holy Spirit (1 Cor. 12:3). The Church invites us to invoke the Holy Spirit as the interior Teacher of Christian Prayer" (*Catechism of the Catholic Church*, n. 2681). As we talk to God through prayer, our love for Him grows, but we also begin to realize the deep mystery of the actual source of prayer, the gift of the Holy Spirit as He lives inside us.

We are told in the Bible to: "Pray without ceasing. In all things give thanks, for this is the will of God in Christ Jesus concerning you all. Do not extinguish the Spirit…" (1 Thessalonians 5:17-19).

Unless we pray, we will not receive the graces necessary for salvation. How do we follow Our Lord's command to pray without ceasing? If we start each day by offering everything we think, say, and do as a prayer to Almighty God, we *can* pray without ceasing. We need to start each day with the Morning Offering, and renew our intention throughout the day if we can. The Morning Offering turns all our thoughts, words, and actions into acts of love throughout the day. This pleases God and gains merit for us. In this way, our entire day becomes an unbroken act of prayer.

"O Jesus, through the Immaculate Heart of Mary, I offer Thee my prayers, work, joys, and sufferings of this day, for all the intentions of Thy Sacred Heart, in union with the Holy Sacrifice of the Mass throughout the world, in reparation for my sins, for the intentions of all our associates, and in particular for all the intentions of this month."

The "intentions" refer to the Pope's intentions. So you could say "… for all the Pope's intentions for this month." Of course, you may have your own intentions also.

We should look to Our Lord Himself, to the Blessed Virgin Mary, to St. Joseph, and to all the saints for their example of praying. As we look over the four Gospels, we can easily see how often Jesus prayed. Remember that He started His public life by first spending forty days in prayer in the desert.

The Blessed Mother, at a very young age, entered the Temple in Jerusalem, where the majority of each day was spent in prayer. St. Joseph received his heavenly messages from an angel, which means he was listening for God's answer in prayer. We can read any of the lives of the saints and be impressed with the amount of time the saints spent in prayer. As busy as the saints were in serving the needs of people, they always found time for prayer. Some of them prayed at night while others were sleeping.

God expects us to spend some time every day in prayer, both in vocal prayer with our family, and in private prayers from our hearts.

St. Gertrude, strong protection of all who venerate you, pray for us.
St. Gertrude, beloved daughter of our heavenly Father, pray for us.

Fill in the Blank

1. Prayer is one of the four basic __foundation__ of the Catholic Church.

2. Prayer is the lifting up of our __minds__ and __hearts__ to God.

3. Over __1000__ references in Scripture tell us that the __heart__ is the source of prayer.

4. __Prayer__ are in vain if our hearts are far from God.

5. The Church invites us to invoke __holy spirit__ as the interior Teacher of prayer.

6. "Pray without __ceasing__."

7. Unless we pray, we will not receive the __Grace__ necessary for salvation.

8. The __rosery__ helps us to offer our daily thoughts, words, and actions to God.

9. We should look to __God__ Himself for an example of praying.

10. Jesus started His public life by spending __forty__ days in prayer.

Prayer is the lifting up of our minds and hearts to God.

Why do we pray? St. Paul gives us four reasons why we are to pray constantly:

1) We pray in order *to adore and to give praise* to God. When we recall the First Commandment, we know that we owe God our primary attention. We are to pray because we are His creation and we owe Him everything. Our very existence and all we have are free gifts of His love. Were it not for God's willing it, no one and nothing would exist. God is pure Love and pure Mercy. Jesus, the Son of God, became Man and died a painful death out of love for us. Our most fitting response to such infinite and divine Love should be prayers of praise and adoration. The Acts of Faith, Hope, and Love are acts of praise and adoration.

2) The second reason we pray is *to thank* our Divine and Loving God for all that He has given us. We can never realize how many things we ought to be thankful for in our lives. The most basic gratitude we owe to God is for our existence. God created each of us from nothing. At the very first second of our existence, He created our souls with a free will and an intellect. God created and sustains us out of pure Love.

"The desire for God is written in the human heart because *man is created by God and for God*; and God never ceases to draw man to Himself... The dignity of man rests above all on the fact that he is called to communion with God. This invitation to converse with God is addressed to man as soon as he comes into being. For *if man exists, it is because God has created him through love, and through love continues to hold him in existence*" (*Catechism of the Catholic Church*, n. 27, emphasis added).

3) We pray *to obtain from God pardon for our sins, and remission of the punishment* due to our sins. Because of our weak and wounded natures, we need to beg our merciful Lord for forgiveness. We must ask God to have mercy on others and on us for all of the times we have not chosen to be obedient to God's laws. We beg Him for the remission of the punishment our sins deserve.

4) We pray *to ask God for graces and blessings,* and for the material things we and others need. Not one of us will ever fully realize how completely dependent we are on God. We humans are weak and truly helpless, especially as we struggle under the disability of sin. We forget that every breath we take and everything we have in our lives is a gift from God. Our families, homes, food, all that we enjoy, and even our illnesses and pains which can be offered up for sins, *everything* is a gift from God.

If God were to suddenly depart from us, we would no longer exist. The continual love of *God keeps us in existence*. Like a good Father, the Lord wants us to ask Him for what we want and need so that we come to know it is our dear Lord Who gives us everything that makes us happy.

When we pray, we should pray with attention and do our best not to be distracted. We should pray with a great desire to please God first. We should pray with loving trust in His goodness. We should pray with perseverance; we should not give up if our prayers do not seem to be answered. God always answers our prayers in the way that is best for us.

We should pray especially for ourselves and our family members, relatives, and friends. Then we should pray for the souls in Purgatory, the Pope, priests, and bishops. We should pray for our president and other officials and leaders in our city, state, and nation.

God always hears our prayers. Our Lord Jesus Christ has promised: "If you ask the Father anything in My Name, He will give it to you." Sometimes we think our prayers have not been answered, but God always answers our prayers in some way, and gives us what is best for us. We should always end our requests with "if it be Thy Will."

There is a difference between what we *want* and what we *need*. Timmy is three years old. He asks Mother for ice cream. She says "no" because he has not had his breakfast yet. Timmy begins to cry. He may have the ice cream later in the day, after lunch perhaps. Does that mean Timmy's request was denied? No, it was just delayed. Sometimes God's answer to a prayer is "yes" but not yet. Other times God's answer to our prayer is "no," because He knows that what we are asking for would not be good for us.

Sometimes we are distracted in our prayers. God understands distractions, and is unhappy only if we willingly are distracted. When we are in Church, or if we are praying before a crucifix, it helps us not to be distracted if we focus on Our Lord on the Cross. Our Church and our home should have pictures and statues to help us focus on our prayers.

St. Gertrude, through your humility, pray for us.
St. Gertrude, devoted to the Sacred Heart, pray for us.

Multiple Choice

_____ a   1. Prayer is
   a) the lifting of the mind and heart to God.
   b) a means of gaining Sanctifying Grace.
   c) one of the Ten Commandments.
   d) one of the Sacraments.

_____ b   2. Prayer comes from
   a) the mind.   b) the heart.
   c) the emotions.   d) the mind and heart.

_____ a   3. "Pray always," comes from
   a) the Bible.   b) the catechism.   c) our parents.

_____ b   4. To "pray always" means
   a) we should say prayers all day.
   b) we should find time to pray every day.
   c) we should always have our wills turned to God.

_____ a   5. The first reason to pray is
   a) to adore God.
   b) to thank God.
   c) to ask God's forgiveness for our sins.

_____ b   6. We adore God because
   a) He is good.
   b) He is God and we are His creation.
   c) we love Him.

_____ c   7. Acts of faith, hope, and love are prayers of
   a) petition.   b) praise.   c) thanksgiving.

_____ d   8. We beg God for His mercy because
   a) we are sinners.   b) we are sorry for our sins.
   c) we need His mercy.   d) a, b and c.

_____ c   9. We should ask God for
   a) only what we need.
   b) only what He wants us to have.
   c) what we need in accord with His will.

_____ a   10. God understands distractions sometimes come in our praying, but He is unhappy only if we are
   a) willingly distracted.
   b) unwillingly distracted.
   c) unhappy to be called away from prayer.

293

Prayer is the lifting up of our minds and hearts to God. We pray mainly to adore God and to thank Him for all the good things He has given us. We also pray to obtain pardon for our sins, to obtain remission of the punishment due to our sins, and to ask for graces and blessings for ourselves and others.

We must pray with attention, with a knowledge of our dependence on God, with a great desire for graces, with loving trust in Him, and with perseverance.

We know that God always hears our prayers, but He may answer us in different ways than we expect. God always knows what we need, even before we ask. He does not need to be informed or persuaded to pay attention. God is omniscient. This mean He knows everything. Why then, do we need to ask? We might make the mistake of thinking, "If God knows all things, He knows what I need, so I should just get what I need without having to ask."

We need to ask Our Lord for what we desire because *in asking, we develop our life of prayer*. Conversation with God is necessary for us, to make us realize the great need we have for God. When we need something from God, it makes us think about how poor we really are; our deficiency stirs up our will to ask for God's help.

God knows from all eternity what we need. This means He always knew, long before we ask, what favor we would be asking Him. God knew, for example, that when you were ten years old

you would be asking Him for healing for your grandmother who was very sick. We are not informing God when we ask Him for what we need. However, God wants us to ask Him for what we need because we need to learn that in asking, we come to understand that we need God's help for everything.

There are two kinds of prayer: our conversation with God can take the form of mental prayer or vocal prayer. Mental prayer is that prayer by which we unite our hearts with God while thinking of His holy truths. For example, when we pray the Rosary, we meditate on the events in the life of Our Lord and Our Blessed Mother. Mental prayer can begin with vocal prayer, which is prayer spoken by the lips. Vocal prayer comes from the heart and mind, but it is spoken aloud.

We can pray familiar Catholic prayers or we may make up our own prayers, or simply talk to God using our own words. We might feel inclined to talk to Our Blessed Mother, the angels, and the saints. All prayer is very pleasing to God, whether we use our own words or those of the Church.

We should pray frequently throughout the day. At the least, we should pray every morning when we start the day, and every night before we go to sleep. Most families pray together at least once during the day, not counting prayers at mealtimes. Students often pray before taking their tests or before starting their lessons. A favorite motto of students is "Pray as if everything depends on God, and work as if everything depends on yourself."

It is important to pray for others, especially for family members, friends, other families in the community or in the parish. It is important to pray for priests and to pray for vocations to the priesthood and religious life. We must pray for the sick and those who have died. Children should pray for their parents, their brothers and sisters, and their grandparents. Jesus said in the Gospel that we should pray for those who persecute us; He meant that we should pray for their conversion. Do you remember that St. Stephen, the first martyr, asked God to forgive those who were stoning him to death? In Mark 11:25, Jesus said that when we pray, we should forgive people who have hurt us.

Prayer is necessary for our salvation. Prayer gains graces for ourselves and others. Without grace, we cannot be saved and obtain eternal life in Heaven. Remember when Jesus asked His Apostles to pray for an hour when He was praying in the Garden of Gethsemane? Most people realize that God expects us to spend at least one hour in prayer each day.

St. Stephen, first martyr, pray for us.
St. Stephen, gentle follower of Christ, pray for us.

Fill in the Blank

1. Prayer is the lifting up of our __minds__ and __hearts__ to God.

2. We pray mainly to __adore__ God.

3. We pray to __thank__ God for all the good things He has given us.

4. We pray to obtain __forgivnes__ for our sins.

5. We pray to obtain remission of the __punishment__ due to our sins.

6. We know that God always __hears__ our prayers, but He may answer us in different ways than we expect.

7. God is omniscient, He __knows everything__

8. Praying helps us to understand that we need God's help for __everything__.

9. There are two kinds of prayer: __vocal__ prayer and __mental__ prayer.

10. __mental__ prayer is that prayer by which we unite our hearts with God while thinking of His holy __truths__.

We have been studying our lesson on Prayer this week. All the saints spent a great deal of time in prayer, many of them learning to pray when they were very young. St. Rose of Lima prayed when she was young, often asking God for little things every day. She loved to pray, and even built herself a little place of prayer in her back yard.

St. Thérèse, the Little Flower, wrote in her autobiography that she had a little altar where she prayed every day. She liked to light the candles on it when she prayed, but her sisters would not allow her it do it alone. She would put fresh flowers on the altar.

Many families have family altars, with a statue or a picture of the Sacred Heart in front of which they pray every day.

What are the prayers every Catholic should know by heart?

Joseph and Margaret have been married for twenty years. They have seven children. From the time the children were very young, they were taught how to pray. The family prays the Rosary together every day. From the youngest to the oldest child, each of them know all the prayers of the Rosary: the Our Father, Hail Mary, Glory Be to the Father, and the Apostles' Creed.

They also know the Acts of Faith, Hope, Love, and Contrition. These are the basic prayers all Catholics should know by heart. These are the prayers that all Catholics should be saying every day. The Act of Contrition should be said before going to bed each night so that we are telling God we are sorry for any sins we committed during the day.

If you do not know some of these prayers, it is well to begin to memorize them right away. They can be found in your catechism. Say them every day and soon you will know them by heart.

We begin and end our prayers with the Sign of the Cross. The Sign of the Cross is the most fundamental profession of the Catholic Faith. The Sign of the Cross is an outward expression of belief in our redemption through Jesus Christ's death on the Cross. In addition, when we pronounce the Names of the Three Divine Persons, we are professing our belief in the Holy Trinity.

The Sign of the Cross is the first of the Church's Sacramentals and can be traced back to the times of the Apostles. We should bless ourselves with the Sign of the Cross whenever we enter or leave Church, whenever we enter or leave our homes, whenever there is some evil taking place, and before and after we pray. Many people make the Sign of the Cross whenever they hear the siren of an ambulance or fire engine, saying a quick prayer for anyone who may be hurt. People make the Sign of the Cross when they pass by a Catholic church in honor of Our Lord Who is in the tabernacle.

Remember that our prayers should be *humble*, because we realize we are God's creatures and we owe everything to Him. Our prayers should be *confident* because we know God is all merciful and all loving, and He wants what is best for us. Our prayers should be *attentive*. We must not willingly give in to distractions. We must strive to overcome distractions.

When you meet a priest and ask him how he happened to become a priest, most of them will tell you that they grew up praying every day in their family. They will tell you that they said the Rosary every day, and that their parents would lead the children in prayer every day. Many priests were altar boys and memorized the Mass prayers.

Recall that Our Lord went out to the desert and prayed for forty days and forty nights before He started His public preaching. Recall the many times Our Lord prayed, especially with Peter, James, and John. Remember the times Our Lord said "Watch and pray." Remember the times Our Lord asked that we pray for those who persecute us.

Remember the time Our Lord said that sometimes we need to fast as well as to pray. Remember when Our Lord threw the moneychangers out of the Temple, saying that His Father's House is a House of prayer. Recall that Our Lord went to the Garden of Gethsemane to pray on the evening before He was to suffer and die on the Cross. We must remember the words of St. Paul: Pray without ceasing!

All you angels, pray for us.
All you saints, pray for us.

Matching

7 — 1. St. Rose of Lima	1. Prayed in front of home altar
1 — 2. St. Thérèse	2. Should be memorized
5 — 3. Rosary	3. Prayer we should say every night
2 — 4. Our Father and Hail Mary	4. Encourages vocations
9 — 5. Sign of the Cross	5. Contains Our Father, Hail Mary, Glory Be, Apostles' Creed
10 — 6. Jesus	6. For those who persecute us
3 — 7. Act of Contrition	7. Built a little house of prayer
4 — 8. Family prayer	8. Not sinful unless deliberate
6 — 9. Our Lord said to pray	9. Recalls the Trinity
8 — 10. Distractions in prayer	10. Prayed for 40 days and nights

Last week, we learned about the importance of prayer. This week, we will discuss the perfect prayer, the prayer given to us by the Son of God, Jesus Christ. Jesus gave us the Our Father.

Jesus was giving His Apostles and disciples the famous Sermon on the Mount, which we can read in the Gospel of Matthew, in chapters five, six, and seven. In chapter six,   Our Lord said, "Therefore thus shall you pray: "Our Father Who are in Heaven, hallowed be Thy name. Thy kingdom come. Thy will be done on earth as it is in Heaven. Give us this day our daily bread. And forgive us our debts [or trespasses], as we also forgive our debtors. And lead us not into temptation. But deliver us from evil. Amen.""

The Our Father is the best of all prayers because it was given to us by the Son of God. It is a prayer of perfect and unselfish love. It is a prayer of perfect and unselfish love because in saying it, we offer ourselves entirely to God. We ask from Him the best things, not only for ourselves but for our neighbor as well.

We address God as "Our Father" because we belong to Him. He created us out of love and continues to watch over us with loving care. He has adopted us as His children when we received a share in His Divine Life through Sanctifying Grace in the Sacrament of Baptism. He desires for us to live with Him in Heaven, our true home.

The Our Father is the prayer the entire Church says every single day at every Mass. We should pray the Our Father frequently every day. We should pray the Our Father primarily as a way to worship, adore, and praise God. The Our Father is the perfect prayer when we have a need. We may be concerned about taking a test; we may be worried about a family member who is sick. It is during times like these that Our Father wants to hear our requests.

There are seven petitions in the Our Father. Like the first three Commandments, the first three petitions of the Our Father are directed towards God. The last four petitions of the Our Father are directed toward ourselves and our neighbor. Our Lord is telling us that our prayers must start by adoring, worshiping, and praising God, by recognizing Him as our Creator and loving Father.

All the saints knew that God is like a loving father who loves them and would help them in all their needs. All the saints knew that God cares for every person in ways no one could ever imagine. The saints expressed their love for God first because He deserves all honor and glory. Therefore, the very first words of the most perfect prayer from the Son of God to His Father begin, "Our Father."

This first petition, addressing God as Our Father, is truly amazing. Why? Recall that Moses, as the first human being after Original Sin to approach God directly, was told to take off his shoes because the ground on which he was standing was holy. God was speaking to Moses from a burning bush. Moses fell to the ground in awe and adoration. But Moses was not allowed to come any closer. All the saints of the Old Testament were kept at a distance from the awesome God!

The Son of God became man about 2000 years ago. As we say in the Mass, Jesus taught us to call God Our Father. When we were baptized, we became children of God and heirs of Heaven. We may now call God, "Our Father!" At Baptism, God the Father adopted us as His sons and daughters. This is how Jesus taught us to pray, so we *dare* to speak the words, "Our Father." The Lord truly is our loving Father!

As our human father cares for us with great love and protection, all the more does our Father in Heaven love us, watch over us, and see to our every need. Unlike our earthly father, our Father in Heaven is our Creator. How completely He understands our every thought! How much He loves us! God the Almighty, the Creator, is truly Our Father Who provides for our every need.

Father of mercy and consolation, have mercy on us.
Father, from Whom all good things come, have mercy on us.

Fill in the Blank

1. The Our Father is the __Perfect__ prayer.

2. The Our Father was given to us by __Jesus__.

3. The Our Father is a prayer of perfect and __unselfish__ love.

4. We ask from God the __father__ things, for our __neighbor__ as well.

5. We address God as Our Father because we __belong__ to Him.

6. He __loves__ us and watches over us.

7. He adopted us as His children in the Sacrament of __baptism__.

8. God desires that we live with Him in __heaven__, our true home.

9. The Our Father is found in the Gospel of __matthew__.

10. The entire Church says the Our Father every day during __Mass__.

Last week, we learned about the importance of prayer. Jesus gave us examples in His own life on earth of the importance of prayer. He spent forty days and forty nights in prayer before He started His public life.

Jesus, Who is the Son of God, gave us the best of all prayers. It is a prayer of perfect and unselfish love. In saying it, we offer ourselves entirely to God, Our Father. We ask from Him the best things, not only for ourselves but for our neighbor as well.

We address God as Our Father because He adopted us as His children when we received Sanctifying Grace in the Sacrament of Baptism. He created us and He continues to watch over us with loving care.

When Jesus wants us to pray "hallowed be Thy name," we are praying that God's name be recognized as holy, with great honor and respect. We pray that God may be known, loved, and honored by all men everywhere in all times. When we say these words, we are acknowledging that *God alone is all holy.* We want everyone to recognize through this prayer that God is all holy.

St. Peter Chrysologus tells us, "We ask that just as the name of God is holy, so we may obtain His holiness in our souls." We are praying that His name be treated with the greatest of reverence. Remember the Second Commandment? "Thou shalt not take the name of the Lord thy God in

vain." Jesus wants us to pray that everyone will respect God's holy name and come to know and love God as their holy and heavenly Father.

When we pray "Thy kingdom come," Jesus wants us to pray that the kingdom of God may be spread throughout the world. We pray that all men may come to know and love His Church, which is His kingdom on earth. We pray that everyone God has ever created and will ever create will enter into the heavenly kingdom of God, at the end of time.

God's Kingdom on earth is the Catholic Church founded by Jesus Himself. When we pray this petition, we are asking:

- That the Church's members become more holy and better at proclaiming the Gospel.
- That more people receive the gift of the Catholic Faith and receive the Sacrament of Baptism.

When we pray for the Kingdom of God in Heaven, we are praying:

- For the grace people need to get to Heaven; and
- For the light people need in their minds and the strength in their wills to obey the Commandments of God.

God Our Father, Who governs all with wisdom and love, have mercy on us.
God Our Father, Who fills all things with blessings, have mercy on us.

Fill in the Blank

1. The Our Father is a prayer of perfect and __unselfish__ love.

2. God adopted us as His children when we received Sanctifying Grace in the Sacrament of __baptism__ .

3. God created us and he continues to __watch__ over us.

4. When we pray "hallowed be Thy name," we pray that God may be known, loved, and __adored__ by all men.

5. We are praying that God's name be treated with the greatest __respect__ .

6. The Second Commandment is: Thou shalt not take the __name__ of the Lord Thy God in vain.

7. When we pray "Thy kingdom come," we pray that the Kingdom of God may be spread throughout the __world__ .

8. We pray that all men may come to know and love His __Church__ on earth.

9. The Our Father is the __best__ of all prayers.

10. The Our Father was taught to us by __Jesus__ .

Jesus, the Son of God, the Second Person of the Blessed Trinity, taught us how to pray. He prayed and fasted in the desert for forty days before starting His public life. Jesus told the Apostles on one occasion that the devil could be cast out only by prayer and fasting. Jesus prayed with His Apostles at the Last Supper as He instituted the Sacrament of the Holy Eucharist. He prayed to His Heavenly Father in the Garden of Gethsemane just before He was captured by the soldiers.

The Apostles were commanded by Jesus to spend the days before the coming of the Holy Spirit in prayer in the Upper Room. From those nine days of prayer, the Church adopted the tradition of novenas, spending nine days in prayer asking for special favors. The Bible itself is a book of prayer, especially such a great prayer book as the Psalms by King David.

Jesus loves us so much that He Himself gave us the perfect prayer, the Our Father. The Our Father is the perfect prayer because it is a prayer of perfect and unselfish love, taught to us by the Son of God. When we pray in the Our Father, "Thy will be done on earth as it is in Heaven," we pray that all men on earth obey the will of God as the saints and angels obey God in Heaven. In Heaven, all the angels and saints are perfect, and are obeying God perfectly.

We might ask, "How is the will of God carried out in Heaven?" The answer is that His will is carried out perfectly! The souls in Heaven see God face to face, and they are deeply in love with Him. They could not possibly love anyone more. This is why they are in Heaven.

However, we here on earth still have the opportunity to use our free wills for good or for evil. Why did God give each one of us a free will? God gives each person He creates an opportunity to choose Him, to choose to be obedient to Him, just as he gave that opportunity to Adam and Eve. God gave us each a free will so that we might freely choose to do His holy will.

Think about this. Suppose you give a birthday party and invited your friends. You like them and they like you and you have a good time together. However, one friend says that he came to the party only because his parents made him come. He really wanted to go to a movie, but was forced to attend your party. How would you feel since your friend did not freely choose to come? God gives us all a chance to say, "Yes, I love You, God, and want to go to Heaven to be with You for all eternity, so I choose to obey Your Ten Commandments." This kind of freely-chosen obedience proves a person's love.

In the Our Father, we pray that people on earth will choose to use their free wills to do God's will. Yet sometimes people either purposefully choose to do evil, or because of a weakness, fail to do what they know they should do. That is why we have this petition in the Our Father. We are desiring with God that everyone on earth do God's will perfectly as do the angels and saints do His will perfectly in Heaven.

The fourth petition of the Our Father is "Give us this day our daily bread." By this petition, we are praying that God will give us each day all that is necessary to support the material life of our bodies, and the spiritual life of our souls.

With this petition, we have a change in focus. The first three petitions are directed towards God and His glory. Just as the Ten Commandments begin with the first three Commandments concerning the glory of God, so the Our Father begins with three petitions venerating God. As the last seven Commandments order proper behavior toward others, so the last four petitions in the Our Father are concerned with our behavior towards our neighbor.

There are three senses in which we ask God for our daily bread. In the first and most important sense, we ask for the daily Bread of the Holy Eucharist. Pope Saint Pius X, in the early part of the twentieth century, said that the daily bread referred to in the Lord's Prayer means the Food for our *souls*, the Holy Eucharist.

The second sense of the meaning of the word "bread" in this petition refers to the Word of God, the Bible. Our *minds* must be nourished with the words of Sacred Scripture and the revealed truths of our salvation so that we may grow in our knowledge of the Faith and trust in God.

The third sense in which we regard this petition of the Our Father is for food for our bodies, as well as other necessary material things as clothing and shelter. We are petitioning for daily bread for all the poor and hungry the world over. We must pray and give all we can to the poor so that they too may be fed in spirit and in body.

O Divine Infant Jesus, have mercy on us.
O Divine Infant Jesus, worshiped by the angels and saints, have mercy on us.

Fill in the Blank

1. When we pray "Thy will be done on earth as it is in Heaven," we pray that all men on earth obey the will of God as the _Angels_ and _Saints_ obey God in Heaven.

2. On earth, obeying God's will means obeying the _ten commandments_.

3. The souls in Heaven see God _face to face_.

4. We are desiring with God that everyone on earth do God's will _perfectly_.

5. The Our Father is the _perfect_ prayer because it was given to us by the Son of God.

6. The first three petitions are directed towards _God_.

7. In the first sense, we are asking for the Bread of the _Eucharist_.

8. _Pope Pius XX_ said the Bread in the Our Father refers to the Bread for our _souls_.

9. The second sense of the meaning of bread refers to the _Word_ of God, to nourish our minds.

10. The third sense of the meaning of bread refers to food for our _bodies_, especially for the _poor_ and hungry the world over.

We are studying the meaning of the perfect prayer, the Our Father, given to us by the Son of God, Jesus Christ.

When we pray in the Our Father, "Forgive us our trespasses as we forgive those who trespass against us," the fifth petition, we pray that God will pardon the sins by which we have offended Him. We also are telling Him that we pardon our fellow men who have offended us.

This petition is a plea to God for mercy. We need to ask God for mercy regarding the forgiveness of our sins. However, God will forgive us our sins only on the condition that we forgive those who have hurt us, wounded our pride, lied about us, or been mean to us.

Jesus told a story about a man who was forgiven by the king a large sum of money which he owed the king. The man was very, very grateful. However, soon after, the man met a poor friend who owed him a much smaller amount of money, but the poor friend could not pay him back right away. The man who was forgiven by the king became very angry and beat his poor friend. Some people who knew the poor friend came and told the king. The king called the man back and said, "I forgave you the large debt you owed me, yet you would not forgive your poor friend. Because of your lack of mercy to your friend, I am going to insist that you pay the huge debt you owe me!" Jesus told this story to show that if we are not kind and generous to each other, we will find that God will not be merciful to us!

Each of us have been forgiven many times for so many sins. God's forgiveness and mercy towards us is so generous! To be perfect, we must forgive others when they hurt us. Just as God loves us, so we must love everyone, even those who treat us badly.

The sixth petition of the Lord's Prayer is "Lead us not into temptation." When we pray this petition, we pray that God will always give us the grace to overcome the temptations to sin which come to us from the world, the flesh, and the devil.

The temptations of the world are the sinful behaviors of people who pressure us to do things which we know are wrong. The temptations of the flesh are the desires of our fallen human nature. The temptations of the devil can make us believe that evil things are attractive.

It is impossible to avoid *all* temptations, but it is possible to avoid *many* temptations. We know that there are persons, places, and things which are temptations we can avoid. We should be constantly on guard to avoid situations which provide temptations.

The saints have given us ways we can protect ourselves from temptations. We should:

- Be on guard against the Evil One; "resist him, steadfast in the Faith" (1 Peter 5:9).
- Examine our consciences every evening. How did we deal with the temptations of the day?
- Thank God for His grace in overcoming temptations.
- Get rid of bad thoughts and desires, and thank God for the good thoughts and desires.
- Take time to think about decisions before acting on them.
- Ask for light for the mind and strength of will to recognize and rebuke temptations.

- Act with humility and prudence in choosing the best course of action.
- Recognize temptations.
- Choose our friends and acquaintances carefully.
- Fear offending our loving God.

The seventh and last petition of the Our Father is "Deliver us from evil." When we pray this petition, we pray that God will always protect us from harm, and especially from harm to our souls.

According to the *Catechism of the Catholic Church*, in this last petition of the Our Father, we are asking God Our Father to protect us from the lies and snares of the devil. "In this petition, evil is not an abstraction, but refers to a person, Satan, the Evil One, the [bad] angel who opposes God" (n. 2851).

The Our Father, as do all prayers, ends with "Amen." We say "Amen" often, but do we know what it means? The word "Amen" means "So be it!" When we speak that word, we are saying that we accept everything in the Our Father, and that we are confident that God will answer all of the petitions.

Now that we have finished this course, may God bless you and keep you in His tender care. May you live very close to Him and His holy Mother so that you will be happy with Him forever.

Please remember in your prayers those who worked on writing this religion book for you. There were several priests, and three lay people. God bless you.

O Divine Infant Jesus, loved as a shining example of obedience, have mercy on us.
O Divine Infant Jesus, adored by the shepherds, have mercy on us.

Matching

__6__ 1. Sixth Petition of the Our Father

__1__ 2. Seventh Petition of the Our Father

__10__ 3. First Petition of the Our Father

__3__ 4. Second Petition of the Our Father

__2__ 5. Fourth Petition of the Our Father

__8__ 6. Third Petition of the Our Father

__9__ 7. Fifth Petition of the Our Father

__7__ 8. World, the flesh and the devil

__5__ 9. Jesus Christ

__4__ 10. Amen

1. "Deliver us from evil"

2. "Give us this day our daily bread"

3. "Thy Kingdom Come"

4. "So be it"

5. Taught us the Our Father

6. "Lead us not into temptation"

7. Three sources of temptation

8. "Thy will be done on earth as it is in Heaven"

9. "Forgive us our Trespasses as we forgive those who trespass against us"

10. "Hallowed be Thy Name"

Take this week to review the lessons from this quarter.

Day 1

Review lessons for weeks 28 and 29.

Day 2

Review lessons for weeks 30 and 31.

Day 3

Review lessons for weeks 32 and 33.

Day 4

Review lessons for weeks 34 and 35.

Day 5

Take the Fourth Quarter Test.

List of Illustrations and Artists

RELIGION 6 FOR YOUNG CATHOLICS ANSWER KEY

Week One: Day 1

1. T
2. T
3. T
4. T
5. F
6. F
7. T
8. F
9. F
10. T

Week One: Day 2

1. D
2. B
3. C
4. A
5. C
6. A
7. C
8. B
9. C
10. A

Week One: Day 3

1. 8
2. 1
3. 5
4. 2
5. 7
6. 10
7. 9
8. 3
9. 4
10. 6

Week One: Day 4

1. Sacred Scripture, Sacred Tradition
2. holy
3. Bible
4. 73
5. inspired
6. Old
7. New
8. Sacred Tradition
9. Sacred Scripture, Sacred Tradition
10. Bible

Week Two: Day 1

1. F
2. T
3. F
4. F
5. T
6. T
7. T
8. F
9. T
10. T

Week Two: Day 2

Across

3. Create
5. Divine
6. Son
7. Inanimate
10. Trinity
11. Free Will
12. Intellect
13. Creature

Down

1. Holy Spirit
2. Rational
4. Existence
8. Animals
9. Loving
11. Father

Week Two: Day 3

1. 7
2. 9
3. 6
4. 5
5. 8
6. 3
7. 4
8. 1
9. 10
10. 2

Week Two: Day 4

1. will
2. good, bad
3. intelligence
4. bodies
5. lure
6. St. Michael
7. Penance, Holy Eucharist, prayer
8. face-to-face
9. guardian
10. day

Week Three: Day 1

1. T
2. T
3. T
4. F
5. T
6. T
7. T
8. T
9. T
10. F

Week Three: Day 2

Across

3. Pelagius
5. Intellect
6. Loved
8. Original Sin
10. Forbidden
11. Die
13. Disobedience
15. Sanctifying Grace
17. Supernatural

Down

1. Carthage
2. Inherited
4. Knowledge
5. Infused
7. Freedom
9. Glorified
12. Perfect
14. Free Will
16. Adam

Week Three: Day 3

1. 2
2. 5
3. 1
4. 10
5. 8
6. 3
7. 9
8. 4
9. 6
10. 7

Week Four: Day 1

1. Paradise
2. Lucifer
3. actual
4. grace
5. merits
6. Sanctifying Grace
7. seriously wrong
8. sufficient reflection
9. consent
10. venial

315

Week Four: Day 2

1. F
2. T
3. T
4. F
5. T
6. T
7. F
8. T
9. T
10. F

Week Four: Day 3

Across

2. Beatitudes
5. Incarnation
7. Gifts
11. Holy Family
12. Jesus Christ

Down

1. Natures
3. Son
4. Perfectly
6. Thirty
8. Virtues
9. Promise
10. Gabriel

Week Five: Day 1

1. 10
2. 1
3. 6
4. 8
5. 2
6. 3
7. 4
8. 5
9. 7
10. 9

Week Five: Day 3

1. third
2. soul, body
3. Limbo, Fathers
4. closed
5. Easter
6. historical
7. soul, body
8. (the Son of) God
9. resurrection
10. happy

Week Five: Day 4

1. F
2. T
3. F

4. F
5. T
6. T
7. T
8. T
9. T
10. T

Week Six: Day 1

1. B
2. C
3. A
4. C
5. B
6. B
7. B
8. A
9. D
10. B

Week Six: Day 2

1. 6
2. 1
3. 4
4. 10
5. 3
6. 9
7. 2
8. 5
9. 7
10. 8

Week Six: Day 3

1. far above
2. Baptism
3. faith, hope, charity
4. God
5. natural
6. intellect
7. rely
8. will
9. God
10. enemies

Week Seven: Day 1

1. 7
2. 10
3. 1
4. 2
5. 8
6. 3
7. 9
8. 6
9. 4
10. 5

Week Seven: Day 2

1. teaches, sanctifies, rules
2. soul
3. Pope
4. Catholic Church
5. Pope, bishops
6. Peter
7. Sacraments
8. dioceses
9. Church
10. work

Week Seven: Day 3

1. F
2. F
3. F
4. T
5. T
6. F
7. T
8. T
9. T
10. T

Week Seven: Day 4

Across

3. God
4. Attribute
6. Evangelium Vitae
8. Authority
9. Govern
10. Infallibility
11. Consummation
12. Bishops

Down

1. Pope
2. Perfect
5. Never
7. Mystical Body

Week Eight: Day 1

1. assurance, conviction
2. Mystical
3. Triumphant, Militant, Suffering
4. Heaven
5. Suffering
6. Militant
7. Corporal, Spiritual
8. Creed
9. body
10. soul

Week Eight: Day 2

1. F
2. T

3. T
4. T
5. T
6. F
7. F
8. T
9. F
10. T

Week Eight: Day 3

Across
1. World
3. Serving
5. Particular
9. Judgment
10. General
11. Consequences

Down
2. Resurrection
4. Goats
6. Righteous
7. Secret
8. Alone

Week Eight: Day 4
1. 7
2. 1
3. 10
4. 2
5. 4
6. 9
7. 5
8. 3
9. 6
10. 8

Week Ten: Day 1
1. A
2. C
3. C
4. B
5. B
6. C
7. B
8. D
9. A
10. D

Week Ten: Day 2
1. T
2. F
3. F
4. T
5. T
6. F
7. F
8. T
9. T
10. T

Week Ten: Day 3
1. law, freedom, morality
2. command
3. nature
4. God's
5. Laws, God
6. God
7. freedom
8. Freedom, law
9. more
10. priesthood, religious

Week Eleven: Day 1
1. 7
2. 10
3. 1
4. 9
5. 3
6. 8
7. 6
8. 2
9. 4
10. 5

Week Eleven: Day 2
1. C
2. B
3. A
4. C
5. A
6. C
7. B
8. A
9. A
10. C

Week Eleven: Day 3
1. F
2. T
3. T
4. F
5. F
6. F
7. F
8. T
9. T
10. T

Week Eleven: Day 4
1. 9
2. 1
3. 6
4. 3
5. 2
6. 4

7. 8
8. 5
9. 10
10. 7

Week Twelve: Day 1
1. T
2. F
3. F
4. T
5. T
6. F
7. T
8. F
9. F
10. T

Week Twelve: Day 2
1. 3
2. 10
3. 1
4. 6
5. 2
6. 9
7. 4
8. 5
9. 7
10. 8

Week Twelve: Day 3
1. God
2. Saturday
3. Sunday
4. rose
5. Apostles
6. Sunday
7. moral
8. participate
9. everything
10. reverence or respect
   or attention or devotion

Week Twelve: Day 4
1. work
2. Servile
3. shopping
4. John XXIII
5. Mater et Magistra
6. Holy Days, Obligation
7. Heavenly
8. Mass or the Holy Sacrifice of the Mass
9. Sunday
10. Policemen / firemen / doctors / nurses / power plant workers (Accept any two of the above or any answer that

is consistent with the teaching found in the Catechism.)

Week Thirteen: Day 1

Across

4. Rule
6. Fourth
9. Existence
10. Jesus
11. Ten

Down

1. Need
2. Our Parents
3. Adoration
5. Bodily
7. Honor
8. Respect

Week Thirteen: Day 2

1. father and (thy) mother
2. authority
3. respect, gratitude
4. God
5. Pontius Pilate
6. above
7. disobedience
8. God
9. obedient
10. cared

Week Thirteen: Day 3

1. 6
2. 1
3. 10
4. 2
5. 8
6. 3
7. 4
8. 5
9. 7
10. 9

Week Fourteen: Day 1

1. Abel
2. fallen
3. own spiritual and bodily well-being, and that of our neighbor
4. neglect
5. sacred
6. life
7. angry
8. God's
9. pray
10. life

Week Fourteen: Day 2

1. Thou shalt not kill.
2. fighting
3. anger
4. revenge
5. drunkenness
6. reckless driving
7. bad example
8. hatred or murder (**Note:** Numbers 2 – 8 need not be in order.)
9. Revenge
10. bad example

Week Fourteen: Day 3

1. Thou shalt not kill.
2. injure
3. save
4. Blackrobes
5. mercy
6. Father Damien
7. self-defense
8. war
9. Ignatius, Francis, George
10. execute

Week Fourteen: Day 4

1. Thou shalt not commit adultery.
2. pure, modest
3. bad, immodest
4. near
5. healthy
6. Pius XI
7. allowed
8. pagan
9. parents
10. frequent the Sacraments

Week Fifteen: Day 1

1. Thou shalt not steal.
2. injustice
3. damaging
4. due
5. defend
6. respect
7. forbidden
8. trust
9. Laws
10. good example

Week Fifteen: Day 2

1. 10
2. 6
3. 1
4. 2
5. 8

6. 4
7. 3
8. 9
9. 5
10. 7

Week Sixteen: Day 1

1. witness
2. truth
3. truth
4. right
5. jumping
6. Calumny (or Slander)
7. damaging (or harming)
8. lie (or secret we are bound to keep)
9. Truth
10. name

Week Sixteen: Day 2

1. T
2. T
3. T
4. T
5. T
6. T
7. F
8. T
9. T
10. T

Week Sixteen: Day 4

1. wife
2. goods
3. pure
4. temptation (or sin)
5. near occasions of sin
6. thoughts and desires
7. guilt
8. Answers will vary.
9. jealous (or envious)
10. Being good; Also accept: Helping others

Week Seventeen: Day 1

Across

3. December
5. Sacrifice
7. Six
8. Mass
10. Saints
12. Assumption
14. Advent
15. Victim

Down

1. Christmas

318

2. Perfect
4. Mortal Sin
6. Calvary
9. Ascension
11. Nativity
12. Assist
13. Present

Week Seventeen: Day 2

1. 9
2. 1
3. 5
4. 2
5. 3
6. 6
7. 10
8. 4
9. 8
10. 7

Week Seventeen: Day 3

1. mortal
2. venial
3. to confess our sins at least once a year
4. mortal
5. frequent
6. holiness
7. Easter
8. Trinity
9. grace
10. Jesus Christ

Week Seventeen: Day 4

1. to contribute to the support of the Church
2. Peter Canisius, responsibility
3. parish
4. priests
5. missionary
6. material
7. to observe the laws of the Church concerning marriage

Week Nineteen: Day 1

1. hear
2. sign, grace
3. symbol
4. material
5. Jesus Christ
6. Sanctifying
7. know, love
8. divine
9. oil

10. water

Week Nineteen: Day 2

1. T
2. T
3. T
4. T
5. T
6. T
7. T
8. T
9. T
10. T

Week Nineteen: Day 3

1. 8
2. 1
3. 9
4. 7
5. 10
6. 3
7. 6
8. 4
9. 5
10. 2

Week Nineteen: Day 4

1. Living
2. know / do
3. grace
4. Augustine
5. religious
6. Confirmation, Eucharist, Sick, Orders, Matrimony
7. mortal
8. sacrilege
9. deed
10. grace or sanctifying grace

Week Twenty: Day 1

1. C
2. A
3. C
4. C
5. C
6. D
7. D
8. A
9. C
10. C

Week Twenty: Day 2

1. 7
2. 5
3. 1
4. 10
5. 4
6. 9

7. 2
8. 6
9. 3
10. 8

Week Twenty: Day 3

1. gives our souls the new life of Sanctifying Grace
2. original sin
3. St. Peter
4. suffering and death
5. love
6. Blood
7. save
8. angels
9. salvation
10. Baptism

Week Twenty: Day 4

1. 7
2. 1
3. 10
4. 9
5. 3
6. 4
7. 8
8. 6
9. 2
10. 5

Week 21: Day 1

1. T
2. T
3. T
4. F
5. T
6. T
7. T
8. F
9. F
10. T

Week 21: Day 2

1. C
2. C
3. D
4. B
5. B
6. A
7. A
8. A
9. B
10. C

Week 21: Day 3

1. 6
2. 1
3. 9

4. 3
5. 2
6. 8
7. 4
8. 5
9. 7
10. 10

Week 21: Day 4

1. Augustine
2. soldiers
3. afraid
4. soul
5. more
6. understand
7. Holy Eucharist (or Holy Communion), Penance
8. character
9. sufferings
10. profess our Faith

Week 22: Day 1

1. T
2. T
3. F
4. F
5. F
6. F
7. T
8. T
9. F
10. F

Week 22: Day 2

1. 8
2. 10
3. 1
4. 2
5. 9
6. 4
7. 3
8. 5
9. 6
10. 7

Week 22: Day 3

1. Jesus Christ
2. defend
3. appearances
4. taste, color, weight (or shape)
5. speck (or particle)
6. drop
7. Consecration
8. Transubstantiation
9. mystery
10. the Holy Eucharist

Week 22: Day 4

1. 6
2. 8
3. 7
4. 2
5. 1
6. 3
7. 9
8. 4
9. 10
10. 5

Week 23: Day 1

1. sacrifice
2. Mass (or the Holy Sacrifice of the Mass)
3. Moses
4. Jesus Christ
5. Divinity
6. Cross
7. "sending"
8. Catholic Church
9. New / Old
10. Mass (or the Holy Sacrifice of the Mass)

Week 23: Day 2

1. T
2. F
3. T
4. T
5. T
6. F
7. T
8. T
9. T
10. T

Week 23: Day 3

1. A
2. C
3. C
4. C
5. C
6. A
7. C
8. A
9. A
10. C

Week 23: Day 4

1. same
2. blood
3. perfect
4. continues
5. infinite
6. priest

7. listen
8. adore
9. thank
10. satisfy (or make reparation)

Week 24: Day 1

1. T
2. T
3. T
4. T
5. F
6. F
7. T
8. T
9. T
10. T

Week 24: Day 2

1. B
2. C
3. B
4. A
5. B
6. A
7. A
8. A
9. A
10. C

Week 24: Day 3

1. 5
2. 1
3. 7
4. 10
5. 2
6. 3
7. 9
8. 4
9. 6
10. 8

Week 24: Day 4

Across

2. Hour
3. Contrite
7. Fifteen
8. Hardon
9. Friday
12. EWTN
13. Fervent
14. Grace
15. Visits

Down

1. Contrition
4. Benediction
5. Daily

6. Spiritual
10. Reverent
11. Mortal Sin

Week 25: Day 1

1. absolution
2. Easter Sunday
3. power
4. humble
5. graces
6. assurance
7. medicine
8. healing
9. forgiven, retained
10. St. John Vianney

Week 25: Day 2

1. T
2. F
3. T
4. T
5. T
6. T
7. T
8. T
9. T
10. T

Week 25: Day 3

1. Baptism
2. Jesus Christ
3. Holy Spirit
4. absolve
5. Sanctifying
6. forgiveness
7. eternal
8. punishment
9. avoid
10. good works

Week 25: Day 4

1. a review
2. Penance
3. conscience
4. daily (or every evening)
5. forgiveness
6. honest
7. Commandments
8. presence
9. forgiveness
10. Contrition

Week 26: Day 1

1. 2
2. 6
3. 1
4. 9
5. 3

6. 10
7. 4
8. 8
9. 5
10. 7

Week 26: Day 2

1. Contrition
2. interior
3. supernatural
4. supreme
5. universal
6. offends
7. Pius XII
8. lead
9. temporal
10. John Paul II

Week 26: Day 3

1. A
2. A
3. B
4. B
5. C
6. A
7. A
8. A
9. C
10. B

Week 26: Day 4

1. hatred
2. sin
3. heart(s)
4. God
5. children
6. Act of Contrition
7. Confession
8. try
9. avoid
10. occasions

Week 28: Day 1

1. priest
2. priest
3. Easter Sunday
4. "Peace"
5. mortal
6. Shepherd
7. conscience
8. forgiven
9. venial
10. month

Week 28: Day 3

1. forgiveness
2. mortal
3. all

4. sacrilege
5. part
6. seal
7. penance
8. avoid
9. confessional
10. Hell

Week 28: Day 4

1. punishment
2. Temporal
3. justice
4. evil
5. warn
6. sufferings
7. Morning Offering
8. all
9. cross
10. Mass, mercy, sufferings

Week 29: Day 1

1. month
2. schedule
3. sins
4. parents
5. improvement
6. regular
7. prayer book
8. sorrow
9. commit
10. sinned

Week 29: Day 2

1. Holy Spirit
2. Cross
3. sinned
4. how long
5. mortal, number
6. sacrilege
7. Communion
8. nearly
9. father
10. children

Week 29: Day 3

1. number
2. past
3. questions
4. clearly
5. advice
6. listen
7. prayers
8. agreed
9. grateful
10. sins

Week 29: Day 4

1. 7
2. 10
3. 1
4. 3
5. 2
6. 5
7. 9
8. 4
9. 6
10. 8

Week 30: Day 1

1. remission
2. Church
3. guilt / punishment
4. guilt
5. temporal
6. Treasury
7. Paul VI
8. Militant
9. Suffering
10. Triumphant

Week 30: Day 2

1. temporal punishment
2. partial / plenary
3. eternal
4. God
5. Catholics
6. confession
7. St. Peter
8. keys / whatsoever
9. loose
10. Treasury

Week 30: Day 3

1. indulgences
2. Treasury
3. Jesus Christ
4. merits
5. Purgatory
6. St. Thomas Aquinas
7. Church
8. Alexander II
9. Crusaders
10. measured

Week 30: Day 4

1. F
2. T
3. T
4. T
5. F
6. T
7. T
8. F
9. T
10. T

Week 31: Day 1

1. Anointing / Sick
2. oil
3. strength
4. death
5. Sanctifying Grace
6. temptation
7. venial
8. health
9. unconscious
10. God

Week 31: Day 2

1. prayer / soul / death
2. Confession
3. Faith, Hope, and Charity
4. ill
5. absolution
6. serve
7. consolation
8. healing
9. despair
10. embrace

Week 31: Day 3

1. grace
2. education
3. rest of his life
4. bishop
5. bishop
6. Sanctifying
7. Sacramental
8. character / supernatural
9. Apostles
10. power / grace

Week 31: Day 4

Across

4. Missionary
7. Reverence
8. Consecrated
10. Jesus Christ
12. Dominicans

Down

1. Philomena
2. Pray
3. Forever
5. Diocesan
6. Priests
9. Damien

Week 32: Day 1

1. Matrimony / bind / grace
2. faithful
3. spiritual
4. death
5. joined
6. children
7. brave / courageous / unafraid
8. sacred bond
9. bad
10. asking / return

Week 32: Day 2

1. baptized / baptized
2. death
3. joined
4. Sacrament
5. husband / wife
6. regulations
7. family
8. one
9. human (or Church)
10. holy

Week 32: Day 3

1. life
2. bishop / priest / deacon (only two answers required)
3. grace
4. duties
5. faithful
6. provide / spiritual
7. marriage
8. Nuptial Mass
9. joy
10. king / queen

Week 32: Day 4

1. Ten Commandments
2. teachers
3. Cana
4. public
5. Sanctifying Grace
6. Sacramental Grace
7. pray
8. parents / confessors
9. Nuptial (or Wedding)
10. perfect

Week 33: Day 1

Across

1. Temporary
3. Sacramentals
6. Kung
7. Catholic
12. Seven
13. Sanctifying Grace
14. Sacraments

Down

2. Actual
3. Sanctifying
4. Medal
5. Sick
8. Additional
9. Prepare
10. Bind
11. China

Week 33: Day 2

1. Sacramentals / spiritual / temporal
2. prayers / devotion
3. Actual
4. venial
5. remission
6. health / material
7. evil
8. Veronica
9. Lourdes
10. Miraculous Medal

Week 33: Day 3

1. F
2. T
3. T
4. F
5. T
6. T
7. T
8. T
9. F
10. F

Week 33: Day 4

1. Actual
2. forgiveness / remission
3. priests
4. Suggested answers include but are not limited to any six of the following: holy water, candles, ashes, palms, crucifixes, medals, rosary beads, scapulars, statues, icons
5. faith
6. Church
7. Heavenly
8. St. Dominic
9. St. Simon Stock
10. St. Blaise

Week 34: Day 1

1. pillars
2. minds / hearts
3. 1000 / heart

4. Prayers
5. the Holy Spirit
6. ceasing
7. graces
8. Morning Offering
9. Our Lord
10. forty

Week 34: Day 2

1. A
2. B
3. A
4. C
5. A
6. B
7. B
8. D
9. C
10. A

Week 34: Day 3

1. minds / hearts
2. adore
3. thank
4. pardon
5. punishment
6. hears
7. knows everything
8. everything
9. mental / vocal
10. Mental / truths

Week 34: Day 4

1. 7
2. 1
3. 5
4. 2
5. 9
6. 10
7. 3
8. 4
9. 6
10. 8

Week 35: Day 1

1. perfect
2. Jesus, the Son of God
3. unselfish
4. best / neighbor
5. belong
6. created
7. Baptism
8. Heaven
9. Matthew (or Luke)
10. Mass

Week 35: Day 2

1. unselfish
2. Baptism
3. watch
4. honored
5. reverence
6. name
7. world
8. Church
9. best
10. Jesus Christ

Week 35: Day 3

1. angels / saints
2. Ten Commandments
3. face to face
4. perfectly
5. perfect
6. God
7. Holy Eucharist
8. Pope St. Pius X / souls
9. Word
10. bodies / poor

Week 35: Day 4

1. 6
2. 1
3. 10
4. 3
5. 2
6. 8
7. 9
8. 7
9. 5
10. 4

Like our books?

You might like our program, too. Seton Home Study School offers a full curriculum program for Kindergarten through Twelfth Grade. We include daily lesson plans, answer keys, quarterly tests, and much more. Our staff of teachers and counselors is available to answer questions and offer help. We keep student records and send out diplomas that are backed by our accreditation with the Southern Association of Colleges and Schools and the Commission on International and Transregional Accreditation.

For more information about Seton Home Study School,

please contact our admissions office.

Seton Home Study School
1350 Progress Drive
Front Royal, VA 22630

Phone: 540-636-9990 • Fax: 540-636-1602
Internet: www.setonhome.org • E-mail: info@setonhome.org